"Chelsea Wakefield is the most luminous new voice in sex therapy. Follow the guidance in this book—your clients will think you're a genius!"
—**Gina Ogden, author of** *Expanding the Practice of*
Sex Therapy **and** *The Heart and Soul of Sex*

"At last, a book about sexuality that is not like all that useless information from the internet and from self-help books that tells you what to do to look sexy. This book tells you how to be a sexual being."
—**Ginette Paris, author of** *Pagan Meditations:*
The world of Aphrodite, Artemis and Hestia

"This book is unique in taking a comprehensive and complex view of female sexuality, emphasizing a challenging, positive view of the role of sex therapy. It would be of particular value for psychodynamic clinicians."
—**Barry McCarthy, co-author (with Emily McCarthy) of**
Rekindling Desire **and** *Sexual Awareness: Your Guide to*
Healthy Couple Sexuality

"This book is an homage to the personal and collective archetypes that comprise each woman's inner 'cast of characters.' Wakefield deftly weaves body psychotherapy and archetypal psychology into an experiential model that transforms ordinary sex therapy into soul work. Embodied stories and 'parts' work bring Aphrodite to life in case examples of women ravaged by heartbreak, sheltered by Eros-inhibiting 'gate keepers' and stunted by one-dimensional sexual scripts. Wakefield writes in a soothing, female-centered voice that celebrates sensuality and desire. Every woman will see herself and feel affirmed in this beautiful guide to becoming a sexually empowered woman."

—Maci Daye, creator of The Passion and
Presence Couples Retreat

"Engaging, illuminating and empowering! Wakefield will energize therapists to go beyond treating sexual dysfunctions in favour of helping each client to awaken the archetypal woman within!"

—Peggy J. Kleinplatz, author of *New Directions in*
Sex Therapy: Innovations and Alternatives

"This book isn't just a gem—it's a whole treasure chest of jewels and golden wisdom—of incalculable value not just to heterosexual women, but to sexual human beings of all genders. The archetypes of the collective unconscious are always 'evading capture,' but here in this book, Dr. Wakefield has persuaded a star-studded group of them to show themselves, and engage in intelligent conversation with her, with each other, and with her readers."

—Jeremy Taylor, author of *The Wisdom of Your Dreams*
and *The Living Labyrinth*

"What a fascinating, enriching, life-affirming book! *In Search of Aphrodite* helps women of all ages to discover—or rediscover—the joys, richness, and complexities of their own individual sexuality and sensuality, of their own erotic identity, as it is expressed in their lives and their intimate relationships. Dr. Wakefield combines scholarly research with a broad range of clinical experience and anecdotal material, to bring us a picture of the road forward into sexual individuation."

—Sidra L. Stone, author of *The Shadow King:*
The Invisible Force that Holds Women Back

In Search of Aphrodite

What does it mean to be "in search of Aphrodite?" For most women, sex is complex, and more than a juxtaposition of body parts. Women sense the possibility of depth, meaning, even transcendence, but in a somatically disconnected, sexually superficial world, it can be difficult for a woman to discover her inner fire, define who she is sexually, and confidently communicate this to her partner.

Part philosophy, part treatment manual, *In Search of Aphrodite* addresses women's sexual problems from an inspiring, creative perspective, integrating Jungian psychology and sex therapy. Readers will deepen their understanding of the sexual psyche and how this realm has an impact on women's lives, as well as what the author calls the "journey of Sexual Individuation™."

Chelsea Wakefield covers a variety of topics such as healing ancient wounds, resolving inner conflicts, exploring sexual essence, identity, scripts, primal instinct, desire, fantasy, longing, and more. She offers pathways to sexual enrichment and improved communication with a partner. Sexual archetypes are introduced and organized around the author's Sexual Essence Wheel. Gatekeepers and Eros-inhibiting archetypes are described, along with what to do when treatment stalls.

This book is appropriate for:

- Clinicians who are nervous about venturing into conversations about women's sexuality
- Clinicians who are comfortable with sexual topics and are curious about new interventions
- Sex therapists who want a treatment model that acknowledges the multidimensional aspects of sexuality
- Jungian analysts and Jungian-oriented practitioners who want helpful tools for addressing sexual issues as an invitation into individuation
- Pastoral counselors and spiritual guidance practitioners who seek to heal souls wounded by sexual trauma and sex-negative teachings
- Women who want to explore their sexual psyche and define their sexual essence, and men who wish to better understand the sexual depths of women

Rich with case histories and an "Inner Cast of Characters" that clients can explore, this resource will help women discover joyful embodiment, innate eroticism, and sexual pleasure!

Chelsea Wakefield, PhD, LCSW is an international teacher and presenter on sexuality and the journey of individuation. She is a Jungian-oriented psychotherapist, couples therapist, AASECT-certified sex therapist, educator, creator of the Luminous Woman® Weekend, and author of *Negotiating the Inner Peace Treaty: Becoming the Person You Were Born to Be.* Chelsea draws from a depth of clinical training and experience in archetypal, transpersonal, psychodynamic, parts psychology, developmental, and somatic methods of working. She facilitates people in moving beyond the wounds of the past, learning more about their unique sexual essence, embracing sexuality as a pathway of growth and individuation, learning how to communicate effectively with partners, and deepening sexual connection, meaning, and pleasure. You can learn more about her work at www.chelseawakefield.com.

IN SEARCH OF APHRODITE
Women, Archetypes and Sex Therapy

Chelsea Wakefield

Routledge
Taylor & Francis Group

NEW YORK AND LONDON

First published 2016
by Routledge
711 Third Avenue, New York, NY 10017

and by Routledge
2 Park Square, Milton Park, Abingdon, Oxon OX14 4RN

Routledge is an imprint of the Taylor & Francis Group, an informa business

Library of Congress Cataloging in Publication Data
Wakefield, Chelsea, author.
 In search of Aphrodite : women, archetypes and sex therapy / by Chelsea
Wakefield.
   pages cm
 Includes bibliographical references and index.
 1. Sex therapy.   2. Psychosexual disorders.   3. Women—Sexual
behavior.   4. Archetype (Psychology)   I. Title.
  RC557.W35 2015
  616.85'83—dc23
  2015029563

ISBN: 978-1-138-81926-9 (hbk)
ISBN: 978-1-138-81927-6 (pbk)
ISBN: 978-1-315-74468-1 (ebk)

Typeset in ITC Legacy Serif
by Apex CoVantage, LLC

Printed and bound in the United States of America by Publishers Graphics,
LLC on sustainably sourced paper.

O FRIEND, UNDERSTAND.

THE BODY IS LIKE THE OCEAN, RICH WITH HIDDEN TREASURES.

OPEN YOUR INNERMOST CHAMBER

AND LIGHT ITS LAMP,

WITHIN THE BODY ARE GARDENS,

RARE FLOWERS, PEACOCKS; THE INNER MUSIC;

WITHIN THE BODY A LAKE OF BLISS,

ON IT, THE WHITE SOUL-SWANS TAKE THEIR JOY.

MIRABAI

CONTENTS

ACKNOWLEDGMENTS

I want to thank the Jungian women, analysts and writers, who have informed my own journey of conscious femininity, and joyful embodiment. Special acknowledgment goes to Polly Young-Eisendrath, whose book, *Women and Desire* opened my eyes. Clarissa Pinkola Estes, Marion Woodman, Jean Shinoda Bolen, Ann Ulanov, Diane Landau, Ginette Paris, and Linda Leonard have all enriched my life and my work with their brilliant writing on women's relational world, embodiment, archetypes, the Goddess Aphrodite, and other aspects of the feminine.

I hold Hal and Sidra Stone in high regard as teachers and encouragers. Hal gave this work a special blessing early on, predicting how many people it would help. Sidra has been a living example of a fully empowered Aphrodite woman, both brilliant and luminous. Thank you for supporting so many other women in their discovery and embodiment of Aphrodite.

I am grateful to Bob Haden and my friends at the Haden Institute, where I began to present this material in its early stages of development, particularly Susan Sims Smith and Jeremy Taylor, who have been enthusiastic encouragers during the gestation and birthing of this book. I thank Jungian analyst, Keith Parker, for his many years of personal soul companioning.

Over my years of presenting and doing workshops about sexuality, I teach, but I also learn a great deal from participants. I am particularly grateful to all of my Luminous Woman® "graduates," who have shared their hearts and souls with me as we journeyed into the deep feminine, grappling with how a woman's journey of individuation differs from a man's.

I am grateful to my father, who gave me my first real introduction to Jung. I was disillusioned about love after my first marriage had ended. My father handed me a copy of Toni Grant's book, *Being A Woman*, and said, "Maybe this will help." That book introduced me to Jung, the world of archetypes, and to Antonia "Toni" Wolff, whose influence on Jung's life and his thinking often goes unacknowledged, and whose model of the feminine inspired my Luminous Woman® Weekends.

My deepest affection and appreciation goes to the brilliant and innovative Gina Ogden, for her pioneering spirit, her generous heart and extraordinary mentoring and friendship. From the first time we met, Gina warmly welcomed me into the field of sexology and supported me in bringing my work to that world. She introduced me to Marta Moldvai, the wonderful editor who grasped the vision for this project, and helped me focus and shape my ideas, with kindness and clarity, so that they could be conveyed to others.

To my husband, Tom, my biggest fan, who has navigated the many requirements for growth and change over our twenty five years together, respecting my Athena mind, and dancing with my Aphrodite soul. You are my dearest friend, and I love you.

INTRODUCTION

When it comes to sex, the old adage goes that we should just "do what comes naturally." Perhaps for some, sex is that simple, but for most, it is not. For most women, sex is especially complex. Although a woman's sexuality can bring deep satisfaction and solace, it is far more common for sexuality to be an area of confusion, discomfort, embarrassment, anxiety, relational power struggling, and punishing consequences. A hundred years ago, women finally got the right to vote in the United States. At that time, only a few radical thinkers were acknowledging that women might be interested in sexual pleasure.

Women have made some good progress in the public arena, but we still struggle in our intimate lives. What do we want, apart from what *others* want and expect from us? Can we express it with confidence and clarity or do we fold at the slightest indication of disappointment or disapproval? Where is the balance in giving and receiving? Can we have both power and pleasure in our lives? Our sexuality is a frontier that we are just beginning to explore in meaningful ways. Women instinctively know that sex is much more than a juxtaposition of body parts. We sense the possibility of depth and meaning, even transcendence, but it often seems like a fairy tale dream. At the same time, we hear the voices of warning in the background, cautioning us, "Being a sexual woman is dangerous, it can lead down the road to ruin."

Information about sexuality seems to be everywhere today. There are entire sections in bookstores devoted to sexual positions, sexual talk, and techniques. The Internet is filled with sexual sites and information. These sources suggest what women ought to *do*, but they don't address what is going on inside of her head and her heart. There is not a lot of help with how to *relate* to another person in bed. Sexuality is not thought of as a *life force energy* that moves through us and can enrich our lives. How does a woman discover her inner fire and define who she really is sexually? If she ever figures this out, how does she confidently communicate this to her partner? Women are taught to *act sexy*, but are not encouraged to become *sexual beings*. How does a woman claim her adult sexuality in a way that feels authentic and life giving? How does a woman learn to be comfortable in her own body when she doesn't look like a movie star or a fashion model? How does she negotiate "safe sex," physically, emotionally, and spiritually? How does her sexuality become an expression of who she is at her most essential level?

The romanticized sexual encounters in the movies seem to flow so easily. We rarely see any sexual negotiations beforehand. We don't see people sticking elbows in each other's eyes, or fumbling with a condom or struggling to get turned on. We do not see the *personhood* or *vulnerability* of the people involved: the hope, anxiety, humor, awkwardness, surprise, disappointment, and delight that make up the spectrum of real-life sexual encounters. Where do people learn how to be present, attuned, patient, compassionate, and playful in bed? These are not skills to be learned; they are personal capacities to be developed! People long for good sexual experiences but don't know how to get there. In a world where sex is behaviorally scripted, sex can become disappointingly rote and predictable.

Women come to sex therapy for help with sexual dysfunction. In recent years, an increasing number of women have come because they are frustrated and confused by the boredom and dissatisfaction that pervades their sexual relationships. Kleinplatz (2001) quotes a young woman who stated, "He plays my body like a violin, and I hate him for it." Sex is clearly more than a behavioral skill set. Women want to be related to, and having an orgasm does not guarantee meaningful sex when the person *within* remains untouched. We also face an age-old, "archetypal" problem of getting the love and the lust in the same bed. Sexologists are interested in this conundrum, and we continue to tackle the problem of how to sustain a passionate connection in a long-term relationship (Leiblum, 2010; Ogden, 2008; Perel, 2007, 2010; Schnarch, 2009). In our sex-saturated culture, there are too many people who "can't get no satisfaction."

What This Book Is About

This book is part philosophy and part treatment manual. The case histories included cover a variety of "diagnoses." This is a book about helping women discover their birthright of joyful embodiment, innate eroticism, and sexual pleasure. It is a book about *sexual subjectivity*, the profound journey of becoming sexually Self-defined and Self-claiming. In the act of looking within, exploring her sexual psyche and embodied experience, a woman will deepen and mature in ways she could not have imagined. This process will empower her and cause her to mature and blossom. It will also require her to take responsibility for her life and her choices. Sensing this, some women hold back, anxious about the implications of undertaking this journey into conscious womanhood, but if her existence has become predictable and unbearably dull, this "call of the wild," will pull her forward. The slumbering instinctual Self will begin to stir. When a woman begins to explore her innate sexuality, it becomes a pathway into greater depth, meaning, and wholeness.

For the past twenty-five years, I have been a student of Jungian psychology, with a fascination for the world of archetypes and the journey of individuation. I have worked at the intersection of psyche, soma, and soul for many years as a psychotherapist, sex therapist, and spiritual guidance practitioner. In my experience, sexuality work *is* soul work. Over the years, I have worked with individuals and couples from all walks of life and a wide range of sexual identities and genders. Many of my clients come because they are suffering from sexual anxiety, shame, confusion, compulsion, frustration, and longing. Some come in search of enriching an already good relationship. I walk with them through their dark and bright experiences, through swamplands of the soul, and celebrations of wholeness and authenticity. I have studied all aspects of sexuality, the history, sociology, religious framing, mythology, and variety of expressions. In all times and in all places, sexuality is of central importance to the human experience.

To live a life of meaning and wholeness, we must ask deep questions of who we are and how we choose to live. One of those important questions is "Who am I as a sexual being?" In my work with women, I help them develop their capacity to look deeply into their experiences, heal what holds them back, understand what lights their fire, develop a capacity for deep encounter, and engage partners in a way that is most likely to result in a meaningful connection. We set about to establish a "center that can hold," healing ancient wounds, negotiating intrapsychic splits, developing emotional regulation capacities, exploring the realm of identity, embodied being, love, creativity, primal instinct, relationship commitments, old scripts, new scripts, fantasy, and longing.

In the process of working with women, I became intrigued by the array of sexual archetypes that exist, and I began to develop my Sexual Essence Wheels (Chapter 7). In working with women to discover their inner sources of desire, I began to identify what I call "Eros-inhibiting archetypes" and "Gatekeepers," who block women's sexual feeling and expression.

As practitioners, we can help women who are in the midst of a somatically disconnected, sexually superficial world. We can help them open up explorations of their embodied experience and create an honored place for mindful sexuality, shared pleasure, and the beauty of *being*. It is time that women began to define their own sexuality; not based on images or ideals promoted by the media, not as *objects* of someone else's script, but as *subjects* of their own stories, operating out of their unique sexual essence. This is the realm of Aphrodite, the ancient Greek Goddess of love, creativity, beauty, sensuality, and sexuality, and we are in search of Aphrodite.

Who Is This Book Written For?

1) Many psychotherapists feel woefully unprepared to assess and address the diversity of sexual issues that clients bring today. Many of our clinical training programs provide only one general human sexuality course. For clinicians who are nervous about venturing into conversations about women's sexuality, this book provides pathways into those conversations and ways of working once you are there. The bibliography is filled with helpful sex therapy references. For those who already feel comfortable in working with sexual issues, this book will expand your sexual perspective and provide helpful interventions. I encourage those who are interested in specializing in sexuality work to become involved with AASECT, the American Association of Sexuality Educators, Counselors and Therapists, where you can pursue professional certification! In the process, your knowledge base will expand greatly, in ways you could never foresee.

I also encourage you, the practitioner, to engage in these explorations yourself. When you have done your own inner work, it makes the work you do with clients more profound and transformational. Clients will go only as deep as you can go.

2) An increasing number of sex therapists believe that sex therapy needs treatment models that acknowledge the multidimensional aspects of sexuality. Human sexuality is far too complex to be confined to a "medical model" (Daniluk, 1998; Ellison, 2000, 2001, 2012; Kaschak & Tiefer, 2001; Kleinplatz, 2001, 2012; Morin, 1995; Ogden, 2006, 2008, 2013; Snell 2001a, 2001b; Snell, Fischer, & Walters, 1993). Leiblum & Rosen (2000) and Kleinplatz (2001, 2012) suggest that the field needs to become more interdisciplinary, integrating medical, behavioral, intrapsychic, interpersonal, and systemic approaches.

Gina Ogden (2013) and Peggy Kleinplatz (2001, 2012) have been tireless promoters of the need to expand the practice of sex therapy. This book is written in that spirit. Although the methods described here can be used in conjunction with "best practice" modalities of the cognitive-behavioral/medical model (Goodwach, 2005a, 2005b), my approach incorporates narrative, experiential, somatic, "parts" psychology and a Jungian perspective on individuation and the world of archetypes. I also outline an effective method for resolving some of those perplexing treatment impasses that frustrate sex therapists. Applying somatic work, parts psychology, and Voice Dialogue provides a zip line into the core of issues, which will appeal to those who want brief therapy interventions. Feminist sex therapists will find this method client centered and empowering for women as they define *their own* experience, restory their lives, and become more joyfully embodied.

Although my way of working is deeply intrapsychic, it is also grounded in the body. Working with the somatic experience of archetypal energies opens up many creative possibilities for exploring the sexual psyche and erotic identity. An archetypal perspective acknowledges the range and multidimensionality of human sexual experience. It provides a way of exploring the inner self system, with its many subpersonalities that are in dynamic interaction. This approach to sex therapy can be applied to all aspects of treatment: intake and assessment, history taking, the conceptualization of sexual problems, treatment planning, and creative interventions.

3) This book will be of interest to Jungian analysts and Jungian-oriented practitioners, who are already working with archetypes, dreams, complex theory, shadow, anima and animus, and the journey of individuation. This work shifts the focus more deeply into the embodied experience of women, and I emphasize how archetypes are experienced somatically. I have coined the term "Sexual Individuation™" because I believe that a consciously integrated sexuality is not just an important aspect of individuation, it is a *path* of individuation. This book introduces the concept of Eros-inhibiting archetypes and broadens our understanding of the many manifestations of Aphrodite and the impact of her archetypal energy on women's lives.

4) This book will also be of help to pastoral counselors and spiritual guidance practitioners. It will assist in addressing the sexual wounds sourced in religious shaming and provide healing remedies for soul-stealing sexual trauma. It is time that we resolve the split between body and soul, between an instinctual human life and the idealized transcendent sphere. Spiritual bypass is not the answer. We need to engage women in a more meaningful discourse regarding soulful sexuality.

5) This book is also for sexual seekers, who would like to explore their sexual psyche. Although this book is written for clinicians and practitioners, if you are familiar with psychological language, you can act as your own "sex therapist" in engaging the work. In the process, you will deepen your sexual Self-understanding, achieve some sexual healing, open new places of discovery, and enrich your sexual experience. If you find that you begin to feel overwhelmed, I suggest that you stop and find a competent therapist who can support you in working through any material that stands in the way of your journey into a joyful sexual wholeness.

6) In the course of writing this book, many men asked me if they might read this work, so that they can better understand the sexual depths of the women they seek to love well. Yes. This book is for you, too.

I have made an effort to be sensitive to the many dimensions and expressions of sexuality. Many of the case histories involve women in heterosexual relationships, but I have tried to include some examples of women who love women. I use the word "partner" often, in an attempt to be neutral about the sexual and gender identities and relationship status of those involved.

A QUICK BOOK TOUR

Part I

Part I provides some background and context for the way in which I have blended sex therapy with a Jungian perspective. Throughout the book, I will always capitalize names that could be considered archetypes. In Chapter 1, I describe the changing perspectives on women's sexuality over the course of history, and I introduce a few key figures in the birth of the field of sexology. In Chapter 2, I offer research on how "the sexual woman" has been defined and the many motivations for why women have sex. In Chapter 3, I outline the Masters and Johnson era, more recent developments in the field of sex therapy, and describe why women come to sex therapy. In Chapter 4, I begin to tie in Jungian psychology by introducing some key concepts originated by Carl Jung, particularly individuation, shadow, anima/animus, and the realm of archetypes. I touch on the relationship and differences between Jung's and Freud's perspectives. I then introduce Aphrodite, the Greek Goddess, whom I have chosen to represent the spectrum of sexual expressions that are possible within a woman's psyche.

Part II

Part II of the book is dedicated to a description of my archetypal approach to working with sexual issues and sexual enrichment in sex therapy. Chapter 5 covers what a sexual practitioner might listen for when taking a client's sexual history, particularly how to listen with "archetypal ears." In Chapter 6, I introduce my model of the "inner cast of characters," a concept detailed in my first book, *Negotiating the Inner Peace Treaty* (Wakefield, 2012). Our "inner cast" carries a variety of archetypal energies and plays out the scripts of a woman's life. In Chapter 7, I introduce my Sexual Essence Wheels, tools I developed to introduce a woman to the many possible expressions of her Aphrodite energy. The two wheels also show ways in which a woman can become stuck in the "sexual shadow lands," and the chapter describes how she can break free. This chapter also covers other ways of understanding one's sexual essence, through "sexual path preferences" and "core erotic themes." Chapter 8 returns to the inner cast of characters and the introduction of Voice Dialogue, a method of getting to know these inner characters and working with them to open new possibilities. I provide a case history that illustrates how dreams can bring the energies that are needed to move a woman forward on her sexual journey. In Chapter 9, I discuss ways that women can learn to "shift states" and develop "archetypal fluency."

Chapter 10 addresses a common problem that practitioners face, those places where treatment stalls or comes to a grinding halt. I offer a reframe for what clinicians often call the "resistant" or "unmotivated" client and introduce the concept of Sexual Gatekeepers. I outline a way of working with these pseudoprotectors, so that clients can move past them into the treasure land of sexual pleasure. In Chapter 11, I discuss how fairy tales shape a woman's world and describe various Fairy Tale Syndromes. In Chapter 12, we look at what it means to move from being a girl into a fully enfranchised woman.

"Women and desire" has become a hot topic in sex therapy today and, in Chapter 13, we will begin to reconceptualize "desire" and understand more deeply what separates women from their innate sense of desire. Chapter 14 covers the meaning, importance, and difficulties related to orgasm. Chapter 15 introduces my concept of Eros-inhibiting archetypes and how they interfere with women's eroticism. In Chapter 16, we look at the impact of trauma on a woman's sexual formation and how the Inner Children who carry this trauma continue to have an impact on a woman's ability to express her Aphrodite Self.

Chapter 17 explores some of the more infamous archetypes of sexuality and what happens when Aphrodite becomes wounded. Chapter 18 looks at women's relationship to their bodies and provides a case history that illustrates that it is the archetypal energy a woman carries that creates her allure. Chapter 19 talks about women's sexuality at midlife and beyond. Chapter 20 looks at the contrast between the icon of the Porn Star and the archetype of the Sexual Priestess.

Chapter 21 defines what a Sexually Empowered Woman really is and offers important foundations for becoming one. It also offers an archetypal perspective on effective sexual communication. Chapter 22 looks at relationships, with each partner housing an inner cast of characters, and many possible bonding patterns. In that chapter, we also look at what long-term partners say about "optimal" sexuality. Chapter 23, the final chapter, describes the woman who has entered the realm of Aphrodite, is on the journey of Sexual Individuation™, and is experiencing the life-giving energy of Aphrodite, enriching and infusing all areas of her life.

BIBLIOGRAPHY

Daniluk, J. (1998) *Women's Sexuality Across the Life Span: Challenging Myths, Creating Meanings*. New York: Guilford.

Ellison, C. (2000) *Women's Sexualities: Generations of Women Share Intimate Secrets of Sexual Self-Acceptance*. Oakland, CA: New Harbinger. www.womenssexualities.com

Ellison, C. (2001) Intimacy-Based Sex Therapy: Sexual Choreography. In P. Kleinplatz (Ed.) *New Directions in Sex Therapy: Innovations and Alternatives* (pp. 163–184). New York: Routledge.

Ellison, C. (2012) Sexual Choreography: "Am I Enjoying This Right Now?" Not "How Am I Doing?" In P. Kleinplatz (Ed.) *New Directions in Sex Therapy: Innovations and Alternatives* (2nd ed., pp. 141–160). New York: Routledge.

Goodwach, R. (2005a) Sex Therapy: Historical Evolution, Current Practice. Part 1. *Australian and New Zealand Journal of Family Therapy*, 26, 3, 155–164.

Goodwach, R. (2005b) Sex Therapy: Historical Evolution, Current Practice. Part 2. *Australian and New Zealand Journal of Family Therapy*, 26, 3, 178–183.

Kaschak E., & Tiefer, L. (Eds.) (2001) *The New View of Women's Sexual Problems*. New York: Haworth.

Kleinplatz, P. (2001) A Critique of the Goals of Sex Therapy, or the Hazards of Safer Sex. In P. Kleinplatz (Ed.) *New Directions in Sex Therapy: Innovations and Alternatives* (pp. 109–131). Philadelphia, PA: Brunner-Routledge.

Kleinplatz, P. (Ed.) (2012) *New Directions in Sex Therapy: Innovations and Alternatives* (2nd ed.). New York: Routledge.

Leiblum, S. (Ed.) (2010) *Treating Sexual Desire Disorders: A Clinical Casebook*. New York: Guilford.

Leiblum, S., & Rosen, R. (Eds.) (2000) *Principles and Practice of Sex Therapy*. New York: Guilford.

Morin, J. (1995) *The Erotic Mind: Unlocking the Inner Sources of Sexual Passion and Fulfillment*. New York: Harper Perennial.

Ogden, G. (2006) *The Heart and Soul of Sex: Making the ISIS Connection*. Boston: Trumpeter.

Ogden, G. (2008) *Return of Desire: A Guide to Rediscovering Your Sexual Passion*. Boston: Trumpeter.

Ogden, G. (2013) *Expanding the Practice of Sex Therapy: An Integrative Model for Exploring Desire and Intimacy*. New York: Routledge.

Perel, E. (2007) *Mating in Captivity*. New York: Harper.

Perel, E. (2010) The Double Flame: Reconciling Intimacy and Sexuality, Reviving Desire. In S. Leiblum (Ed.) *Treating Sexual Desire Disorders: A Clinical Casebook* (pp. 23–43). New York: Guilford.

Schnarch, D. (2009) *Intimacy & Desire: Awaken the Passion in Your Relationship.* New York: Beaufort.

Snell, W., Fischer, T., & Walters, A. (1993) The Multidimensional Sexuality Questionnaire: An Objective Self-Report Measure of Psychological Tendencies Associated With Human Sexuality. *Annals of Sex Research, 6,* 27–55.

Snell, W. E., Jr. (Ed.) (2001a) *New Directions in the Psychology of Human Sexuality: Research and Theory.* Cape Girardeau, MO: Snell. http://cstl-cla.semo.edu/snell/ books/sexuality/sexuality.htm

Snell, W. (2001b) Multidimensional Sexual Self-Concept Questionaire. In Fisher et al.'s (Eds.) *Handbook of Sexuality-Related Measures* (pp. 537–540). New York: Routledge.

Wakefield, C. (2012) *Negotiating the Inner Peace Treaty: Becoming the Person You Were Born to Be.* Bloomington, IN: Balboa.

Part I

History and Backstory

Sexology and Jungian
Psychology—Strange Bedfellows

Chapter 1

ANCIENT HISTORY AND NEW VIEWS

"Your body knows its heritage and its rightful need and it will not be deceived."

Kahlil Gibran

In Ancient Times, Sexuality Was Revered

There was a time in antiquity when women's bodies were viewed as divine vessels with magical powers that corresponded with the rhythms of the moon. During her moon cycle, a woman's body could bleed without dying. A woman's body brought life into being, and then sustained that life with the milk of her breast. The nearness of a woman's body could cause a man's sexual organ to rise, and her capacity to give and experience pleasure had no limit (Eisler, 1996). There was a time when sexuality was revered as a mystery and viewed as a source of cleansing, having magical powers to heal. Sexuality could elevate consciousness, even enlighten. Sexual union with a temple priestess was seen as having the power to recivilize, reinstate humanity, heal the wounds of war, and make men whole. From what we know about these prepatriarchal times, there were few restrictions around women's sexual expression. Sex was not burdened with territoriality or shame. Children born during that time were considered a gift of the Divine Mother rather than the property of a particular man. Children were raised and cared for by the community at large and no child was considered illegitimate (Eisler, 1996; Gimbutas & Dexter, 1999; Qualls-Corbett, 1988; Savage, 1999).

As the monotheistic religions gained supremacy, our deep connection with the Great Mother was undermined and made taboo. The concept of property became established, and women became part of that property system. The right of sexual access to women's bodies was considered a reward for conquering warriors and for those who held power. As this happened, women's sexuality became increasingly conscripted, and over time, the rights of women to determine anything in their own lives was abolished. The lineage line became increasingly important for the inheritance of property. Virginity and sole sexual fidelity (for the woman, not the man) gave men the assurance that their fortune was passing to a child of their own bloodline. Heavy punishments were enacted for the woman who dared stray outside the dominion of her father's governance, and then her husband's. By the time the Greeks began to record their epic stories, women and their bodies had been conquested and demoted from sacred chalice to male property for the purposes of either procreation or recreation.

The church became a powerful force in the subjugation of sexuality, the denigration of the body, and the distrust of all things instinctual. Pleasure for the sake of pleasure alone became vilified and strictly forbidden. Virginity became elevated to the highest state and women were split into two categories, Madonna (exemplified in the celibate nun) and Whore. Riane Eisler's (1996) *Sacred Pleasure* is a master work that provides a sweeping history of the cultural, economic, and religious forces that have shaped the fear and prohibition of pleasure and conscripted women's sexuality. Another excellent treatise on our fear of the body and the senses is *Coming to Our Senses*, by social philosopher Morris Berman (1990).

Philosopher and social theorist Michel Foucault (1990a, 1990b) has written definitive works on the social control of sexuality and pleasure. He emphasizes that pleasure must be discouraged in a society where efficiency and productivity hold the highest value. St. Augustine formulated the theology of "original sin," and named woman as entirely responsible for the fall of man. Sexuality was deemed a necessary evil, only allowable for the purpose of procreation. During the middle ages, women were viewed as decidedly corrupt and filled with insatiable lust, which needed to be strictly controlled. Celibacy and the cloistered monastery became a place of protection from these dangerous temptresses.

The promotion of desexualized purity (even for married women), reached its height of idealization in the Victorian period. During that time, no decent woman would express any interest in sexual pleasure. Amid their placid, sedentary lives, many women suffered from a malady called "hysteria." The symptoms were thought to be caused by a "wandering uterus." The cure became wildly popular among respectable Victorian women. It involved a manipulation of the genitals until "paroxysm" was achieved. The waiting rooms of the doctors who practiced this cure were filled to capacity. During this same period, there was a growth of prostitution among the working class, whose clientele consisted of wealthy Victorian men (Maines, 1999; Slick, 2007).

THE BIRTH OF SEXOLOGY

Sexuality has been a central part of our human experience since the dawn of time. When it comes to sex, we all speak the same universal language as we did at the dawn of time: moans, grunts, gasps, laughter, tears, panting, screams, and sighs. Sexuality is laced with archetypal themes, and the joys and sorrows related to sex are a central part of the human story. Sex has always been a focus of curiosity, confusion, conflict, and conversation. It has been studied by philosophers, theologians, scientists, doctors, artists, and poets, who have pondered it from every conceivable direction.

The scientific study of human sexuality and sexual dysfunction became established in the mid-1800s. The most significant work of that era was Richard von Krafft-Ebing's *Psychopathia Sexualis*, published in 1886. Havelock Ellis was another important sexologist who published a six-volume series in 1936 entitled *Studies in the Psychology of Sex*. Radical for his time, Ellis's work asserted that women were sexual beings who had sexual needs and desires just like men (Berman, Berman, & Bumiller, 2005). Margaret Sanger forwarded women's sexual freedom and opened the first clinic to disseminate information about what she called "birth control." She did this in an era when it was illegal to do so and was arrested for violating "indecency" laws, which only served to escalate public awareness regarding ways in which women could choose whether to become mothers. The work of Ellis and Sanger began a pendulum swing away from the virtuous, asexual Victorian Woman, as people began to consider that women might have sex for the purpose of pleasure. In the 1950s, Alfred Kinsey conducted face-to-face interviews with 12,000 people and compiled a massive amount of data about the diversity and frequency of human sexual behaviors, which showed that the private behaviors of ordinary Americans was significantly different from the publicly promoted "norms" (Berman et al., 2005; Masters, Johnson, & Kolodny, 1995).

Freud

Sigmund Freud entered the scene towards the end of the Victorian era and began to publish works related to sexuality in the early 1900s. His ideas regarding psychosexual development continue to have vast influence on psychological theory today. He believed that the sexual drive (libido) was the primal motivating force that underlies all of life (albeit largely unconscious). Sexual instincts were always seeking gratification, and the conscious "ego" and the regulating "super-ego" served to redirect these animalistic lower drives ("id") into civilized outlets. The inner tension created by this conflict was always seeking discharge. When repressed, it produced neurosis, when sublimated (redirected), it led to the creation of great art and civilization (Stein, 1998).

Freud was a voice in the wilderness of suppression advocating pleasure as an important component of life. He made it possible to have open conversations about sex, but he also did significant sexual disservice to women. First, there was his theory of penis envy. He then generated a powerful mythology regarding what he considered the "mature" and "immature" orgasm. With a lack of knowledge regarding female anatomy, he considered the clitoris to be the immature focus of sexual pleasure, which would be abandoned by healthy adult women, when they shifted their interest to the "proper organ of receptivity," the vagina, and graduate into the "mature" vaginal orgasm. Freud engendered untold misery for two generations of women, who thought they were neurotic or repressed because they could not achieve an orgasm through intercourse alone. Unfortunately, there are still women who suffer under this false paradigm even though William Masters and Virginia Johnson established that *all orgasms originate through either direct or indirect clitoral stimulation* (Berman et al., 2005), and Shere Hite's (1976) research showed that only about one third of women ever reach orgasm through simple intercourse alone.

The Sexual Self

In 1973, John Gagnon and William Simon wrote a seminal text that began to explore the phenomenon of the Sexual Self as a central building block of our identity. The Sexual Self is socially constructed through the interaction of socialization and sexual experiences. Although sex involves instinctual drives, it also involves the enactment of a complex set of cultural meanings, which Gagnon and Simon referred to as "sexual scripts." Our sexuality is governed by these elaborate scripts, which tell us what to do, who the actors are, what part we play, and why, how, and when the events should unfold. Sexual scripts have a performance aspect (governing the sequence and acts of sexual behavior) and a cognitive aspect (shaping thoughts, fantasies, and attitudes). Sexual scripts define what is normal, functional, moral, and acceptable. They are internalized from our early environment and continue to be shaped by media, culture, religion, peer group, and life experiences. Scripts operate on three levels: cultural (social), interpersonal, and intrapsychic (Gagnon & Simon, 1973; Kimmel, 2007).

THE SEXUAL REVOLUTION

The "sexual revolution" of the 1960s turned the virtuous sexual script on its head. For the first time in patriarchal history, women were encouraged to experience pleasure and to be sexually free. Although this released women from sexually oppressive scripts of the past, it did not help all women to become more sexually empowered. It did not teach women how to say no to unsafe sex (physically, emotionally, and spiritually), and it did not help women make more discerning choices about who they would "freely" share their precious bodies with.

Naomi Wolf (1997) writes about her journey into adulthood during the sexual revolution and how she navigated the dicey line between Prude and Slut. She suffered continually with an anxious awareness that winding up on the wrong side of that hard-to-discern line would be costly. It was a confusing time.

Shere Hite (1993) suggests that the sexual revolution merely put pressure on women to have more of the same kind of sex, rather than helping them redefine what kind of sex they really want to have. Sex is strongly intertwined with economic provision and Hite emphasizes that "you cannot decree women to be sexually free when they are not economically free; to do so is to put them into a more vulnerable position than ever, and make them into a form of easily available common property" (p. 91).

Bernard Apfelbaum (1995) cites an ironic downside of the sexual revolution, "response anxiety." Women now feel pressure to respond

17

positively (rather than authentically) to whatever a partner is doing, and return the favor, rather than just receive. This has created a whole new form of performance anxiety. "Producing" an orgasm has become the "gold standard" of a man's sexual skills, and many women admit to faking or amplifying their orgasmic response in an effort to validate their man's sexual skills or simply to end the effort. If orgasm is the only dimension of sexuality a woman knows, then not having one can be frustrating. If the woman has never had an orgasm, it becomes an elusive experience (Cass, 2007) that she feels deprived of, or sexually inferior about. Although the ability to have an orgasm is important to women, it is not the be-all, end-all of sexual experience, and having an orgasm does not necessarily define women's most meaningful sexual and erotic memories (Kleinplatz et al., 2009; Ogden, 2006).

SEX IN THE 21ST CENTURY

Very few people have been given any useful direction for harnessing the power of primordial instincts. Instead, our instinctual lives have been shamed and condemned. For centuries, the only sex education that people had was an exhortation towards denial and prudence. The result of this is to send our instincts into the shadow lands, where they become like feral animals that begin to stalk us and break out in distorted ways.

Currently, in the 21st century, sex is everywhere. Our media-oriented culture is filled with images and story lines that tell women they *should* be sexual. Entire sections of bookstores are devoted to sexual information and how to have the hottest, best sex ever. Sexually explicit websites pervade the Internet along with sites to facilitate private hook-ups for every conceivable sexual fantasy or desire. Virtual worlds such as Second Life allow people to create characters of their own design, who can explore the outer reaches of sexual imagination online.

Amid this sexual free-for-all, the number one presenting complaint of women in sex therapy is a lack of sexual desire. An increasing number of men are coming to sex therapy because they don't know how to relate or cannot become aroused in the presence of a *real* woman. There is a disturbing lack of awareness that real women are not porn stars (Maltz & Maltz, 2010).

Under the veneer of our pleasure-promoting society, we still have a lot of anxiety around pleasure. People are particularly at a loss regarding how to make *real-time intimate connections* (Resnick, 1997, 2012). Women continue to hear the vague whisperings of stern, tight-laced ancestors, whispering in the background, warning of "the road to ruin." It is difficult for women to find the Goldilocks zone, where their "porridge" is not too hot, not too cold, but just right.

BIBLIOGRAPHY

Apfelbaum, B. (1995) Masters and Johnson Revisited: A Case of Desire Disparity. In R. Rosen & S. Leiblum (Eds.) *Case Studies in Sex Therapy* (pp. 23–45). New York: Guilford.

Berman, M. (1990) *Coming to Our Senses: Body and Spirit in the Hidden History of the West*. New York: Bantam.

Berman, J., Berman, L., & Bumiller, E. (2005) *For Women Only: A Revolutionary Guide to Reclaiming Your Sex Life* (2nd ed.). New York: Henry Holt.

Cass, V. (2007) *The Elusive Orgasm*. Cambridge, MA: Da Capo.

Eisler, R. (1996) *Sacred Pleasure: Sex, Myth, and the Politics of the Body—New Paths to Power and Love*. San Francisco: HarperCollins.

Foucault, M. (1990a) *The History of Sexuality: Vol. 1, An Introduction*. New York: Vintage. (Originally published in 1978 through Random House)

Foucault, M. (1990b) *The Use of Pleasure: Vol. 2, The History of Sexuality*. New York: Vintage. (Originally published in 1985 through Random House)

Gagnon, J., & Simon, W. (1973) *Sexual Conduct: The Social Sources of Human Sexuality*. Chicago: Aldine.

Gimbutas, M., & Dexter, M. (1999) *The Living Goddesses*. Berkeley and Los Angeles: University of California Press.

Hite, S. (1976) *The Hite Report: A Nationwide Study of Female Sexuality*. New York: Seven Stories.

Hite, S. (1993) *Women as Revolutionary Agents of Change: The Hite Reports and Beyond*. Madison: University of Wisconsin Press.

Kimmel, M. (Ed.) (2007) *The Sexual Self: The Construction of Sexual Scripts*. Nashville, TN: Vanderbilt University Press.

Kleinplatz, P., Menard, A. D., Paquet, M., Paradis, N., Campblee, M., Zuccarino, D., & Mehak, L. (2009) The Components of Optimal Sexuality: A Portrait of 'Great Sex.' *Canadian Journal of Human Sexuality, 18*, 1–2, 1–13.

Maines, R. (1999) *The Technology of Orgasm*. Baltimore, MD: The Johns Hopkins University Press.

Maltz, W., & Maltz, L. (2010) *The Porn Trap: The Essential Guide to Overcoming Problems Caused by Pornography*. New York: Harper.

Masters, W., Johnson, V., & Kolodny, R. (1995) *Human Sexuality* (5th ed.). New York: HarperCollins College Publishers.

Ogden, G. (2006) *The Heart and Soul of Sex: Making the ISIS Connection*. Boston: Trumpeter.

Qualls-Corbett, N. (1988) *The Sacred Prostitute: Eternal Aspect of the Feminine*. Toronto, ON: Inner City.

Resnick, S. (1997) *The Pleasure Zone: Why We Resist Good Feelings and How to Let Go and Be Happy*. Berkeley, CA: Conari.

Resnick, S. (2012) *The Heart of Desire: Keys to the Pleasures of Love*. Hoboken, NJ: Wiley and Sons.

Savage, L. (1999) *Reclaiming Goddess Sexuality: The Power of the Feminine Way*. Carlsbad, CA: Hay House.

Slick, W. (Director) (2007) *Passion & Power: The Technology of Orgasm* [DVD]. US: Wabi Sabi Productions.

Stein, M. (1998) *Transformation: Emergence of the Self*. College Station: Texas A&M University Press.

Wolf, N. (1997) *Promiscuities: The Secret Struggle for Womanhood*. New York: Random House.

CHAPTER 2

WHO IS "THE SEXUAL WOMAN?"

"The body is like the ocean, rich with hidden treasures."

Mirabai

JOYFUL EMBODIMENT—A WOMAN'S BIRTHRIGHT

I am at the beach with Susie and her three girls. The four-year-old is twirling, eyes closed, smiling, her face raised to the sun. The seven-year-old is dripping wet sand onto the turret tower of her sandcastle. The ten-year-old is wading out into the waves, squealing as the cold water hits her body. They are reveling in their senses, carefree, and joyfully embodied. This is a woman's birthright. Down the beach is an older woman who is just coming out of the water after a swim. She looks to be in her seventies. She looks healthy and vibrant, and I observe her walking, hips swinging easily. She stops to watch the little girls playing and smiles. We exchange a look of sweet reminiscence.

Women are sensual creatures. We love beautiful surroundings filled with pleasing colors and textures. We love bouquets of bright flowers, the flicker of firelight, the taste of delicious food, and the creamy texture of ice cream. We love soft fabric on our skin, the fragrance of candles, and the sensation of slipping into warm, bubbly, scented bath water. Our natural inclination is to connect. We savor the breathless anticipation of a lover's soft kiss and the touch of loving hands caressing our bodies. We will seek out skin-to-skin contact with a lover who appreciates and understands us and is attuned to our needs and desires. We enjoy exchanging pleasure, and when we feel safe and free, we express a wide range of emotions through our bodies. All this is our natural heritage, unless it has been toxified. Oh, that we could remain in that state of bliss that came so naturally when we were little girls on the beach, but somewhere along the line, we get very self-conscious about our bodies and become separated from this birthright of joyful sensuality.

Sexual Identity—What Defines the "Sexual Woman?"

The phrase "sexual identity" has most often been associated with *partner preference*. In recent years, the spectrum of sexual *identities* has become so numerous that we no longer have enough initials to include them (e.g., LGBTQ). We are coming to understand that sexual identity is unique to the individual and that we cannot confine it to the boundaries of fixed categories (Schwartz & Rutter, 1998). A woman's sexuality shifts and changes over the course of her lifetime in response to different situations and partners. The construct of "sexual fluidity" is becoming part of our cultural lexicon, as we begin to acknowledge the uniqueness of individual sexuality and a wide spectrum of identities, templates, desires, and patterns of expression (Diamond, 2008).

In 1973, Gagnon and Simon created the construct of the Sexual Self. In 1994, Andersen and Cyranoski conducted research in which they asked women to describe the positive qualities of "the sexual woman." The words that women used were: arousable, stimulating, passionate, feeling, warm, loving, romantic, direct, experienced, straightforward, revealing, open minded, and uninhibited. The sexual woman is also "one who experiences passionate and romantic emotions and who evidences a behavioral openness to sexual experiences, romantic experiences, or both; such a woman suffers little from embarrassment or conservatism regarding sexuality" (p. 1087). Not surprisingly, women who claimed the description of "sexual woman" had greater levels of satisfaction and enjoyment in their sexual lives. The same group was asked to describe the "non-sexual woman." She was described as embarrassed, conservative, cautious, self-conscious, timid, cold, inexperienced, and prudent. Women who describe themselves in this way were less romantic and had fewer passionate emotions. They were also less likely to attempt to engage in romantic or sexual relationships.

Over the years, I have collected more words to describe the qualities of a sexually empowered, sexually Self-claiming woman. She is assertive, imaginative, responsive, authentic, soulful, rapturous, free, present, bold, embodied, passionate, compassionate, playful, magnetic, intuitive, radiant, erotic, expressive, spontaneous, curious, adventurous, courageous, creative, having a sense of humor, generous, confident, able to go deep, able to negotiate, warm, inviting, intimate, and comfortable in her body. These are Luminous Women (Wakefield, 2009), in touch with their Aphrodite energy. These women have a greater sense of self-esteem and sexual agency. Their eyes are alive, and they have a particular sparkle. Like Aphrodite, they understand themselves as erotic beings and as creative, inspired women who express their sensuality in their loving and in their living.

WOMEN AS SEXUAL BEINGS ACROSS THE LIFESPAN

Women are sexual beings across the lifespan, and a woman's sexuality is a continually evolving, developmental process. As a woman enters every era of her life, her sexuality must be repeatedly redefined.

Our sense of being happily embodied and comfortable with sexuality begins from the early days of infancy. Sexuality and a capacity for closeness is greatly affected by our early interactions with caregivers and the safety we felt in early attachments (Cozolino, 2006; Poole Heller, 2008; Siegel, 1999). If a girl is raised in an environment that communicates a positive view of her body and budding sexuality, if she is given a positive frame for menarche (first menstruation) and puberty, some good sexual education, including communication skills, and if she has a positive sexual initiation with a caring partner (awkwardness allowed), her transition into adult sexuality should be fairly positive and smooth. If she values herself and her sexuality, she will be more likely to say no to unsafe sex. She will feel deserving of love, pleasure, and respect, and her choice of partners will be more discerning. If she chooses to marry and have children, she will adjust to family life, balancing caring for others with caring for herself, continuing to value her sexuality throughout family life into her postmenopausal years and on into later life (Daniluk, 1998; Foley, Kope, & Sugrue, 2012).

The prevalence of unaddressed sexual abuse, violence, and trauma in this culture interfere significantly with a woman's positive sexual formation. Trauma shapes identity. It leaves an indelible mark on how a woman values herself, whether she experiences others as safe or threatening, and how she views her place in the world. There is also a subtle message in the culture that women who are raped or sexually abused as children somehow "asked for it." Women pick up the message that to be sexually empowered or sexually curious is dangerous (Levine, 2010; McCormick, 1994; Pesso, 2013).

WHO DO YOU THINK YOU ARE?—ATTENDING TO THE SEXUAL SELF

Many women have never explored themselves as sexual beings. They have never defined or attended to their Sexual Self (Bennet & Holczer, 2010; Foley et al., 2012). These women may not even think of themselves as sexual beings, certainly not in their own right. Most women view sexuality as something that takes place in a relationship. They are *sexual responders, not initiators*. In their orientation toward pleasing others, women often fail to notice their individual arousal templates and pleasure maps.[1] Some women are fortunate because they pick partners who are good love matches, attuned to them, and interested in the process of discovery that makes for a great sexual relationship. Even women who are enjoying a positive sexual experience may have never thought about the distinct qualities they embody in their sexuality, their unique *sexual essence*.

As a sex therapist, I find it amazing how few women really understand their sexual anatomy or have ever looked at their genitals in a mirror, to actually see what is "down there." They do not understand how their bodies respond or know anything about the function of arousal or how orgasms actually occur. It is easy for them to pathologize themselves as "sexually dysfunctional." Because of this lack of sexual knowledge, the Kinsey Institute has estimated that one in ten women have never had an orgasm (Reinisch, 1991).

SEXUALITY AS AN INTEGRATION OF HEART, MIND, BODY, AND SPIRIT

Women's fight for their own sexual pleasure was an important aspect of the women's movement, but having an orgasm does not mean a woman is having "great sex." In the late 1990s, Ogden (2006, 2008, 2013) began a groundbreaking research project, "Integrating Sexuality and Spirituality

(ISIS)," that diverged from counting the number of times a woman had sex, or how often she had an orgasm, and began to explore the *meaning* that sex held for women. The women in Ogden's research began to talk about the *multidimensionality* of great sexual experiences. Out of this research, Ogden developed the "ISIS wheel of sexual integration," which explores dimensions of heart, mind, body, and spirit. Ogden also looks into the rich narratives and symbolic meaning that women bring to their sexuality as ultimate determinants of arousal and satisfaction beyond the genital matrix. Women love orgasms, but women also want intellectual stimulation, eye contact, partner exchanges of self-disclosure, and whole-body sensuality.

Why Do Women Have Sex?

If we are to understand the scope of women's sexuality, we need to look at sexual motivation. Meston and Buss's (2009) research showed that the primary motivations for women to have sex are to express love, to seek connection, and to provide comfort and nurturance. Women also have sex to feel valued, boost their egos, and to ensure themselves that they are still appealing. They have sex out of duty and because they feel guilty. Women also have sex to capture a mate (or to "poach" someone else's). Women have sex to "mate-guard," hoping that a partner satisfied at home will not seek satisfaction elsewhere. Women have sex for a sense of adventure. Just like men, they get curious about sex with another partner, wondering what it would be like with someone else, wondering if they would respond differently or learn something new. On the darker side, women engage in sex for revenge or to break up a relationship (their own, or someone else's). They have sex as a means of "trading up," to capture a man they view as superior to their current catch. Although women are reticent to discuss sex in such "crass" terms, women barter sex for goods and services, everything from household repairs, specialized assistance, the go-ahead to spend money on a large purchase, or the promise of career advancement. Women sometimes have sex when what they really want is companionship for an evening, or just a nice restaurant meal. Women marry and have sex with men they don't particularly like in exchange for financial security, or a lifestyle, which no one considers prostitution, whereas the direct exchange of money for sex will get a woman thrown in jail (while the "john" goes free).

What Do Women Really Want?

Sex researchers Kleinplatz et al. (2009) conducted a research project in which they interviewed long-term couples who were still having what she calls "optimal sex." The participants represented a variety of sexual orientations and sexual arousal templates but, regardless of this, their answers were similar. The kind of sex described in this research mirrors the kind of sex that women in my practice long for, if they only knew how to make it happen. What these researchers found was that wonderful sex begins with being fully embodied, in the present moment, connected, and in sync with another person. There is interpersonal risk-taking, permission to explore, and a sense of fun. Partners are able to be transparent, authentic, and vulnerable, and can surrender themselves into the experience. All of this leads to erotic intimacy and a sense of bliss and peace. This kind of sex can open up the realms of transcendence, which results in experiences of healing and transformation. It is important to note that nowhere in this study did the researchers find that the participants had to have perfect bodies, or know a lot of exotic sexual positions, or have an amazing sexual skill set. Age, illness, or disability did not preclude the achievement of these experiences, and orgasm, although a frequent outcome, was not considered the most important factor.

Note

1 John Money (1993) was the first to discuss how we each have a highly individual arousal template, which he referred to as a "love map."

Bibliography

Andersen, B., & Cyranowski, J. (1994) Women's Sexual Self-Schema. *Journal of Personality and Social Psychology, 67*, 6, 1079–1100.

Bennet, L., & Holczer, G. (2010) *Finding and Revealing Your Sexual Self: A Guide to Communicating About Sex*. Lanham, MD: Rowman & Littlefield.

Cozolino, L. (2006) *The Neuroscience of Human Relationships: Attachment and the Developing Social Brain*. New York: W. W Norton.

Daniluk, J. (1998) *Women's Sexuality Across the Life Span: Challenging Myths, Creating Meanings*. New York: Guilford.

Diamond, L. (2008) *Sexual Fluidity: Understanding Women's Love and Desire*. Boston: First Harvard University Press.

Foley, S., Kope, S., & Sugrue, D. (2012) *Sex Matters for Women: A Complete Guide to Taking Care of Your Sexual Self*. New York: Guilford.

Gagnon, J., & Simon, W. (1973) *Sexual Conduct: The Social Sources of Human Sexuality*. Chicago: Aldine.

Kleinplatz, P., Menard, A. D., Paquet, M., Paradis, N., Campblee, M., Zuccarino, D., & Mehak, L. (2009) The Components of Optimal Sexuality: A Portrait of 'Great Sex.' *Canadian Journal of Human Sexuality, 18*, 1–2, 1–13.

Levine, P. (2010) *In an Unspoken Voice: How the Body Releases Trauma and Restores Goodness*. Berkeley, CA: North Atlantic.

McCormick, N. (1994) *Sexual Salvation: Affirming Women's Sexual Rights and Pleasures*. Westport, CT: Praeger.

Meston, C., & Buss, D. (2009) *Why Women Have Sex: Understanding Sexual Motivations—From Adventure to Revenge (and Everything in Between)*. New York: Times Books.

Money, J. (1993) *Lovemaps*. Buffalo, New York: Prometheus Books.

Ogden, G. (2006) *The Heart and Soul of Sex: Making the ISIS Connection*. Boston: Trumpeter.

Ogden, G. (2008) *Return of Desire: A Guide to Rediscovering Your Sexual Passion*. Boston: Trumpeter.

Ogden, G. (2013) *Expanding the Practice of Sex Therapy: An Integrative Model for Exploring Desire and Intimacy*. New York: Routledge.

Pesso, A. (2013) *Presentations & Lectures by Albert Pesso on Pesso Boyden System Psychomotor Therapy (1984–2012)*. Kindle edition.

Poole Heller, D. (2008) *Healing Early Attachment Wounds: The Dynamic Attachment Re-patterning Experience-Module 1* [manual]. Louisville, CO: Author.

Reinisch, J. M. (1991) *The Kinsey Institute New Report on Sex: What You Must Know to Be Sexually Literate*. New York: St. Martin's Press.

Schwartz, P., & Rutter, V. (1998) *The Gender of Sexuality*. Thousand Oaks, CA: Pine Forge.

Siegel, D. (1999) *The Developing Mind: How Relationships and the Brain Interact to Shape Who We Are*. New York: Guilford.

Wakefield, C. (2009) *What Is a Luminous Woman®?* http://www.chelseawakefield.com/programs/the-luminous-woman/

CHAPTER 3

MASTERS AND JOHNSON
AND BEYOND

"One of the curious elements of sexual myths is that they are so easily
believed, despite the lack of evidence to substantiate their existence . . .
worst of all, people who latch onto myths about sex often use them
as excuses for giving up on changing their sex lives for the better."

Masters, Johnson, and Kolodny (1982, pp. 450–451)

Before I outline my own archetypal approach to sex therapy (in Part
II), providing some brief backstory will be helpful. This information
will be familiar to sex therapists, but it was not familiar to me before
I entered the field. Therefore, I offer it to practitioners and others who
are beginning to learn more about the history of sexology. This chapter
also describes some of the new viewpoints and innovative practices in
sexology and how I am aligning myself with them.

THE MASTERS AND JOHNSON ERA

The field we now call "sex therapy" began with the pioneering efforts of
William Masters and Virginia Johnson (1966, 1970). Masters and Johnson conducted the first "in vivo" laboratory study of what actually happens to the body during sex, which was considered radical research for its
time. Their research was particularly helpful in dispelling a lot of myths
about sexuality, including Freud's unenlightened perspective on the
"mature" vaginal orgasm versus the "immature" clitoral orgasm. Masters

and Johnson's research clarified that *all* orgasms are ultimately sourced from direct or indirect clitoral stimulation. Their treatment approach was female friendly, effective, and affordable for the average American.

In 1976, Shere Hite published the results of her massive research project on female sexuality in *The Hite Report* (over 48 million copies sold worldwide). Rather than asking women *if* they reached orgasm, she asked them *how*. Her research showed that only about one-third of women achieved orgasm through intercourse alone. The rest required some form of additional stimulation. The same statistic holds true today (Cass, 2007; Foley, Kope, & Sugrue, 2012).

Masters and Johnson (1966, 1970; Masters, Johnson, & Koldony, 1982) provided sex education for the masses in an era where accurate information was difficult to obtain. Prior to that time, "normal, decent people" did not talk about sex, even in intimate relationships. Most people assumed that sex was supposed to "just happen" and a lack of awareness regarding sexual anatomy and the human sexual response cycle (excitement, plateau, orgasm, and resolution), led to many disappointing experiences. Many women found sex uncomfortable, even painful. Orgasm was a mystery. Sex was viewed as an obligatory duty. Most people with sexual problems suffered in ignorance and silence or avoided sex altogether. Masters and Johnson stabilized and enriched many relationships and significantly reduced the collective sexual anxiety that existed in a repressive society.

The most famous exercise of Masters and Johnson (1970), which is still in use today, is Sensate Focus. This exercise is designed to help people move out of "spectatoring," the disembodied watching and self-critical judging that so many people engage in during sex. This series of progressive "non-demand" touching exercises takes the pressure off pleasing or performing and steers people away from the "target zones" of sex. It encourages people to move out of their heads and into their senses to become more present as they experience touching and being touched. Sensate Focus is also used to improve sexual communication and relax rigid sexual scripts. Iasenza (2010) suggests that sensate focus can be reframed as a mindfulness practice. She asks clients to engage their Observer (rather than the critical Spectator) in order to become aware of their thoughts, feelings, body sensation, and breathing while they are touching.

Helen Singer Kaplan (1974, 1979, 1983) was another significant sex therapist during the Masters and Johnson period. She adopted many of their ideas, but unlike Masters and Johnson, who screened out troubled couples, Kaplan worked with couples who were having interpersonal difficulties. Kaplan's writing describes how toxic couple dynamics interfere with sex therapy goals. She advocated deeper psychodynamic work with troubled couples and individuals in order for treatment to proceed successfully. Kaplan offered her own triphasic sexual response model of desire, arousal, and orgasm. Some of her most important work was focused on the role of *desire*. Kaplan wrote a series of excellent sex therapy books and trained hundreds of sex therapists.

Kaplan (1983) introduced an important practice called the "Sexual Status Exam" (I dislike this term and prefer to think of this practice as an "Intimate Inquiry"). In an Intimate Inquiry, the sex therapist asks the client to describe a recent sexual encounter in detail, looking at what transpired during each stage of the sexual response cycle (including the invitation into sexual activity), noting how each partner is relating to the other, and bringing to light how *outer behaviors are intersecting with inner responses*. Microtracking an encounter can help the practitioner to discover the exact places where things go "off the rails," and to explore more deeply what happened there. (In my approach to sex therapy, I am also looking at the archetypal bonding patterns between the two partners.)

The major components of sex therapy are permission giving, education, normalizing individual desires, reducing shame, and encouraging exploration of needs, fears, desires, and expectations through improved communication and touch. Sex therapists try to ascertain problems that may be caused by health and hormonal issues and refer people for medical evaluations. They dispel unrealistic myths about sexual performance and rework inhibiting scripts. Sex therapists offer education and interventions that address specific difficulties like early ejaculation or problems with reaching orgasm (anorgasmia). They also coach clients in skill sets that enable them to become more satisfied and sensitive lovers (Goodwach, 2005a, 2005b; Kaplan, 1974, 1979; Kleinplatz, 2001, 2012; Leiblum & Rosen, 2000; Masters et al., 1982).

AASECT (American Association of Sexuality Educators, Counselors and Therapists) is the primary certifying body for sex therapists and educators, with a strict code of ethics and professional qualification standards.[1] AASECT continues to work toward educating the public about what sex therapists do, and seeks to bring the field into greater legitimacy (for example, sex therapy is a clothing-on talk therapy). An

AASECT-certified sex therapist must hold a medical or mental health license, which will prohibit sexual contact. AASECT also advocates for a number of sexual health, sex education, and sexual justice issues.

How Women Have Been Framed

Over the years, sexual disorders and dysfunction have been defined and redefined by the *Diagnostic and Statistical Manual of Mental Disorders* (American Psychiatric Association, 2013), which is commonly referred to as the "DSM." Although sexual health is certainly important, the increased medicalization of the field has reinforced a perspective that sex is something we *do* and that *function*, as defined by the *DSM*, is the focus of sex therapy. Many feminist sexologists feel that women have been "framed" by these definitions, and that the *DSM* pathologizes women in unfair ways. Basson et al. (2003), Ellison (2000, 2012), Kleinplatz (2001, 2012), McCormick (1994), Ogden (2006, 2008, 2013), and Tiefer (2004, 2012) have all written about the need to reconceptualize women's sexuality in a way that acknowledges the relational, sociocultural, and situational realities of women's lives. These factors are not considered in the *DSM* diagnostic criteria, but they affect women's sexual attitudes, feelings, and "function" across the lifespan. Another objection to the *DSM* standard of "functional sex" is that it focuses on penetrative intercourse leading to the "production of orgasms." This focus marginalizes meaningful sexuality for those who do not consider penetrative intercourse important.

The New View Campaign

In 2000, a group of eminent sexologists gathered to create a more holistic conceptualization of women's sexual functioning that frees most women from the *DSM*'s pathologizing frame. They called this work the "New View Manifesto" (the entire text can be found in the Appendix). This reconceptualization acknowledges the realities of women's lives, incorporates the many dimensions in which women experience and express sexuality, includes the importance of a woman's relational world, acknowledges the realm of subjective meaning, and empowers women to define sexual meaning, satisfaction, and pleasure for themselves (Kaschak & Tiefer, 2001).

Sexuality Is a Multidimensional Phenomenon

Sex is much more than a successful progression through a sexual response cycle of desire, arousal, orgasm, and resolution. Sexuality is a *multidimensional phenomenon* (Snell, 2001a, 2001b; Snell, Fischer & Walters, 1993). Ogden (2006, 2013) emphasizes that sexuality includes dimensions of heart, mind, body, and spirit, and that we need to move beyond counting and measuring orgasms. Sexuality is imbued with symbolic meaning, and it is this subjective realm that determines whether sex is satisfying (Gagnon & Simon, 1973; Kleinplatz, 2001, 2012). Kleinplatz (2012) asserts that we focus too much on parts and not enough on people, whose "subjective, sexual/erotic meanings are as distinctive as fingerprints . . . intricate, complex, subtle and powerful" (p. 103). Perel (2010) states, "the erotic landscape is vastly larger, richer, and more intricate than the physiology of sex or any repertoire of sexual techniques" (p. 29). The greatest predictor of real sexual satisfaction occurs when partners experience a good match-up of deep symbolic material and meaning and a coordinating intersubjectivity (Bader, 2002; Daniluk, 1998; DeLamater & Shibley Hyde, 2004; Ellison, 2000, 2001; Iasenza, 2010; Kleinplatz, 2001, 2012; Morin, 1995; Ogden, 2006, 2008, 2013; Tiefer, 2004).

Some Post–Masters and Johnson Theorists

The kinds of issues that today's clients bring into sex therapy differ from those that Masters and Johnson treated. In their day, the most common disorders were premature ejaculation and anorgasmia[2] (Rosen & Leiblum, 1995). In recent years, the most common disorder that brings women (and an increasing number of men) into treatment is mismatched or low sexual desire, which has been found to be far more challenging to treat (Basson, 2000; Leiblum & Rosen, 2000).

Kleinplatz (2001) suggests that we are in a Post–Masters and Johnson era, having progressed far beyond their cognitive behavioral foundations.[3] A cognitive behavioral model is by far the most common approach to sex therapy, and although it can provide education, address skill sets, rework limiting scripts, and dispel unrealistic myths, it cannot address problems that are driven by unconscious processes. Material in the unconscious realm is by its very nature outside of awareness and cannot be identified or explored as "cognitive" (Emmerson, 2003). To understand processes that are largely unconscious, we must move to the intrapsychic realm where arousal templates and sexual desire originate. The intrapsychic realm houses the seedbed of our archetypal potential. Here is where our "inner cast of characters" resides with their various scripts and agendas, which can compete and collide. Each of these "inner characters" has an archetypal resonance, which can be felt in the body, influencing our thoughts, decisions, and reactions (Wakefield, 2012).

WHY WOMEN COME TO SEX THERAPY

Women come to sex therapy with a variety of issues. They come on their own, but often they are referred by someone: a health practitioner, a gynecologist, a clergy person, and psychotherapists who feel unqualified to address sexual issues. Women will often become motivated to come to sex therapy when their sexual issues begin to overshadow their intimate relationships. Sometimes a partner will bring a woman in, hoping that I will "fix" her. In these cases, I often see the woman sitting across from me, eager to please, anxious that something is fundamentally wrong with her, or feeling hurt and angry at being made "the problem." The number one reason today that women come to sex therapy is because they have no sexual desire.

When I meet with women individually, they often reveal that they don't know how to deal with a partner who has clumsy sexual skills paired with a fragile ego. The partner may be struggling with his own sexual dysfunction and blaming it on the woman. If he has been "sex educated" through pornography, he may be critical of her because she doesn't meet those "standards." Sometimes her partner is narcissistic, insensitive, demanding, or controlling, and she feels unseen, unheard, insecure, intimidated, and understandably inhibited.

Most women receive deplorably insufficient sex education. They don't understand how their bodies work or the sexual response cycle. They don't know that the arousal stage serves a lubrication and engorgement function, which makes intercourse comfortable. They have rigid scripts or unrealistic expectations that sex will be like the movies. Women experience pain or discomfort during intercourse that they have never discussed with anyone, including their gynecologist. They grit their teeth and endure their discomfort, wondering what is wrong with them. They may have other health issues that are affecting their sexuality, but they have little money to afford the health care they need. When they feel safe enough to speak about it, they reveal humiliating early experiences and haunting memories of childhood sexual abuse that cause them to go numb or leave their bodies entirely during sex. They despair of ever feeling good enough in bed. They worry about being compared with other partners or to porn. They come with guilt over past actions or concerns about their present actions, which feel out of control. They have concerns about sexually transmitted diseases/infections or don't know how to tell a partner that they have one. They worry about being used or opening themselves up to hurt. They come in the midst of passionate, illicit affairs that are tearing their lives apart, or on the verge of an affair with an overwhelming attraction. They are desperately searching for meaning and satisfaction in a long-term sexual relationship that has gone stale. They want things in bed that they have never revealed to anyone. They lack self-esteem and self-confidence. They have no sense that they can make the changes they desire. They don't feel entitled to ask for what they want. They don't know what they want. They have a lot of anxiety about their bodies, especially their aging bodies. They are unable to find or keep a desirable partner. They have long-standing sexual identity or gender identity issues. They are exhausted. They have an inkling that sex could hold pleasure or meaning, but are completely mystified as to how they might get there. These are the sexual issues that women struggle with . . . and more.

When women come to sex therapy, I experience them in a search for themselves, adrift in a sea of other people's scripts and confusing messages about who and how they should be. They are disconnected from their empowering depths and at odds with their bodies. In our work together, they will begin to discover who they are as sexual beings, their unique sexual essence. They will establish a relationship with their bodies and define their individual path into the land of sexual meaning and pleasure. In their search to resolve their sexual problems, they have inadvertently entered into a growth process, what Carl Jung called the "journey of individuation," what I now call the journey of Sexual Individuation™.

In the next chapter, I will introduce some important concepts found in Jungian psychology, for those who may not be familiar with them. In particular, I will describe Jung's ideas about individuation and the realm of archetypes, which are essential to understand before I enter Part II, to describe my archetypal treatment approach.

NOTES

1 Other important organizations that are devoted to sexology are the Society for the Scientific Study of Sexuality (SSSS), the Society for Sex Therapy and Research (SSTAR) and the Kinsey Institute.

2 Anorgasmia refers to an inability to reach orgasm.

3 Kleinplatz's (2001, 2012) two publications of *New Directions in Sex Therapy* offer a number of alternative approaches to sex therapy other than cognitive behavioral. They include narrative, systemic, solution-focused, feminist, experiential, and other postmodern modalities. Green and Flemons (2004) provide an excellent collection of post–Masters and Johnson treatment perspectives in their book, *Quickies: The Handbook of Brief Sex Therapy*. Ogden is the editor of *Extraordinary Sex Therapy* (2015), with chapters describing a number of innovative treatment approaches, including my own (Wakefield, 2015).

BIBLIOGRAPHY

American Psychiatric Association (2013) *Diagnostic and Statistical Manual of Mental Disorders, Fifth Edition: DSM-V*. Washington, DC: Author.

Bader, M. (2002) *Arousal: The Secret Logic of Sexual Fantasies*. New York: Thomas Dunne.

Basson, R. (2000) The Female Sexual Response: A Different Model. *The Journal of Sex and Marital Therapy, 26*, 51–65.

Basson, R., Leiblum, S., Brotto, L., Derogatis, L., Fourcroy, J., Fugl-Meyer, K., . . . Weijmar Schultz, W. (2003) Definitions of Women's Sexual Dysfunction Reconsidered: Advocating Expansion and Revision. *Journal of Psychosomatic Obstetrics and Gynecology, 24*, 221–229.

Cass, V. (2007) *The Elusive Orgasm*. Cambridge, MA: Da Capo.

Daniluk, J. (1998) *Women's Sexuality Across the Life Span: Challenging Myths, Creating Meanings*. New York: Guilford.

DeLamater, J., & Shibley Hyde, J. (2004) Conceptual and Theoretical Issues in Studying Sexuality in Close Relationships. In J. Harvey, A. Wenzel, & S. Sprecher (Eds.) *Handbook of Sexuality in Close Relationships* (pp. 7–30). Mahwah, NJ: Lawrence Erlbaum.

Ellison, C. (2000) *Women's Sexualities: Generations of Women Share Intimate Secrets of Sexual Self-Acceptance*. Oakland, CA: New Harbinger. www.womenssexualities.com

Ellison, C. (2001) Intimacy-Based Sex Therapy: Sexual Choreography. In P. Kleinplatz (Ed.) *New Directions in Sex Therapy: Innovations and Alternatives* (pp. 163–184). New York: Routledge.

Ellison, C. (2012) Sexual Choreography: "Am I Enjoying This Right Now?" Not "How Am I Doing?" In P. Kleinplatz (Ed.) *New Directions in Sex Therapy: Innovations and Alternatives* (2nd ed., pp. 141–160). New York: Routledge.

Emmerson, G. (2003) *Ego State Therapy*. Carmarthen, Wales: Crown House.

Foley, S., Kope, S., & Sugrue, D. (2012) *Sex Matters for Women: A Complete Guide to Taking Care of Your Sexual Self*. New York: Guilford.

Gagnon, J., & Simon, W. (1973) *Sexual Conduct: The Social Sources of Human Sexuality*. Chicago: Aldine.

Goodwach, R. (2005a) Sex Therapy: Historical Evolution, Current Practice. Part 1. *Australian and New Zealand Journal of Family Therapy, 26*, 3, 155–164.

Goodwach, R. (2005b) Sex Therapy: Historical Evolution, Current Practice. Part 2. *Australian and New Zealand Journal of Family Therapy, 26*, 3, 178–183.

Green, S., & Flemons, D. (Eds.) (2004) *Quickies: The Handbook of Brief Sex Therapy*. New York: W. W Norton.

Hite, S. (1976) *The Hite Report: A Nationwide Study of Female Sexuality*. New York: Seven Stories.

Iasenza, S. (2010) What Is Queer About Sex? Expanding Sexual Frames in Theory and Practice. *Family Process, 49*, 3, 291–308.

Kaplan, H. S. (1974) *The New Sex Therapy: Active Treatment of Sexual Dysfunctions*. New York: Brunner/Mazel.

Kaplan, H. S. (1979) *Disorders of Sexual Desire*. New York: Brunner/Mazel.

Kaplan, H. S. (1983) *The Evaluation of Sexual Disorders: Psychological and Medical Aspects*. New York: Brunner/Mazel.

Kaschak E.,& Tiefer, L. (Eds.) (2001) *The New View of Women's Sexual Problems*. New York: Haworth.

Kleinplatz, P. (2001) A Critique of the Goals of Sex Therapy, or the Hazards of Safer Sex. In P. Kleinplatz (Ed.) *New Directions in Sex Therapy: Innovations and Alternatives* (pp. 109–131). Philadelphia, PA: Brunner- Routledge.

Kleinplatz, P. (Ed.) (2012) *New Directions in Sex Therapy: Innovations and Alternatives* (2nd ed.). New York: Routledge.

Leiblum, S., & Rosen, R. (Ed.) (2000) *Principles and Practice of Sex Therapy*. New York: Guilford.

Masters, W., & Johnson, V. (1966) *Human Sexual Response*. New York: Bantam.

Masters, W., & Johnson, V. (1970) *Human Sexual Inadequacy*. Boston: Little, Brown.

Masters, W., Johnson, V., & Kolodny, R. (1982) *Sex and Human Loving*. Boston: Little, Brown.

McCormick, N. (1994) *Sexual Salvation: Affirming Women's Sexual Rights and Pleasures*. Westport, CT: Praeger.

Morin, J. (1995) *The Erotic Mind: Unlocking the Inner Sources of Sexual Passion and Fulfillment*. New York: Harper Perennial.

Ogden, G. (2006) *The Heart and Soul of Sex: Making the ISIS Connection*. Boston: Trumpeter.

Ogden, G. (2008) *Return of Desire: A Guide to Rediscovering Your Sexual Passion*. Boston: Trumpeter.

Ogden, G. (2013) *Expanding the Practice of Sex Therapy: An Integrative Model for Exploring Desire and Intimacy*. New York: Routledge.

Ogden, G. (Ed.) (2015) *Extraordinary Sex Therapy: Creative Approaches for Clinicians*. New York: Routledge.

Perel, E. (2010) The Double Flame: Reconciling Intimacy and Sexuality, Reviving Desire. In S. Leiblum (Ed.) *Treating Sexual Desire Disorders: A Clinical Casebook* (pp. 23–43). New York: Guilford.

Rosen, R., & Leiblum, S. (1995) *Case Studies in Sex Therapy*. New York: Guilford.

Snell, W., Fischer, T., & Walters, A. (1993) The Multidimensional Sexuality Questionnaire: An Objective Self-Report Measure of Psychological Tendencies Associated with Human Sexuality. *Annals of Sex Research*, 6, 27–55.

Snell, W. E., Jr. (Ed.) (2001a) *New Directions in the Psychology of Human Sexuality: Research and Theory*. Cape Girardeau, MO: Snell. http://cstl-cla.semo.edu/snell/books/sexuality/sexuality.htm

Snell, W. (2001b) Multidimensional Sexual Self-Concept Questionaire. In Fisher et al.'s (Ed.) *Handbook of Sexuality Related Measures* (pp. 537–540). New York: Routledge.

Tiefer, L. (2004) *Sex Is Not A Natural Act & Other Essays* (2nd ed.). Boulder, CO. Westview.

Tiefer, L. (2012) The "New View" Campaign: A Feminist Critique of Sex Therapy and an Alternative Vision. In P. Kleinplatz (Ed.) *New Directions in Sex Therapy: Innovations and Alternatives* (pp. 21–36). New York: Routledge.

Wakefield, C. (2012) *Negotiating the Inner Peace Treaty: Becoming the Person You Were Born to Be*. Bloomington, IN: Balboa.

Wakefield, C. (2015) In Search of Aphrodite: Working With Archetypes and an Inner Cast of Characters in Women With Low Sexual Desire. In G. Ogden (Ed.) *Extraordinary Sex Therapy: Creative Approaches for Clinicians* (pp. 31–51). New York: Routledge.

CHAPTER 4

SEXUAL INDIVIDUATION—WHAT'S JUNG GOT TO DO WITH IT?

"Through the assimilation of unconscious contents, the momentary life of consciousness can once more be brought into harmony with the law of nature from which it all too easily departs, and the person can be led back to the natural law of his or her own being."

Carl Jung

"To become—in Jung's terms—individuated, to live as a released individual, one has to know how and when to put on and to put off the masks of one's various life roles."

Joseph Campbell

CARL JUNG

Carl Jung, 1875-1961, was the Swiss psychiatrist who founded the field of Analytical Psychology. He developed psychological theories and concepts that continue to inform depth psychology thinking and practice today. These include complexes, archetypes, shadow, individuation, the collective unconscious, anima and animus, introvert, extrovert, and synchronicity (Campbell, 1971). Jung introduced the underlying personality typologies that evolved into the Myers-Briggs Type Indicator. Many of his concepts have become commonly known as part of our cultural lexicon.

FREUD AND JUNG

Jung was once considered Freud's "golden boy" and heir to his empire, but their diverging viewpoints on sexuality and human development eventually caused a breach in their relationship. Freud believed that developmental psychosexual stages were basically fixed by puberty. He believed that the energy originating from the human sex drive undergirded all of psychological life and that civilization and culture were a result of redirecting (sublimating) primitive sexual impulses (the chaotic "id") into something of a "higher order."

Jung firmly believed that human beings grow and change across the lifespan. He emphasized the process of transformation instead of Freud's sublimation. Jung believed that a spiritual force undergirded all of life and that sexuality was one possible path of expression for spiritual energy (Stein, 1998). Jung also became interested in how erotic attractions function to awaken the psyche and move it towards greater development. He believed that the primary source of these attractions came from unconscious contra (opposite) sexual forces which he called *anima* and *animus*. The *anima* sources from the undeveloped female aspects in the male psyche, and the *animus* sources from the undeveloped male aspects of the female psyche. When individuals project these aspects of the psyche out onto others, they will find themselves inexplicably attracted to that person who is said to "carry" their "anima or animus projection." Jung was interested in the lifelong process of growth and transformation which he called "individuation." Individuation is directed by an orchestrating archetype at the center of the psyche, which Jung referred to as the "capitol S" Self, as opposed to the "little s" self, which referred to the ego identity. The Self operates to forward our individuation by bringing undeveloped, unconscious, and disowned (shadow) material into life, through dreams, synchronicities, and our mysterious attractions. These grow the person into the fullest expression of who he or she was born to be (Singer, 1972/1994). An analogy that has been used a lot in the Jungian world is that oak trees grow from acorns and cedar trees are not unsuccessful oaks (Hillman, 1996)!

The development of the "little s" self (the personal ego identity) is an important part of a woman's developmental life, as women are heavily socialized to refer to *others* in defining themselves. The "capital S" Self is the self-actualizing, growth-generating force that drives the individuation process. It emanates from the depths of a woman's being and will energize her creative and erotic life. The Self orchestrates things behind the scenes in a way that can seem almost mystical to the "ego," but the Self is always seeking to bring balance into areas where we have gotten stuck or overidentified with something limiting or extreme. The Self pushes us toward the integration of opposites, balance, growing our unawakened potential, embracing a larger whole, and reaching greater conscious awareness.

The Archetypal Realm

Whereas Freud believed that we have one level of the unconscious, composed almost entirely of things forgotten or repressed, Jung believed that there were two primary levels of unconscious material. The personal unconscious holds our *complexes*, those emotionally charged areas of our lives that shape personality and drive much of our behavior, as well as being the repository of things pushed out of awareness, such as forbidden impulses or rejected parts of self. Jung also believed that in addition to the *personal unconscious*, there is a deeper level of the psyche, the *collective unconscious*, which acts as a repository of all human experience, including repeating patterns, which he called *archetypes*. Each of our personal complexes has an archetype at its core, which is why complexes are so powerful (Jung, 1959). Jung believed that archetypes are part of the innate structure of the human psyche, "inherent organizing forms for the expression of what is enduring and archaic in human nature" (Young-Eisendrath, 1984, p. 29). Archetypes have recognizable patterns of action and thought that organize human instinctual-emotional responses. They are universal prototypes found in all places, throughout history. Archetypes are more than roles or categories, they are systems of energy that move through the psyche and motivate behavior, thought, feeling, perception, and interpretation of experience (Young-Eisendrath, 1984).

Jung spent a major portion of his life studying archetypal patterns, particularly those found in archaic images, myths, and fairy tales, which he thought of as expressions of the collective unconscious of humankind. He incorporated the concept of archetypes into his psychological theory and looked for them in people's dreams and life stories. An archetype might lie dormant in the seedbed of the psyche until it is activated by developmental passages or by the requirements of an environment or experience. Jung emphasized that archetypes could not be grasped by intellect alone. An archetype carries a strong feeling tone and when constellated as a psychic entity, has the ability to activate and transform the contents of consciousness. Archetypes are felt in the body as energy and emotion. He emphasized that ultimately, in order to understand an archetype, it has to be experienced (Johnson, 1986; Stevens, 1982).

Various writers have created lists of archetypes and typologies to help us understand our personalities and human experience (Grant, 1988;[1] Leonard, 1982, 1993; Myss, 2003; Pearson, 1991; Shinoda Bolen, 1984). In my previous book, I created a list of archetypes that I have encountered, (Wakefield, 2012), but I emphasize that there is no definitive or comprehensive list of archetypes.

What Carl Jung was describing by the word *archetype* is currently being explored and demonstrated in the field of neuropsychology, as we can now see distinct clusters of neural pathways that "fire" in response to particular human experiences and create impulses that drive behavioral responses. We no longer consider the word *energy* to be "new age," because we can now see that the brain is filled with organized pathways of travelling energy (Cozolino, 2006; Siegel, 1999).

OUR "COMPLEXED" WORLD

Jung was the originator of the term "complex." A complex is a tangle of emotional reactivity: thoughts, feelings, memories, and sensations organized around an archetypal core. These patterned ways of reacting develop from early life experiences and developmental junctures. The most intense of these complexes consist of primitive defenses that protect us in situations where we feel like our very existence is in danger. Complexes have a life of their own. They hijack us and cause us to go unconscious. When we are under the spell of a complex, we are not aware of it. We have lost our capacity to reflect on our choices and behaviors. We are activated and driven by internal energies (Ulanov, 1971). Everything we think, feel, say, and do feels entirely justified. When we calm down, we may feel differently. A good way to become more aware of our "complexes" is to spend the day noting when the body feels particularly energized or activated. When we do healing work to untangle our "complexed" reactivity, the world may begin to look like an entirely different place, and we may interpret people's actions and intentions differently.

The more inner work we do, the more we realize that "identity," what we think of as "me," is a construction of protective mechanisms developed from painful past experiences and scripts handed to us by others.

When we adopt other people's scripts, instead of being who we are, we send aspects of ourselves into the shadow. Shadow selves seek integration because they are part of the Self. They intrude in "shadow outcroppings," at which times people say things like, "I don't know what overcame me. I wasn't myself." For many women, sexuality work feels like dark shadow work. That makes sexuality work challenging and of immense importance. Through this shadow work, we retrieve something that is essential in the journey to become "whole."

Shadow—Our Seeds of Potential

Until an archetype is awakened, these seeds of potential lie fallow. They can be considered "shadow" aspects of the psyche. Shadow material can also include aspects of the personality that were split off and disowned at some point because they were punished by an authority figure or deemed unacceptable by an affiliative group. Although most people tend to think of shadow as something "dark," shadow can just as easily be "bright." The highest and best stuff in human beings is sometimes too beautiful or brilliant for the people around us to accept or even tolerate. When this happens, these positive qualities can become disowned and sent into the unconscious where they become "bright shadow." Each of us will develop only a portion of the archetypal spectrum of our human possibility. The rest will remain in the unconscious, as undeveloped potential.

If we view sexuality from an archetypal perspective, it becomes evident that we all have sexual potentials that remain undeveloped, "sleeping" in the seedbed of the psyche. When people begin to cooperate with the journey of individuation, sexuality becomes part of that journey because our sexuality is such a fundamental component of our identity. When we begin to move sexuality beyond the behavioral realm, beyond the "ego identity," and consider it an expression of the Self, it becomes a *pathway* of individuation. In this way, we might refer to a journey toward a conscious sexuality, a journey of Sexual Individuation™.

Lovers and Other Strangers

There is a good deal of writing in Jungian literature regarding Jung's concept of anima and animus, and how these contra-sexual forces in the psyche create powerful external attractions (Hannah, 2011; Hollis, 1998;

Johnson, 1983; Landau, 2011; Luke, 1995; McNeely, 1991; Paris, 1986; Pinkola Estés, 1992; Qualls-Corbett, 1988; Shinoda Bolen, 1984, 1990; Ulanov A., Ulanov B., 1994; Woodman, 1985, 1990; Young-Eisendrath, 1984, 1993, 1999).[2] We can certainly acknowledge that erotic attractions begin with idealized projections onto the object of our desire. Often, in reading the Jungian literature, I do not see reference to the powerful undertow, the deeply felt eroticism that is awakened by these attractions. Much of the writing seems to convey that the most valuable use for these compelling experiences is in how they open up undiscovered country of the woman's projective psyche. An example is Helen Luke's definition of "animus," in which she states that the positive function of the animus is to act as a guide to the unconscious and to the creative images within. The writing often takes on a lofty, psychologized, even spiritualized quality.

From my perspective, there is insufficient inquiry into the *instinctual* nature of these experiences and how they are felt in the body. The analytic, arms-length tone of the animus literature somehow diminishes the power that these enchantments hold for a woman, for the profound awakening and potential wreckage they can portend. They are more than "material" projected out from the unconscious realm of the psyche. They draw her forward out of her previously defined box. In the erotic nature of the experience, she awakens, her body comes to life as she revels in the taste, smell, touch, sound, and sight of the beloved.

Jungian literature provides little advice regarding how not to be swept downstream, once one has been "struck by lightning" and is actively experiencing the intense body sensations and overwhelming hunger for union with the beloved. When our clients are in the throes of such an experience, what seems most pressing are admonitions to remain circumspect until the force of the "projection" dies down. As clinicians, we often have concerns that our clients might blow up their existing lives, jumping off into the unknown.

The prevailing relationship therapy literature leans heavily toward interventions that heal and maintain *established* relationships. There is little writing regarding how the Self sometimes orchestrates a forceful awakening and a dramatic but purposeful reordering of a woman's life. We need to consider that the deconstruction of her current life is not always a terrible mistake. Likewise, there is also not enough writing about how the disruptive nature of these third-party experiences might be beneficial in the long run, jump-starting a stagnated marriage or a stalled out individuation. Might it be possible that these love affairs sometimes bring a wrecking ball to a relationship that has long needed to be deconstructed, in order for one or both of the parties to move forward into a more purposeful life? How might the presence of a threatening third party forward the development of the existing couple? If the relationship survives, how might this grow them up and deepen them in the long run? There is nothing like sexual attraction to challenge our banal reality and shallowly considered rules for living. A truly individuated life is not disconnected from the body or from the instincts. The instincts are felt and considered in the context of the whole life. Although I generally warn women against reckless or impulsive acts, I also encourage women to tune in deeply to what these experiences stir in them. How is she experiencing herself differently in the midst of this attraction? What is opening up in her? What is the story she is telling herself about what this means? How is this changing her perspective on life? Is this awakening inviting her to become more embodied, to expand her life, or dare something new, or to nurture an aspect of her slumbering psyche that has just awakened?

In my own way of working with the "inner casts" of women, I have found it useful to personify a woman's animus energy as an "inner character" that plays a part in her emerging story and identity. Her animus characters may appear in her dreams, or they may appear as attractive manifestations in her waking life.

ENTER APHRODITE

When we begin to look at myth and legend, there have always been goddesses of love and sexuality. Inanna of Sumer, Ishtar of Babylon, and Isis of Egypt all held places of honor and significance in prepatriarchal times. As the monotheistic religions displaced the earth religions, these Goddesses were branded as "harlots" and campaigns of denunciation and denigration were launched that split body from soul and frightened future generations from any association with their realm or rites (Eisler, 1996; Hall, 1991; Hillel, 1997; Taylor, 1998). Because these Goddesses were vilified so thoroughly by Christianity, most modern women are not familiar with their names. Because Western civilization has valued the Greek classical era, we are more familiar with Aphrodite and her place in the classical Greek Pantheon of Goddesses. Jean Shinoda Bolen (1984) helped to familiarize a wider audience of women with these Greek Goddesses and how they represent *archetypal potentials that reside in the psyches of all women*.

Aphrodite was the self-defining, empowered, alchemical Goddess of love, pleasure, desire, sensuality, beauty, creativity, and eroticism. She was free spirited and did not concern herself with the opinions of others. She maintained her own authority, entering relationships that pleased her and exiting relationships that no longer served her. Her consciousness could move from a sharp focus on the object of her desire, to a soft, intuitive, sensuous receptivity. We know an Aphrodite woman when she enters the room. Women who carry this energy have a lot of "juice" flowing through them, and this brings everything they touch to life. Aphrodite women tend to have a lot of suitors. When the archetype of the goddess of love (Aphrodite energy) is constellated, a woman is imbued with vitality, love, beauty, sexual passion, and spiritual renewal (Qualls-Corbett, 1988; Shinoda Bolen, 1984).

The quality and form of Aphrodite expression will differ from woman to woman, because every woman has a unique sexual essence, her "signature perfume" (which I describe in my Sexual Essence Wheels). It is important to emphasize that the sparkle and life energy of Aphrodite is not dependent on having a partner and is not limited to genital sexuality. It is based on a woman's capacity to be passionately engaged with her life.

A woman's Aphrodite potential can lie unawakened in her archetypal seedbed. It can be starved and stunted, frightened into hiding by traumatic experiences or a culture that tells her it is dangerous to shine too much. Before they become self-conscious about their bodies, you can see Aphrodite in the delight of little girls exploring and reveling in their senses. They run naked down the hall after baths, squealing with delight, pet fuzzy caterpillars, play in the mud, gather wild flowers, chase butterflies, and eat ice cream without guilt. Aphrodite twinkles in the girl of four or five, with her wide open smile, snuggling, flirting, and melting the heart of her beloved daddy. She is just beginning to understand the power of her feminine wiles, just beginning to test her capacity to capture attention, to charm and enchant, all dimensions of Aphrodite's power. This innocent flirtation is the reason it is so important that we protect girls at this age, so that they can continue to explore and grow into the full flower of their Aphrodite Self, without anyone crushing the bloom.

Landau (2011), Leonard (1993), Paris (1986), and Shinoda Bolen (1984) have written eloquently about the gifts and quandaries of women who carry Aphrodite energy. In Clarissa Pinkola Estés's (1992) landmark book *Women Who Run With the Wolves*, she writes of the necessity of a woman's connection to her wild, instinctual nature, in order for her to grow into her full personhood. Pinkola Estés brings her message home as she illustrates, in story after story, the importance of remaining connected to instinct, and how this connection will affect all areas of a woman's life. It is an absolute necessity for her to become a fully sexual being. In Pinkola Estés's (1993) *How to Love a Woman*, she reconstructs some of the erotic poetry of Sappho and explores the depths of a woman's sexual psyche. Marion Woodman (1982, 1985, 1990, 1993) devoted a good deal of her career to the topic of conscious femininity, the necessity for women to move beyond the archetype of Daughter, and the central importance of embodiment in becoming a sexual woman. In Sidra Stone's (1997) important book *The Shadow King*, she writes about the inner struggle that women feel in openly claiming intelligence and sexuality in a patriarchal culture. Power is still viewed as "unfeminine" or emasculating, but women are even more ambivalent about claiming the independent, vibrant, life-giving power of Aphrodite.

ARCHETYPES OF SEXUALITY

Sexuality is an important component of what is "enduring and archaic in human nature," so it follows that there are multiple, diverse archetypes of sexuality. These archetypes energize and inform the Sexual Self. When the unique archetypal template of a woman's sexuality is in conflict with socially accepted scripts, the core aspects of her sexuality are likely to become disowned and relegated to "shadow." The developing Sexual Self would be forced into conformity with outer scripts rather than developing as an authentic expression of the deep Self. This misalignment and disconnection from the authentic Self will lead such a person to feel out of synch, unfulfilled, and sexually unrealized for their entire life.

When we talk about sexual identity, we are talking about a great deal more than partner preference and gender identity, or even preferred sexual activities. It takes great courage to claim who you are and to live in alignment with that luminous core of the Self, but this is the path to a conscious, emotionally, physically, and spiritually fulfilling life.

ROLES AND ARCHETYPES

It is important to distinguish between roles and archetypes. They are easily confused, but a role refers to a position that a person occupies within a social or family system. Roles have norms and expectations associated with that position. People assume and fulfill roles and those who do not comply with role expectations are punished. Although people may comply outwardly, they may also harbor forbidden longings or find ways to live secret lives (Longres, 1995). In these cases, the role and the archetype are mismatched.

We could almost say that roles operate from the outside in, whereas archetypes generate from the inside out. People can carry out a role from a number of archetypal orientations. A Responsible Mother can help a child with homework from Encourager or Critic, two very different energies. A woman can give a lover feedback about what she prefers, and it will be received very differently when communicated from Critical Mother or Playful Kitten. This is why the same words spoken from a different archetypal stance will have a very different effect on the listener.

NOTES

1 It was through Toni Grant's book *Being a Woman* that I was introduced to the important work of Jung's colleague Toni Wolff and her structural forms of the feminine psyche, arranged under the rubric of four primary archetypes: Amazon, Hetaera (Courtesan), Mother, and Medial Woman. Wolff's thinking has been a "jumping-off" point for much of my own work in archetypes of the feminine, including this work.

2 There are those who object strongly to the problems that arise from the heterosexual and gender biases inherent in Jung's original "contra-sexual" formulations of anima and animus in sexual attractions. Bradley TePaske (2008) is a Jungian analyst who provides a more enlightened "post-Jungian" perspective of how these concepts can apply to a wider array of sexual orientations and gender identities.

BIBLIOGRAPHY

Campbell, J. (Ed.) (1971) *The Portable Jung*. New York: Penguin.

Cozolino, L. (2006) *The Neuroscience of Human Relationships: Attachment and the Developing Social Brain*. New York: W. W. Norton.

Eisler, R. (1996) *Sacred Pleasure: Sex, Myth, and the Politics of the Body—New Paths to Power and Love*. San Francisco: HarperCollins.

Grant, T. (1988) *Being a Woman: Fulfilling Your Femininity and Finding Love*. New York: Random House.

Hall, N. (1991) *The Moon and the Virgin: A Voyage Towards Self-Discovery and Healing*. London: The Woman's Press.

Hannah, B. (2011) *The Animus: The Spirit of Inner Truth in Women*. Wilmette, IL: Chiron.

Hillel, R. (1997) *The Redemption of the Feminine Erotic Soul*. York Beach, ME: Nicolas-Hays.

Hillman, J. (1996) *The Soul's Code: In Search of Character and Calling*. New York: Random House.

Hollis, J. (1998) *The Eden Project: In Search of the Magical Other*. Toronto, ON: Inner City.

Johnson, R. (1983) *We: Understanding the Psychology of Romantic Love*. San Francisco: HarperCollins.

Johnson, R. (1986) *Inner Work: Using Dreams and Active imagination for Personal Growth*. San Francisco: HarperCollins.

Jung, C. G. (1959) *The Archetypes and the Collective Unconscious*. The Collected Works of C. G Jung (Vol. 9, Part 1). Princeton, NJ: Princeton University Press.

Landau, A. (2011) *Tragic Beauty: The Dark Side of Venus Aphrodite and the Loss and Regeneration of Soul*. New Orleans, LA: Spring Journal.

Leonard, L. S. (1982) *The Wounded Woman: Healing the Father-Daughter Relationship*. Boston: Shambala.

Leonard, L. S. (1993) *Meeting the Madwoman: Empowering the Feminine Spirit*. New York: Bantam.

Longres, J. (1995) *Human Behavior in the Social Environment*. Itasca, IL: John Peacock.

Luke, H. (1995) *The Way of Woman: Awakening the Perennial Feminine*. New York: Doubleday.

McNeely, D. A. (1991) *Animus Aeternus: Exploring the Inner Masculine*. Toronto, ON: Inner City.

Myss, C. (2003). *Sacred Contracts: Awakening Your Divine Potential*. Carlsbad, CA: Hay House.

Paris, G. (1986) *Pagan Meditations: Aphrodite, Hestia, Artemis*. Woodstock, CT: Spring.

Pearson, C. (1991) *Awakening the Heroes Within: Twelve Archetypes to Help Us Find Ourselves and Transform our World*. San Francisco: HarperCollins.

Pinkola Estés, C. (1992) *Women Who Run With the Wolves: Myths and Stories of the Wild Woman Archetype*. New York: Ballantine.

Pinkola Estés, C. (1993) *How to Love a Woman: On Intimacy and the Erotic Life of Women*. [CD Series]. Boulder, CO: Sound True.

Qualls-Corbett, N. (1988) *The Sacred Prostitute: Eternal Aspect of the Feminine*. Toronto, ON: Inner City.

Shinoda Bolen, J. (1984) *Goddesses in Every Woman: A New Psychology of Women*. New York: Harper Perennial.

Shinoda Bolen, J. (1990) *Gods in Everyman: A New Psychology of Men's Lives and Loves*. New York: HarperPerennial.

Siegel, D. (1999) *The Developing Mind: How Relationships and the Brain Interact to Shape Who We Are*. New York: Guilford.

Singer, J. (1994) *Boundaries of the Soul: The Practice of Jung's Psychology*. New York: Random House. (Original work published 1972)

Stein, M. (1998) *Transformation: Emergence of the Self*. College Station: Texas A&M University Press.

Stevens, A. (1982) *Archetypes: A Natural History of the Self*. New York: William Morrow.

Stone, S. (1997) *The Shadow King: The Invisible Force That Holds Women Back*. Lincoln, NE: iUniverse.

Taylor, J. (1998) *The Living Labyrinth: Exploring Universal Themes in Myths, Dreams and the Symbolism of Waking Life*. Mahwah, NJ: Paulist.

TePaske, B. (2008) *Sexuality and the Religious Imagination*. New Orleans: Spring Journal.

Ulanov, A. (1971) *The Feminine in Jungian Psychology and in Christian Theology*. Evanston, IL: Northwestern University Press.

Ulanov, A., & Ulanov, B. (1994) *Transforming Sexuality: The Archetypal World of Anima and Animus*. Boston: Shambhala.

Wakefield, C. (2012) *Negotiating the Inner Peace Treaty: Becoming the Person You Were Born to Be*. Bloomington, IN: Balboa.

Woodman, M. (1982) *Addiction to Perfection: The Still Unravished Bride*. Toronto, ON: Inner City.

Woodman, M. (1985) *The Pregnant Virgin: A Process of Psychological Transformation*. Toronto, ON: Inner City.

Woodman, M. (1990) *The Ravaged Bridegroom: Masculinity in Women*. Toronto, ON: Inner City.

Woodman, M. (1993) *Conscious Femininity: Interviews With Marion Woodman*. Toronto, ON: Inner City.

Young-Eisendrath, P. (1984) *Hags and Heroes: A Feminist Approach to Jungian Psychotherapy With Couples*. Toronto, ON: Inner City.

Young-Eisendrath, P. (1993) *You're Not What I Expected: Learning to Love the Opposite Sex*. New York: Morrow.

Young-Eisendrath, P. (1999) *Women and Desire: Beyond Wanting to Be Wanted*. New York: Three Rivers.

Part II

Sex Therapy From an Archetypal, Inner Self System Perspective

Working With Archetypes, the Inner Cast of Characters, Scripts, and Sexual Essence

CHAPTER 5

INTAKE AND ASSESSMENT—WHAT ARE WE LISTENING FOR?

"Identity is the story we tell ourselves about ourselves."

Stone, Patton, and Heen (1999, p. 112)

WOMEN'S SEXUAL STORIES

We find archetypes embedded in the great myths and stories of the world, and Jung recognized that we each have an individual myth that we live. Jung also understood that the meaning we bring to the events of our lives is more important than the events themselves (Singer, 1972/1994). In the 1970s, Michael White and David Epson developed a method of therapy that focused on the stories that people tell about their lives. Called "Narrative Therapy," it offers a way to work with the personal narratives that shape our client's realities. White and Epson became fascinated by how, in the vast territory of lived experience, certain events stand out as "important," while others recede into the background. These defining events become the proof text for how clients conceptualize themselves, others, and life itself. One of the valuable principles of Narrative Therapy is to encourage clients to externalize a problem so that "the person is not the problem, the problem is the problem." This opens up a space to *develop alternative story lines*, *draw different conclusions*, and *construct preferred identities* (Freedman & Combs, 1996; White, 2007).

Laird (1991) emphasizes that "women are part of a gendered myth-making process in which they are rarely the authors" (p. 448). Women's stories have often been trivialized, because they center on the domestic sphere rather than matters of "world importance," as if what happens in the home did not have an impact on the world. This is why it becomes all the more important to allow a woman to tell her story and interpret her own experience. Laird calls this "restorying" her life.

As sex therapists, we can help clients develop richer narratives and "preferred identities" as they "restory" their lives. When we do this, whole realms of possibility open up that were previously occluded by the lenses through which the client was viewing things. White encourages clients to talk about their *relationship to* a problem rather than speaking of it as a core component of their identity. So often in therapy, people get "labeled" and then begin to think of themselves in terms of that label. *Having* a sexual problem is quite different from *being* sexually dysfunctional. Changing the interpretation and the meaning of a situation can cause a "problem" to disappear altogether (Freedman & Combs, 1996; White, 2007).

ASSESSMENT

Taking a Sexual History—Her Story

Taking a sexual history is a cornerstone of treatment evaluation and Masters and Johnson (1966, 1970), Hartman and Fithian (1972), and Kaplan (1983) devote a great deal of time to this endeavor. The method and complexity of history gathering differs with the practitioner today. The general purpose is to understand the client's family and religious background, sexual education and formation, past relationships and significant sexual experiences, level of self-esteem and feelings about the body. If there is a current partner, we also want to know the client's feelings about the partner, her sense of trust, comfort with touch, desires, and turn-ons and turn-offs in sexual interactions. We are also assessing if the problem is due to a lack of education or skill set. Is it interpersonal or intrapsychic, and is there a medical component requiring a referral (Bennet & Holczer, 2010; Kaplan, 1974, 1983; Masters & Johnson, 1970)?

Although taking an in-depth history can provide a wealth of important information, a formal history can take several sessions and the scope of information may or may not be directly applicable to the presenting problem. The desire for "brief treatment" has increased client impatience with lengthy intake protocols (Green & Flemons, 2004). Clients want help fast, and practitioners are looking for ways to make history taking more efficient. There is growing support for a narrative approach to history gathering, which allows information relevant to the immediate problem to be revealed in the context of the client's unfolding story (Ogden, 2013; White, 2007).

I have found a narrative means of taking a history more effective than asking a list of questions on a sexual history form. Certain questions are difficult for many women to answer in early sessions. If the question elicits shame, or the content is surrounded by protective defenses, the answer may be dismissive or intellectualized, without revealing emotional content. Allowing a woman to reveal very intimate information in the flow of her own narrative is a kinder and gentler means of gathering history.

Listening With Archetypal Ears

How we listen to a client makes a difference. When a woman enters my office and begins to tell her story, I am listening on multiple levels. I am listening to her narrative. In doing so, I am gathering the factual details of her history, but *I am listening beyond the words*. I want to understand the meaning of the events. I am sensing the *archetypal resonance* from which she is speaking. I want to know what part she is playing in her story. What roles does she play in her life today, and *from what archetypal stance does she fulfill them*? If she is here with a sexual problem, I want to know how she is experiencing it and how it is affecting her life. Why is she seeking help right now? Where is her Sexual Self in this story line? Do I hear one? If not, why not? In terms of this problem, what solutions has she tried, and *from what archetypal stance has she tried them*? What has worked or not worked? A good solution attempted from a disempowered archetypal stance will fail. What else is going on in her life?

As I listen, I am making mental notes as well as some written notes. I am formulating my own internal hypothesis about the situation, her stage of development, her inner world. Who do I already hear in terms of her inner cast of characters, and how are they interfacing with the problem? Which of these inner selves brought her into my treatment room and what does this inner self want? The "who" versus the "what" question becomes very important, and it differentiates my approach from others. I want to know if I am sitting with an exhausted Caregiver, with

55

added responsibility of looking after aging parents, or an Empty-Nest Mother, whose identity is adrift after her last child went to college. Is she an ambitious Career Woman, with a tidal wave of stressful demands, or a Betrayed Wife, who recently discovered her husband's affair? "Who" brought her in to sex therapy, and what does a "solution" look like from this inner character's perspective? It is also important to wonder who else might be looking in from the wings.

Working from an archetypal/inner self system perspective changes the way a sexual history is gathered and can provide a "zip line" into the core of the problem. For example, if the problem is lack of desire, is it her inner Pleasing Partner who brought her in? Is she a passive protagonist in someone else's script? Did she ever have an inner Pleasure Seeker? If not, why not? If so, where did this Pleasure Seeker go, and who took her place? Are there contextual circumstances that are extinguishing her flame? Is this an identity issue or a role-overload issue? I want to understand her operating rules for being sexual and "who" enforces them? Where is Aphrodite?

If I am speaking to a Polished Professional Woman, I will probably meet her "persona" and hear a particular kind of history. Later on, I may meet a more vulnerable self. A Sexually Abused Child may emerge from behind the curtain of her persona, and I will hear a very different story, one she may not even have remembered when she was operating as the Polished Professional Woman. A sexual history should be viewed as a prism, a multidimensional puzzle, rather than as a time line of factual events. I am always aware that I am seeing only the initial presentation of the person sitting in front of me. I try to sense her archetypal energy. Is this a Good Girl, a Waif, an Armored Amazon, a Dutiful Wife, a Seductress?

Throughout the session, I am also tuning in to shifting states, each representing a different member of her inner cast. I am noting the non-verbal cues: body language, changes in the voice, language, breathing, and skin tone. How much eye contact is the client making? I am noting the "main characters" who are front and center as well as the "supporting cast" and the "not-so-supporting cast." I am also aware that I have yet to meet the "kids behind the curtain" (Wakefield, 2012). If this client is to truly bloom into the fullness of her sexuality, it is important to understand the other players in her inner cast. Do some of them consider her sexuality to be a threat? Are there Gatekeepers who block her entry into this realm, Voices of Warning who remind her of past hurts and restrictive scripts? Has she become overtaken by Eros-inhibiting archetypes that will not allow any space for an Aphrodite Self?

What Else to Listen For

Early sessions of sex therapy are devoted to understanding the presenting problems, establishing trust and confidence in the process, and outlining a path of treatment. In our conversation, I am listening for the following qualities and asking eliciting questions to determine the following factors.

Insight and Self-Awareness

How *Self-aware* is she? Is she tuned in to her internal processes? Does she have an *Observing Self* that can step back and reflect on situations and how she operates in her life? How *curious* is she about herself, and how *motivated* is she to learn and grow?

Developmental Milestones and Life Stages

I also listen for things that indicate *important developmental markers* along the way: experiences in family life, her parents' relationship, other key figures in her early life, early body experiences, difficult losses, sources or absence of secure attachment, nurture and support, her experience of menarche (first menstruation), early love relationships, sexual initiation, how she fit in during high school and college, adult sexual relationships, significant love affairs, work life and career development, pregnancies in and out of marriage, abortions, marriages, children, menopause, retirement.

Systems and Interpersonal Dynamics

I want to grasp how Self-defined she is as a person and how *differentiated* she is from others. What kind of *systems* is she embedded in: religious, cultural, family, friendship networks, career? Does she know who she is and can she maintain that sense of Self in close relationships? How well does she maintain her sense of Self when others put pressure on her to be different? What kind of insight does she have into *interpersonal dynamics*?

What are the ongoing conflicts? Is there a threat of loss? What about *safety*? Is it safe for her to be herself, or does she live under some threat of danger? Do her relationships supply security, support, and nurturance?

Emotional Regulation Skills

How are her *emotional regulation* skills? Does she have the capacity to handle strong emotions, to center, ground, and comfort herself? Does she disconnect from herself emotionally or fall into reactive patterns that are destructive to herself or her relationships? Might there be some developmental trauma that is feeding into this? Does she do a lot of projecting and mind reading? Do the stories she is telling me indicate that she can manage herself in difficult situations in a way that moves the relationship forward? Can she center herself and calm herself down in the midst of stressful situations? Can she state her wants and needs clearly and confidently? Can she hear what others are trying to communicate and respond in ways that move the communication and cooperation process forward, seeking to understand and negotiate, or does she shut down or devolve into tears, anger, or manipulation? Can she continue to value her own experience, even when others don't? Is she easily swayed or drawn into other people's emotional reactivity?

Inner and Outer Resources

How is her sense of *agency* and *self-esteem*? Does she have a confident sense of options in her life? Does she demonstrate curiosity and seek out information? Can she evaluate things and problem solve? Does she have a sense that she can implement the changes she desires and determine her direction? How *economically independent* is she? Can she sustain herself (and any children) financially? How *intelligent* is she? What is her level of *education*? Is she undereducated for her native intelligence?

Time, Energy, and Health

If I created a pie chart of her life, where are her time and energy going? Is she conscious of this? Looking at this through the perspective of the "inner cast," who do I see operating? Is she directing this, or is this in response to the demands of others? What is my overall sense of her life energy? Does she have any known health issues? Has she had a medical evaluation lately? Is she on medications that have an impact on sexuality?

Self-Care and Inspiration

How is her *self-care*? Where does she draw her *inspiration* and *replenish* herself? How is she creative? Do I hear something in her life that brings her joy and pleasure? How much capacity for happiness and goodness does she seem to have? Where are her deep sources of meaning? Does she have a source of *spiritual renewal*, or is her religious affiliation a source of diminishment and suppression?

Sexual Empowerment

How sexually self-empowered is she? Do I sense a *Sexual Self*? Can she speak from this Self? How does she feel about her body? Is she *in* her body? Is she attuned to her senses and bodily sensations as a feedback system? What is her level of relevant sex education? Does she seem to understand her arousal template: who she's attracted to, what motivates her sexually and gets her motor running? What is her fundamental sexual essence, and how she likes to express herself sexually? Where do I sense that she is on the Sexual Essence Wheels (more on this in Chapter 7)? What are her core erotic themes and her sexual path preference? Is she performance oriented, or is she seeking pleasure and connection? Do I hear an alignment (or splits) among heart, mind, body, and spirit? Does she know what she wants, and can she communicate this in a way that is likely to evoke a positive response? Has she resolved any difficult personal experiences that were suppressive, shaming, or traumatic?

UNDERSTANDING THE WOMAN . . . OR THE GIRL

The aforementioned assessment questions seem like a lot to think about, but over time, as a clinician, you hold these reference points in awareness, as you are listening to the flow of the narrative and asking follow-up questions. Obviously, you will not ask *all* of these questions, certainly not in one or two sessions. The goal is to understand the woman herself, who she is right now. When you understand her, and she feels understood, it may be the first time she has ever experienced this. She will have revealed herself and been seen and known, which is a crucial foundation for achieving a satisfying sexuality. This is a good starting point for your work together. Understanding where you are starting from will tell you how to proceed. You may see things she is not even aware of, as you track the movements of her inner self system, watching "who" is front and center, and "who" is emerging. Is there a noticeable lack of an organizing adult self? You will formulate treatment goals on the basis of what she comes in with, but your treatment goals may change as she develops as a woman. It is a good idea to revisit them occasionally.

Chronological vs. Psychosexual Age

A client's chronological age is no indicator of psychological or sexual development. Assessing a client's psychosexual age and stage of development is an important aspect of a sexual assessment. Do I sense a full-grown woman sitting in front of me, or is she still a girl? It is also important to note that this "age" may shift as she moves from topic to topic, across her portfolio of inner selves. Some can be significantly younger than the client's chronological age. Some are older, wiser, even ageless. As you observe this client's facial expressions, gestures, posture, and choice of language, ask yourself "who" is speaking right now and how old are they? A few possibilities include Obedient Child, Scared Little Girl, Rebellious Teenager, Hovering Mother, Sophisticated Seductress, or timeless Wise Woman.

As you watch a client, does she appear to regress at certain times during the session? Some clients come in appearing very confident and adult like, but when they begin to speak about their sexuality, they exhibit considerable embarrassment, become silly, or sullen. This client may be stuck along the time line somewhere. Why is this? Did something happen to her at that age that arrested her development? I might bookmark this as a future exploration or I might ask, "How old do you feel at this moment?" A woman may pause at this question, but then she will look in and come up with an answer. This process helps her to develop the Observing Self, that part of our psyche that becomes so crucial to insight and Self-awareness. If she answers, "About twelve," I might follow up with, "Tell me more about you at twelve." Now she is more attuned to that inner twelve-year-old, and I will learn some important history.

Economic Independence and Sexual Self-Determination

Emotional maturity, self-awareness, curiosity, openness to change, intelligence, education, and self-confidence give women options. Shere Hite (1993) emphasized that you cannot decree a woman to be sexually free when she is not economically free. As sex therapists, we need to keep in mind that a woman's sexuality is entangled with her economic status. It is a sad thing to acknowledge, but a woman who is unable to support herself or her children on her own will never have equal power or equal voice in a relationship, and her sexuality will reflect this. Women throughout history have exchanged sexual access, in loveless relationships, for provision and protection. That is not to say that a woman who has chosen to be a Home Maker or a Stay-at-Home Mom (both archetypes) can't have a voice or be empowered, but this requires both a solid sense of Self and a more conscious relationship.

If a woman is in a relationship with someone suffering from addiction, or if there is domestic violence, what she needs is support and resources for dealing with these important issues first, before dealing with her sexual issues.

MAY I HAVE A WORD WITH THE DOCTOR?

Very few women feel comfortable talking about sex with their doctors, and so many sexual problems have an intersecting health, medication, and hormonal component. Women comment that doctors always seem to be in such a hurry, and yes, they are. Doctors operate under tight reimbursement parameters. I urge women to bring up sexual issues as a fundamental entitlement! Many gynecologists don't inquire about a women's sex life. There may be an "Are you satisfied with your current sex life?" yes/no box on the intake form, but this is not adequate! Checking "yes" might mean satisfied that she is successfully *avoiding* a sex life she never enjoyed, or my *partner* is satisfied, or I'm *resigned* to my present difficulties. Many doctors receive very little education on human sexuality beyond anatomy courses, and they often feel inadequately prepared to address the types of sexual issues that women face. Some are dismissive about women's sexual concerns. Cancer patients are rarely educated about how treatment will affect their sexual health and functioning (Katz, 2009). Many postmenopausal women begin to avoid sex because of changes in their uro-genital health that lead to decreased pleasure and increased discomfort. They don't understand what is happening because their doctors have never explained it to them, and they are completely unaware that viable solutions exist for these problems (Northrup, 2012). It is important to ask what medications a woman is on, as some of them have significant sexual side effects. For example, many women have been placed on SSRI anti-depressants for stress and premenstrual syndrome. They are surprised to learn that this may be the source of their utterly flattened libido. Their doctor never mentioned this side effect. It is important for sex therapists to have an excellent referral network with practitioners who are up to date and really invested in women's sexual health.

BIBLIOGRAPHY

Bennet, L., & Holczer, G. (2010) *Finding and Revealing Your Sexual Self: A Guide to Communicating About Sex*. Lanham, MD: Rowman & Littlefield.

Freedman, J., & Combs, G. (1996) *Narrative Therapy: The Social Construction of Preferred Realities*. New York: Norton.

Green, S., & Flemons, D. (Ed.) (2004) *Quickies: The Handbook of Brief Sex Therapy*. New York: Norton.

Hartman, W., & Fithian, M. (1972) *Treatment of Sexual Dysfunction: A Bio-Psycho-Social Approach*. Long Beach, CA: Center for Marital and Sexual Studies.

Hite, S. (1993) *Women as Revolutionary Agents of Change: The Hite Reports and Beyond*. Madison: University of Wisconsin Press.

Kaplan, H. S. (1974) *The New Sex Therapy: Active Treatment of Sexual Dysfunctions*. New York: Brunner/Mazel.

Kaplan, H. S. (1983) *The Evaluation of Sexual Disorders: Psychological and Medical Aspects*. New York: Brunner/Mazel.

Katz, A. (2009) *Woman, Cancer, Sex*. Pittsburgh, PA: Hygeia Media.

Laird, J. (1991) Women and Stories: Restorying Women's Self-Constructions. In M. McGoldrick, C. Anderson, & F. Walsh (Eds.) *Women in Families: A Framework for Family Therapy* (pp. 427–450). New York: Norton.

Masters, W., & Johnson, V. (1966) *Human Sexual Response*. New York: Bantam.

Masters, W., & Johnson, V. (1970) *Human Sexual Inadequacy*. Boston: Little, Brown.

Northrup, C. (2012) *The Wisdom of Menopause: Creating Physical, Emotional Health During the Change*. New York: Bantam.

Ogden, G. (2013) *Expanding the Practice of Sex Therapy: An Integrative Model for Exploring Desire and Intimacy*. New York: Routledge.

Singer, J. (1994) *Boundaries of the Soul: The Practice of Jung's Psychology*. New York: Random House. (Original work published 1972)

Stone, D., Patton, B., & Heen, S. (1999) *Difficult Conversations: How to Discuss What Matters Most*. New York: Penguin.

Wakefield, C. (2012) *Negotiating the Inner Peace Treaty: Becoming the Person You Were Born to Be*. Bloomington, IN: Balboa.

White, M. (2007) *Maps of Narrative Practice*. New York: Norton.

CHAPTER 6

TREATMENT FOUNDATIONS

"The privilege of a lifetime is to become who you truly are."

Carl Jung

THE TREE, THE ONION, AND THE ARCHEOLOGICAL DIG

It would be wonderful if fixing a sexual problem were a linear process. Sometimes simple interventions like education and permission giving go a long way. More often, the source of a woman's difficulties is more deeply embedded in self-limiting scripts, unconscious decisions made early in life, and an inner cast of characters in conflict with her Aphrodite Self.

I have a number of metaphors for how I work with clients. Sometimes it is like a decision tree. What we discover will determine where we go next. We might have a number of options, and we might loop back to revisit the branches not explored in previous sessions. Sometimes it feels like peeling the layers of an onion. The client feels like she is circling around the same old problem, but we have not really been at this place before. We are going deeper, gaining more understanding. Sometimes working with sexuality feels like an archeological dig; slowly, carefully, we are excavating layers of hardened cultural edicts and negative experiences. A skeletal Sexual Self will begin to emerge, but she will need flesh on the bones and life breathed into her to become the Goddess Aphrodite. The woman I am working with may be living as Sleeping Beauty or Cinderella, caught in a Fairy Tale Syndrome (see Chapter 11), in which case, we will work with her story line. We may be looking for a missing puzzle piece or a key to unlock the door. Clients themselves will give you metaphors. Use them!

First Order and Second Order Change

When I work with women from an archetypal perspective, I am not just coaching women on sexual skills or how to "act" sexy. Changing behavior is "first order change." I am interested in what Paul Watzlawick called "second order change." Second order change occurs at the level of *identity*. It's not just what we do, but *who we experience ourselves to be* (Fraser & Solovey, 2007; Watzlawick, Weakland, & Fisch, 1974). What flows from that will be authentic, feel right, and sustain a woman in an ongoing process of sexual Self-discovery.

When second order change occurs, there is an actual change in the brain. Ecker, Ticic, and Hulley (2012) describe how this works. The therapist surfaces implicitly held beliefs about an "old reality," then juxtaposes a "new reality." This new reality can be drawn from their lived experience, the therapeutic relationship, or any intervention that shifts a client into a new state of being. What is important is that the new reality has a *strong emotional resonance*. By placing the old and new realities side by side, the client can now *see* the disparity and *feel* the dissonance. As the "felt sense"[1] of a new reality takes hold, old neural paths unlock and new connections are made. It's as if the train track of sparking neurons switches away from the old line and creates a new route. Ecker's work is called "Coherence Therapy," and he refers to the process of changing the emotional brain as "memory reconsolidation."

When this sort of change takes place it is different from a "reframe," or countering of old thought patterns with positive self-statements. This is a transformation, an axial shift, where the world turns. New contextual realities have been established and thoughts and behaviors flow from this place. Neuroscience can actually show us these new neural networks which have been built to supplant the old ones. Both positive and negative experiences imprint the brain, but the brain is far more changeable than we once thought. Neurons turn out to be highly polyamorous, they do not mate for life. This is how we heal the negative experiences of the past. This is how we construct "preferred identities." This is how good therapy changes lives (Cozolino, 2006; Ecker et al., 2012; Levine, 2010; Siegel, 1999).

THE PRACTITIONER'S ARCHETYPAL STANCE

Because this book is about working from an archetypal perspective, I suggest that it is valuable for you to take a look at your own "archetypal identity." From what archetypal stance do you do your work?

When I think of Masters and Johnson, I think of the archetype of Scientist and Pioneer. Many sex therapists operate out of the archetypes of Educator, Empathic Listener, Consultant, and Permission Giver. Some practitioners consider themselves to be Healers. In reading Carol Ellison's writing (2000), I was struck by how she refers to herself as a Detective, Problem Solver, Choreographer, and Bridge Builder. Clearly she knows what her archetypal orientation is. Here are some other possibilities to reflect on: Catalyst, Encourager, Hope Builder, Facilitator, Expert, Collaborator, Script Consultant, Vision Holder, Wise Woman, Sage, Advocate, even Anthropologist. The archetypal orientation from which you source your work will shape what you see, how you interpret it, and how you intervene!

When you begin with yourself, take a look at the Sexual Essence Wheels in Chapter 7, and determine which archetypal energies *you* feel more or less at home with. Do you have a sense of growth and emergence in your own sexual experience? Is there movement around the wheel in your *own* sexual expression? Keep in mind that you too can develop more archetypal fluency and an awareness of your own shifting states. Being able to occupy a variety of states and perspectives will make you a better clinician, better able to match the archetypal orientation of your clients and to meet them where they are coming from. If you find yourself stuck in one archetype, you might want to experiment with how your work changes when you shift states! For example, Cora is a clinician I once supervised whose practice changed significantly when she shifted from the archetype of Behavioral Coach to Transformative Space Holder.

WHAT DOES IT MEAN TO "HOLD SPACE?"

The American Psychological Association has done research on what happens when *transformational* change takes place in therapy. Despite the emphasis on "evidence-based treatment," we return again and again to the importance of the relationship between practitioner and client (Fraser & Solovey, 2007). As practitioners, our capacity to create a space where clients feel safe to reveal themselves without judgment or agenda is crucial to all healing work, and particularly in regard to a woman's sexuality. In order to do this, we need to have worked through our own triggering material. This enables us to listen and walk with our clients through difficult experiences without being swept downstream by our own emotional reactivity or becoming hyper-rational in defense. We need to be able to model being grounded in the body, as a non-anxious, compassionate presence. We need to become good at "bi-location" (Ogden, 2013), being focused and emotionally attuned to what the client is experiencing, and yet able to reference our clinical perspective, with one foot in the client's world and one foot firmly in our own.

It is important for a practitioner to resist the inner pressure to address *everything* that goes by, attempting to get as much done as possible in one session. You can "bookmark" ideas for future work and revisit this at a later date if it still seems relevant. This can be hard in an insurance-driven world, but what clients need is a non-anxious presence, not pressure! Helping a client to embody a new way of *being* is more important than imparting large amounts of information. Clients can learn information from books. Remember that one axial shift can change everything. What clients often need the most help with is how to *be*.

One of the requirements of becoming a certified sex therapist is to attend a Sexual Attitude Restructuring class in which the practitioner evaluates his or her own attitudes, values, wounds, and assumptions about sexuality. These tend to be outside of our conscious awareness, and as practitioners we can *unconsciously* impose these on our clients. The more personal work we do as practitioners, the clearer we become and the deeper our clients can go with us.

Spontaneous Awakenings—Deepening the Experience

Clients will have moments of spontaneous awakening (Finley & Myss, 2009), when a new reality breaks through. These moments may happen *in or out of session* (we do like it when they happen *in session*). When these shifts occur, things become possible that were not possible before. I had been working with a client for months, with very little progress, and one day she burst into the session, telling me how suddenly in the grocery aisle, her world turned on its axis, and everything seemed different. Another client had a life-changing shift while she was folding the laundry. We don't always have to be on the top of a mountain for a profound experience to happen!

As practitioners, we can easily let these golden moments of potential slip by in our enthusiasm to do more work. When a client has one of these big "aha" moments, take some time! If it happens in the midst of a session, pause, and help her deepen the experience. Ask her what it feels like in her body and continue to encourage her to become more aware of the "felt sense" of this new reality. Help the roots deepen. The next time she comes in, return to this experience again to see if she has kept this in her awareness. How has this new reality changed her experience of living, loving, and being a woman?

EARLY SESSIONS—INTRODUCING THE MODEL: OUR INNER CAST OF CHARACTERS AND HOW THEY OPERATE

If we view the Sexual Self through a Jungian lens, we can think of that Sexual Self as carrying a variety of archetypal energies, shaped by culture, family, and historical experiences, burdened by scripts and complexes, but holding great creative potential to carry the energies of Aphrodite.

Having a sexual identity that feels authentic is foundational to a woman's satisfying sexuality. The woman who identifies as a Sexual Woman can speak readily about sexual aspects of her experience. She is anchored in her Aphrodite energy.

I begin to introduce the concept of the inner self system early on in my work with clients, even during intake. The metaphor of the "inner cast of characters" is easily relatable to clients who are already talking about their inner contradictions, saying things like, "A part of me wants to do this, but another part wants to do that." I might begin by saying, "It sounds like being a Mother is very important in your life. Each of us has multiple facets of self. Tell me about who you are in other areas of your life." I might say, "Have you ever noticed that these conflicted parts each have a specific feeling to them?" I am helping her tune in to the "felt sense" of her inner characters. "What if we gave these parts names?" Or I might say, "I hear what a Caring Daughter you are to your aging mother. It sounds like you become guilty and concerned when you don't have much energy left for your husband. It sounds like the Caring Daughter and the Guilty Wife are in quite a struggle."

My previous book, *Negotiating the Inner Peace Treaty* (Wakefield, 2012), will provide a more thorough overview of how to work with a woman's inner cast of characters. This is a method of personifying the inner self system, the parts or subpersonalities that live in us. We can name these parts of self, dialogue with them, and get to know them. We can gather them around an "inner round table" and negotiate with them to resolve inner conflicts. We can engage in an ongoing process of growth and discovery as we develop an Observing Self and use the insights brought to us by dream work and shadow work. Each of our inner characters has their own recognizable feel in the body. When we begin to recognize this, we can identify "who" is on the stage of our lives at various times. In having this conscious awareness of our inner workings, we come to understand that the way we see the world and how we interpret events is largely determined by which inner character's eyes we are looking through.

Other theorists have referred to these aspects of self as subpersonalities (Assagioli, 2000) and ego states (Watkins & Watkins, 1997). Fritz Perls (1969/1992), originator of *Gestalt Therapy*, externalized two inner selves, placing them in two opposing chairs and having them dialogue with each other. This has come to be known as the "two chair technique." Hal and Sidra Stone (1989) began a process of interviewing a range of "inner selves" called Voice Dialogue. Richard Schwartz (1995), creator of *Internal Family Systems* interviews "parts" (Noricks, 2011). Eric Berne (1961) creator of *Transactional Analysis*, was particularly interested in the shifting subjective ego states in two person "transactions." Berne contributed greatly to the understanding that we move through ego states that operate at different ages. He was interested in whether a person was relating from a Parent (Critical or Nurturing), Child (Adapted or Free), or clear-thinking Adult state[2] (Stewart & Joines, 1987). Identifying and working with "states" is relevant to all interpersonal "transactions," including those which are sexual.

Our "inner cast" was primarily formed early in life. Some of these inner characters are internalized versions of early caregivers and authority figures.[3] Other inner characters carry early decisions we made about how we were going to protect ourselves and get our needs met. We have a whole set of "inner selves" that formed around our sexuality, and they carry the scripts that shape how we relate to others.

As a woman begins to think about her inner cast of characters, she will begin to see their conflicts. This is the natural process of developing an Observing Self, that neutral aspect of the psyche that will allow her to lift out of her inner dynamics and reflect on her life. My goal is for her to develop an Inner Director, who can be more at choice about "who" should be center stage at what time, and for how long. Although I might offer names for a woman's inner characters, I find it best for her to name them herself. This is how a woman begins to define her inner world. One of her inner characters is the Sexual Self, which may or may not carry *any* Aphrodite energy when you first begin to work with her.

Developing her Sexual Self will require a "recalibration" of the inner self system. When a woman begins to develop her Aphrodite Self, she will need to move aside other dominant inner characters, who often do not want to share the stage. A woman needs to create a protected space for her Aphrodite Self. Aphrodite does not like being relegated to a bit part.

TRACING THE VOICES BACK

One way of discovering a woman's inner cast is to trace her scripts backward to where they originated. In doing so, the character who holds that script will begin to take shape. Differing scripts can be held by different inner characters, and those scripts can be in conflict. Each script is held with total conviction, as if it were the only script worth living. This is why women can be so conflicted and confused about their sexuality. Working with the inner cast in this way can help practitioners unlock some of the most confounding impasses in treatment.

NOTES

1 The term "felt sense" originated with Eugene Gendlin (1978). It refers to a knowing or realization that is deeply felt in the body.

2 In my work, I break down the parent, child, and adult states even further into nuanced expressions of each.

3 In other psychological theories, these "inner characters" have been referred to as "introjects."

BIBLIOGRAPHY

Assagioli, R. (2000) *Psychosynthesis: A Collection of Basic Writings*. Amherst, MA: The Synthesis Center.

Berne, E. (1961) *Transactional Analysis in Psychotherapy*. New York: Grove.

Cozolino, L. (2006) *The Neuroscience of Human Relationships: Attachment and the Developing Social Brain*. New York: Norton.

Ecker, B., Ticic, R., & Hulley, L. (2012) *Unlocking the Emotional Brain: Eliminating Symptoms at Their Roots Using Memory Reconsolidation*. New York: Routledge.

Ellison, C. (2000) *Women's Sexualities: Generations of Women Share Intimate Secrets of Sexual Self-Acceptance*. Oakland, CA: New Harbinger). www.womenssexualities.com

Finley, J., & Myss, C. (2009) *Transforming Trauma: A Seven-Step Process for Spiritual Healing*. [Audio CDs] Sounds True.

Fraser, J. S. & Solovey, A. (2007) *Second-Order Change in Psychotherapy: The Golden Thread That Unifies Effective Treatments*. Washington, DC: American Psychological Association.

Gendlin, E. (1978) *Focusing*. New York: Bantam.

Levine, P. (2010) *In an Unspoken Voice: How the Body Releases Trauma and Restores Goodness*. Berkeley, CA: North Atlantic.

Noricks, J. (2011) *Parts Psychology: A Trauma-Based Self-State Therapy for Emotional Healing*. Los Angeles: New University Press.

Perls, F. (1992) *Gestalt Therapy Verbatim*. Gouldsboro, ME: Gestalt Journal Press. (Original work published 1969)

Schwartz, R. (1995) *Internal Family Systems Therapy*. New York: Guilford.

Siegel, D. (1999) *The Developing Mind: How Relationships and the Brain Interact to Shape Who We Are*. New York: Guilford.

Stewart, I., & Joines, V. (1987) *TA Today: A New Introduction to Transactional Analysis*. Nottingham, UK and Chapel Hill, NC: Lifespace.

Stone, H., & Stone, S. (1989) *Embracing Our Selves: The Voice Dialogue Manual*. Novato, CA: Nataraj.

Wakefield, C. (2012) *Negotiating the Inner Peace Treaty: Becoming the Person You Were Born to Be*. Bloomington, IN: Balboa.

Watkins, J., & Watkins, H. (1997) *Ego States: Theory and Therapy*. New York: Norton.

Watzlawick, P., Weakland, J., & Fisch, R. (1974). *Change: Principles of Problem Formation and Problem Resolution*. New York: Norton.

CHAPTER 7

EXPLORING SEXUAL ESSENCE

"I'm every woman, it's all in me."

Chaka Khan

THE SEXUAL ESSENCE WHEELS

The Sexual Essence Wheel charts shown on the following pages developed out of my observation of the many ways in which women carry the energies of Aphrodite. The two charts, used together, cover a possible range of qualities and archetypes. I have grouped them under four main categories of sexual essence: Romantic, Nurturer, Seductress, and Mystic/ Muse (see Figures 1 and 2 and larger versions of these in the appendix).

Here is a tool for opening conversations and sparking imagination about sexual possibilities. It is a tool for exploring romantic, sensual, and erotic identity. Although the word *erotic* has become closely linked with the world of pornography, the root of the word is *Eros*. Eros represents that irresistible energy which invites us into the dance of life, into an appreciation of the senses, and into soul-to-soul encounters that can open us up to new places in the psyche (Haule, 1990). Reclaiming the word *erotic* is part of becoming a sexually empowered woman.

The Sexual Essence Wheels are designed like flowers, with four overlapping petals that draw us around the circle, symbolizing the movement of the psyche through many different expressions. The petals of each wheel also symbolize the process of emergence and unfolding that goes on throughout our entire lives. A sexual identity that exists in only

71

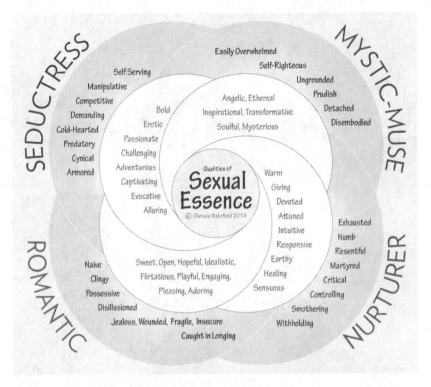

Figure 1: Qualities of Sexual Essence (see appendix for larger version)

one quadrant of these wheels, to the negation of the others, becomes stagnant like water that has ceased to move. Anytime we become ove-ridentified with *anything*, we become calcified and stuck. The Self is always seeking growth, movement, and emergence. Looking at sexual energy is a hologram for looking at how *life energy* moves through a woman.

The petals of the wheels represent four realms of sexual expres-sion. The *Romantic* quadrant holds sweetness, hope, play, idealism, and open-hearted experience. The *Nurturer* represents our capacity for grounded sensuality, sexual generosity, responsiveness, and attunement. The realm of the *Seductress* fills us with a sense of adventure, boldness, passion, and instinctual eroticism. The realm of the *Mystic or Muse* repre-sents the place of mystery, inspiration, soulfulness, and potential trans-formation. Every woman has a unique sexual essence, a blend of qualities and an archetypal resonance that represent her "native land."

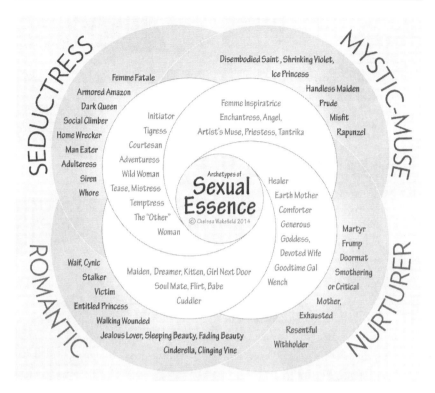

Figure 2: Archetypes of Sexual Essence (see appendix for larger version)

Each of these categories has a bright and dark aspect. When a woman moves too far into any one of these categories and neglects to balance it with elements of the others, she is likely to experience its "dark" side. The remedy usually involves her activating her interior "passport" and venturing out to travel to other lands. She can always return to her native land, but she will come home bearing gifts, enriched and restored by the new energies she now carries. Figure 3 shows all of the qualities and archetypes in table form, in both their bright and dark manifestations.

SHADOW REMEDIES—THE POISON WE MOST NEED

In working with the Sexual Essence Wheels, the solution for a woman's life often resides in the integration of qualities and archetypes from other quadrants. Initially, she may view these qualities with some suspicion and judgment, an indication that they are indeed "shadow." We get very attached to our current "ego identities," and a shadow remedy from

Types	Bright Manifestations		Dark Manifestions	
	Qualities	Archetypes	Qualities	Archetypes
Romantic	Sweet, Open Hopeful, Idealistic Flirtatious, Playful Engaging, Pleasing, Adoring	Maiden, Dreamer Kitten, Girl Next Door Soul Mate, Flirt Babe, Cuddler	Naive, Clingy, Possessive Disillusioned, Jealous Wounded, Fragile, Insecure Caught in Longing	Waif, Cynic, Entitled Princess Walking Wounded, Stalker Jealous Lover, Clinging Vine Victim, Sleeping Beauty Fading Beauty, Cinderella
Seductress	Bold, Erotic, Passionate Challenging, Adventurous Captivating, Evocative Alluring	Initiator, Tigress, Courtesan Adventuress, Wild Woman Mistress, Temptress, Tease The "Other" Woman	Self-Serving, Manipulative Competitive, Demanding Predatory, Cynical, Armored Cold Hearted	Femme Fatale, Siren Armored Amazon, Whore Dark Queen, Social Climber Home Wrecker, Man Eater Adulteress
Mystic/Muse	Angelic, Ethereal, Inspirational Transformative, Soulful Mysterious	Femme Inspiratrice Enchantress, Angel Artist's Muse Priestess, Tantrika	Easily Overwhelmed Self-Righteous Ungrounded Prudish, Detached Disembodied	Disembodied Saint, Prude Misfit, Shrinking Violet Ice Princess, Rapunzel The Handless Maiden
Nurturer	Warm, Giving, Devoted Attuned, Intuitive Responsive, Earthy, Healing Sensuous	Healer, Earth Mother, Comforter, Generous Goddess Devoted Wife, Wench Goodtime Gal	Exhausted, Numb, Resentful Martyred, Critical, Controlling, Smothering Withholding	Martyr, Frump, Doormat Exhausted-Resentful Withholder, Smothering or Critical Mother

© Chelsea Wakefield 2014

Figure 3: Sexual Essence Table

some foreign realm often looks like poison, but it is the very poison we most need to bring us out of an imbalance, enlarge the life, and bring it into greater sense of wholeness. For example, my client Betsy was an Exhausted Martyr. She couldn't stand the idea of setting limits on serving and pleasing. Taking some "me" time seemed impossible to her. Integrating just a bit of Wild Woman energy woke her up out of her martyred coma and freed her from the grip of that archetype. Initially, this looked reckless and self-serving to the Martyr, but it took the counterbalance of the Wild Woman energy to move her forward. With an infusion of this new energy, she began to feel revived as a woman.

A Disembodied Saint will be frightened to death by anything too earthy or sensuous. She may never have learned to play or care for her body. She has become imbalanced in the direction of heaven and needs some earth to ground her in the here and now and allow her to engage with mere human beings. The shy Romantic, who is too timid to ask for what she wants, will see the Bold Seductress as brash and aggressive, but she needs a bit of that boldness. The Rebellious Wild Girl won't open her heart, out of fear that she will be too vulnerable and wind up wounded. The Seductress is convinced that becoming nurturing will turn her into a Doormat. The Frump cannot imagine that she could be mysterious or alluring to anyone. The Fading Beauty, who has always relied on her superficial appearance, will resist the idea that going inward, deepening her soul, and becoming a woman of substance is a pathway to a meaningful relationship in later life. Each needs something that is offered in other quadrants.

Hal Stone and Sidra Stone (1989) use the analogy of homeopathic tinctures, where we imagine turning some shadowy quality into an infusion and taking just a few drops of it. This imaginary tincture contains the "poison" we most need to cure what ails us, to move us toward great wholeness. All of the energies represented on the Sexual Essence Wheels exist in the seedbed of the psyche, as shadow and light. Every woman carries these potentials. Some may be developed, some are like seeds lying dormant in the ground having never been watered or cultivated.

Both the qualities and archetypes found on the wheels are merely jumping-off points for conversations. It opens up discussion about the story a woman wants to live. What qualities seem impossible for her to carry? How might she begin to travel to these foreign lands? If she embodied more of a certain archetype in the bedroom, how would it change her experience? How would it be if she embodied more of that energy in the rest of her life? What would she be doing that she is not doing right now? What would she stop doing?

Ways to Use the Sexual Essence Wheels[1]

When I am using the sexual essence wheels in my practice, the process might look like this:

1) Hand the charts (I copy them front-back on one sheet of paper) to a client and let her study them. I remain silent for a good long time and allow her to take in the ideas. As she begins to respond, we move into a conversation about the qualities and archetypes represented there.

2) Where does she find herself on the wheels? I may have her circle the qualities she feels most familiar with. In my experience, I find that most women live in the realms of Romantic and Nurturer. Is she experiencing the "dark" manifestations in any of these realms? If she is in my office, it is likely that she has. For example, has the Nurturer become a Smothering Mother or a Sexual Martyr? Has the Romantic become a Wounded Woman or a Clinging Vine? Some women have absolutely

nothing in the Seductress and Mystic quadrants, and this sudden awareness surprises or awakens them. I emphasize that it is perfectly OK to inhabit *any* of these quadrants as a "homeland," but a complete vacancy in other quadrants tells me she is only accessing a portion of her erotic potential and has become constrained in some way.

3) She may not like *any* of the words I have chosen to describe qualities or archetypes. That's just fine. I then ask her to describe herself, to name her own qualities and archetypes. This is an act of Self-definition and agency. I want that.

4) Does she like where she is on the wheel? If not, where would she like to be? I may ask her to put a star next to the qualities or archetypal energies she would like to explore and possibly integrate into her sexual identity. Later on, we may employ some of the methods described in this book to "try on" the energy, to see how it feels.

5) I may ask her to talk about qualities and archetypes that make her uncomfortable. This conversation will reveal much about her sense of identity, her history, sexual scripts, wounding, and current relationship quandaries. Many women develop pervasive complexes based on experiences where they were wounded or shamed. They begin to avoid things in life that remind them of those memories. Sometimes they are unconsciously compelled to repeat an experience, trying to figure out what happened or "rework" the outcome. Trauma shuts down pleasurable possibilities and inner Protectors and Gatekeepers develop to prevent further vulnerability.

6) If the charts spark curiosity or imagination, we may talk about the "foreign lands" on the charts. How might she integrate shadow energies as part of her journey of individuation? How would this challenge her? What might this expansion open up for her? I may invite her to imagine how her *entire life* would be different if she integrated just a little bit of that quality or archetype.

Connie's Case

Connie was a sweet, young Romantic, easy-breezy at the outset of her relationships, she could purr like a Kitten. She was looking for her Prince Charming, who would rescue her from her boring life. Filled with longing, she often became a Fool for Love, idealizing the men she dated. Well-practiced in romantic projection, she was always sure this was "the one," but insecure about her ability to capture and hold a man, she rushed headlong into bed, hoping this would deepen the relationship. When she discovered that she had encountered another guy who just wanted an easy fling, she was shattered, and she would sit in my office weeping, the Wounded Innocent. After several rounds of this, I suggested we look at some other alternatives for relating. In looking at the Sexual Essence Wheels, the Muse caught her eye. She so wanted to be sought after and idealized. We talked about how the Muse was a cooler archetype than Connie's "home base" of Romantic. In Connie's imagination, the Muse hung back and allowed herself to be admired from afar. She did not reach for a man; she was sought after, carrying a more detached archetypal energy, not anxious, definitely more self-contained. The Muse does not hand herself over on a platter. She takes her time before giving her heart away. Connie liked this idea, and we began to work with the felt sense of this energy. In doing so, she began to feel more grounded in herself, more confident, and more valuable. She began to sit back during a first date. Rather than leaning in and gushing forth to tell all, she began to listen and watch the men she was interested in. In doing so, she began to catch her romantic projections and to see who she was really dealing with. The "players" began to fall away and about a year later, she met a quiet guy who was not quite as flashy as her previous amours, but turned out to be a person of emotional depth, who appreciated her warm heart and was interested in becoming her Soul Mate.

OTHER WAYS OF EXPLORING ESSENCE

Archetypes are systems of energy that originate in the psyche, are felt in the body, and shape values, perceptions, emotions, needs, and agendas. We can integrate new archetypal energies, and in doing so, expand our identities, so that our lives can become more fulfilling.

Actress Archetypes

One venue in which such a wide range of sexual archetypes is portrayed is film: the Sex Kitten in Marilyn Monroe, the Saucy Vamp in Mae West, the Femme Fatale in Angelina Jolie, the Romantic idealism and vulnerability of Ingrid Bergman, the Girl Next Door in Doris Day and Julie Andrews, the Playful Pixie in Meg Ryan, the cool, distant (Muse like) beauty of Grace

Kelly, the fiesty, sultry, earthy Goddess in Sophia Loren. Every generation has its leading ladies, and they carry a spectrum of sexual archetypes. This is why they become such great "projection screens" for women and is part of the reason why we love the movies. Ask your clients about the women in film that they are drawn to and discuss the quality of the energies these women hold. Have them imagine being "her" and explore how it would feel to carry that energy in their own bodies.

Tigress or a Shy Doe?

Another way of exploring sexual essence is to ask a woman, "In terms of your sexuality, if you were an animal, what kind would you be?" I enjoy asking this question in workshops and hearing the wide variety of animals in the room, a veritable zoo: shy does, tigresses, otters, praying mantis, scared rabbits, doves, eagles, monkeys. Experiment with changes of animal and see how this shifts her state. Have her imagine being various creatures and see how it feels. What would she do in the "essence" of this creature that she is not doing now? How would she engage her partner differently? How would she engage life differently?

What Is Your Elemental Essence?

Exploring the elements is another way for a woman to understand herself. If she were a force of nature, what would she be? If she were a landscape, how might she describe herself? Is she a tornado or a summer breeze, an ocean of love or a parched desert, the frozen tundra of Russia or a teeming rain forest? Is her fire blazing or banked down? Is she earthy or airy? How does she experience herself in relationship with her partner? How might she want to change this? If she is in touch with her essence, has she been able to reveal this to her partner? If not, why not? What does her partner long for? Is this in her? If not, would she be interested in expanding her sexual expression while retaining who she is at her core?

Music, Movement, and Private Dancing

Moving and dancing in the privacy of her home are great ways to open up a constricted energy field. It is a way of exploring sexual essence. Middle Eastern and Tribal dancing, Tango, Salsa, Flamenco, Hip Hop, or even

Pole-Dancing classes are wonderful ways for women to explore embodiment, eroticism, sexual tension, the interplay of challenge and surrender, celebration, boldness, instinct, freedom, and transcendence. For the woman who might be too shy to be seen in a pole-dancing class, a home DVD like Laurie Conrad's (2001) *The Art of Erotic Dancing for Everyday Women* might help her find her inner beauty through sensual movement. In doing so, she will come up against the inner Voices of Warning, and she can trace them back to their source and examine if she really wants to live under their "rule." This is not about "acting sexy." It is about expanding a woman's sense of internal freedom and her range of external expression. Part of empowering a woman in her sexuality is for her to know that she has *choices*. She can choose if, when, and how she wants to activate *any* of her archetypal energies.

Questions to Ask

When a woman is "trying on" an archetypal energy, here is a list of questions you might ask her. Be careful not to barrage her with questions. Ask only the ones that seem relevant and give her time to really tune in to her inner experience, the sensual orientation of the energy. If she appears to be returning to a thinking state, ask her about sensations in her body again.

- What does this energy feel like? (You are looking for body sensations)
- What does the world look like from here?
- How would you dress or decorate your home from this place? What kind of car would you drive? Where would you go on vacation? (You can engage in additional "how would you be different" questions. Your client will sit, gesture, and move differently from this place. It can be valuable to have her move around the room, to become accustomed to new ways of moving and being.)
- When you are in this new energy, what do you want to experience or express?
- If you carried this energy, what would you be doing that you are not currently doing? What would you stop doing that you are currently doing?
- Is there anyone in your inner cast who would object or feel anxious about you expressing this energy? (We are looking for

Gatekeepers, Inner Critics, Script Monitors, Reputation Police, Vulnerable Children, or Voices of Warning. More on this in Chapter 10.

- If this were more of your "homeland," how would you engage a partner differently? How might your partner respond to you in this new place? This will raise both hopes and vulnerabilities to be explored later. She doesn't even have to inform her partner, she might just "carry the energy" and see what happens. Remember that differing archetypes evoke differing responses.

- When working with clients in search of a partner, ask her, "What kind of partner would you choose to engage with from this place?" This begs the question of "who" in us picks our partners! It is wise to look at potential partners through a variety of lenses within the inner cast, before deciding that this is "the one." Likewise, carrying a different archetypal energy as "front-runner," might be the key to *attracting* the partner the woman really wants!

This experience may have been wonderfully exciting and expansive, but it might also have stirred up anxiety or shame. Process this. Find out "who" in her is anxious or ashamed. This can be the basis for another dialogue to explore these concerns. One important point about dialoguing is that we don't "argue" with restrictive inner voices, we respectfully consider their viewpoints and concerns (Wakefield, 2012). I have found it helpful, in working with anxious inner selves, to assure them that it is the client's *conscious choice* regarding when, how, and where she will express any new archetypal energy.

Sexual Path Preferences

Women also have what Mosher (1980) called a Sexual Path Preference. When a woman learns about her preferred path, it can enlighten her regarding partner mismatches. The three paths are *sexual trance, partner engagement,* and *role enactment.*

Women who enjoy *sexual trance* like to move inward. They enjoy becoming absorbed in their sensuality and focus on their inner experience and all the pleasurable sensations. They often close their eyes to avoid the distractions around them. Asking them a question or even speaking to them may break their sexual trance. Their interior experience can be quite mystical or spiritual. They want their sexual experiences protected and insulated from the world and enjoy atmospheres that help "take them away." Women can also travel into their interior world when they are unhappy with their current partner, imagining being far away with a dream lover.

Women who like *partner engagement* are usually high Romantics. They love eye contact, intimate exchanges, the communication of feelings and sensations during their love-making. They may also enjoy "lusty" talk. A sense of attunement and communion is one of their main motivations for sex, the desire for sensual connection to strengthen the bond of love. They might object vehemently to the discovery that their lover is imagining another woman while making love to them. They want the focus to be here and now, on each other. Women who blend Romantic and Mystic on the Sexual Essence Wheels will find Tantric sexual practices (Dunas, 1997; Stubbs, 1999) particularly fulfilling.

Role enactment is a style of sexual engagement that involves an exploration of fantasy scripts and scenarios. These women can have a field day with explorations of sexual archetypes, moving around the wheel into all kinds of different pairings and creative expressions. If she finds a partner to play with, the couple may plan out highly scripted dramas to enact. Sexual skills are valued by these lovers, but imagination is valued even more. They employ the use of erotica, costumes, mirrors, sex toys, lingerie, unusual settings, lusty talk, and anything that creates novelty and heightens sensory and dramatic intensity.

Some women really enjoy enacting fantasies; some fantasies lose their magic when played out. Making love on a deserted beach may seem romantic, until sand gets introduced into the mix. For the bold and adventurous woman who wants to bring fantasies to life, Deborah Addington (2003) has written a guidebook for erotic role-play.

DONELLA'S DILEMMA

Donella came to work with me because her partner, Samantha, had called her a "dead fish" in bed (definitely one of those negative sexual archetypes). Donella was confused, "I don't understand. I love the way she touches me. I close my eyes and float away because it's paradise! I have these enormous orgasms. What does she want from me?" Donella was describing her own sexual path preference of *sexual trance*. I asked,

"Does she want you to look into her eyes?" "Yes!" she said, "and it's so distracting. I can't stay turned on!" Her partner's path preference was clearly *partner engagement*.

I began to talk to Donella about archetypes and sexual path preferences. We looked at the Sexual Essence Wheels together, and I asked her where she felt most at home. She pointed to the quadrant of the Mystic. For her, sex transported her into the spiritual realm. She was having her own private mystical experience, with a sweetheart of a partner who longed for terms of endearment and intense engagement. The light bulb came on for Donella. She finally understood. We began to talk about sexual cooperation and how this Mystic could become more engaged.

Mismatched sexual path preferences can lead to untold grief for partners who have great sexual skills but can't seem to "meet" each other in bed. Both think their way of being sexual is best and they are often hurt by or critical of the other, taking their partner's style as a personal rejection. As Donella and I talked about the Sexual Essence Wheels, I asked her what realm she might be comfortable exploring outside of her "native homeland." She decided she could definitely be an Earth Mother, moving into the quadrant of the Nurturer. We began to explore ways she could do this. "I guess I could tell her that I love her!" We laughed. What now seemed obvious was not so obvious before. She suddenly felt the stirring of a much younger self, a Humiliated Teen, struggling with her sexual orientation. She recalled an earlier experience where she had expressed feelings for someone and had been shamed and rebuffed. She recalled making a vow that she would never openly express herself again. When we surfaced that memory, we were able to work with it to reduce the lingering charge, opening more capacity to express.

Donella planned a special evening, where she set up a blanket in front of the fireplace with some sensuous music and massage oil. She had prepared a plate of delicious fruits to enjoy, and gave her partner a terrific massage, making engagement the central point of the experience. For the first time, she became aware of how much that Humiliated Teen had kept her walled off from the love that her partner offered her. Her evening of sensual delights was very well received, and she found herself truly enjoying the engaging Earth Mother she had activated inside. Making eye contact became easier, and when she explained sexual path preferences to her partner, she invited her partner to just receive pleasure instead of feeling so pressured to always be giving. Walking in each other's preferred paths opened up new awareness for both of them, and enriched their loving relationship.

CORE EROTIC THEMES—ARCHETYPES AND THE EROTIC IMAGINATION

When you begin to explore a woman's sexual imagination, you will discover what Jack Morin (1995) called "core erotic themes." *The Erotic Mind* is a book I recommend to my clients, because imagination is at the center of eroticism, and women who understand this are more likely to have emotionally meaningful and erotically satisfying sex. Morin did research on "peak erotic experiences" analyzing their core components.

Although Morin does not frame his work archetypally, these core erotic themes can easily be viewed through an archetypal lens. Two people in a matchup of core erotic themes will experience the most compelling sex of their lives. When women begin to reminisce about some past sexual experience that was particularly memorable, spend some time exploring the subjective experience. What archetypal energy was she in? How did the scene unfold, and what part did she play? What part did the partner play? Was this a "Mt. Olympus" experience, or something that sustained in a lingering relationship? Where has she felt most sexually free? What contributed to this? Where does she typically live (her archetypal stance) with her current partner? If she has never had such an experience, what has she imagined and who is she in that scenario? How is she different there than in real life? What would happen if she began to bring more of this fantasy energy into her life? If she is denying it or suppressing it, why?

FANTASY AND REALITY

Nancy Friday is the author of a string of books that explore private erotic imagination. She began to interview women at a time when women did not talk about their fantasies. Her early work, and most famous book, is *My Secret Garden* (Friday, 1973). Her work shows that normal people have wildly imaginative and unusual fantasies.

Fantasies are not meant to be taken literally. They are like waking dreams, filled with symbolic material and archetypal inhabitations. The most controversial fantasy that many women have involves being forced into sexual acts, sometimes being forced to experience pleasure.

Do women secretly want to be raped? They do not. Marion Woodman (1982, 1985) asserts that fantasies in which a woman is "raped" or forced to experience pleasure "against her will" are mischaracterized. She emphasizes that these scenes actually convey a longing in women to be *ravished*, broken open by a profound experience and swept away. This is why women become fascinated with the archetype of the Pirate, the Outlaw, and the Bad Boy. They want to be in contact with something wild that will break them free of the boring, well-behaved Good Girl. Women who can't access their own wildness want to be taken out of their heads, into their deep feminine nature, their innate sexuality, rooted in the instinctual body.

Bader (2002) believes that sexual fantasies reflect a complex reworking of internal fears and longings. They offer an arena for women to be free, selfish, narcissistic, vengeful, and aggressive (shadow qualities for most women). In their fantasies, women can play out these impulses without guilt, shame, or the fear of being punished. In fantasies of being dominated, a woman doesn't have to take care of anyone or be sensitive to anyone's feelings. Fantasies allow the woman who has been rejected or overlooked to compensate. She can imagine herself as a sought-after, high-priced Call Girl, or a mysterious Muse, capturing an artist's imagination and inspiring great art.

Sex therapist Wendy Maltz (Maltz & Boss, 1997) names the most common themes in women's fantasies (which are all archetypes): Pretty Maiden, Victim, Wild Woman, Dominatrix, Beloved, and Voyeur. Although Maltz addresses the downside of women who live in fantasy (avoiding real-life relationships), she encourages women to use their fantasy life as a doorway into deeper Self-understanding.

Note

1 If you would like a color copy of the Sexual Essence Wheels, contact me through my website and I will happily send you a PDF copy.

Bibliography

Addington, D. (2003) *Fantasy Made Flesh: The Essential Guide to Erotic Roleplay.* Emeryville, CA: Greenery.

Bader, M. (2002) *Arousal: The Secret Logic of Sexual Fantasies.* New York: Thomas Dunne.

Conrad, L. (2001) *The Art of Exotic Dancing for Everyday Women, Video 1* [DVD]. Philadelphia Films.

Dunas, F. (1997) *Passion Play: Ancient Secrets for a Lifetime of Health and Happiness Through Sensational Sex*. New York: Riverhead.

Friday, N. (1973) *My Secret Garden: Women's Sexual Fantasies*. New York: Pocket.

Haule, J. (1990) *Divine Madness: Archetypes of Romantic Love*. Boston: Shambhala.

Maltz, W., & Boss, S. (1997) *In the Garden of Desire: The Intimate World of Women's Sexual Fantasies*. New York: Broadway.

Morin, J. (1995) *The Erotic Mind: Unlocking the Inner Sources of Sexual Passion and Fulfillment*. New York: Harper Perennial.

Mosher, D. L. (1980). Three Dimensions of Depth of Involvement in Human Sexual Response. *The Journal of Sex Research, 30*, 1, 1–42.

Ogden, G. (2013) *Expanding the Practice of Sex Therapy: An Integrative Model for Exploring Desire and Intimacy*. New York: Routledge.

Stone, H., & Stone, S. (1989) *Embracing Our Selves: The Voice Dialogue Manual*. Novato, CA: Nataraj.

Stubbs, K. (1999) *The Essential Tantra: A Modern Guide to Sacred Sexuality*. New York: Tarcher/Putnam.

Wakefield, C. (2012) *Negotiating the Inner Peace Treaty: Becoming the Person You Were Born to Be*. Bloomington, IN: Balboa.

Woodman, M. (1982) *Addiction to Perfection: The Still Unravished Bride*. Toronto, ON: Inner City.

Woodman, M. (1985) *The Pregnant Virgin: A Process of Psychological Transformation*. Toronto, ON: Inner City.

CHAPTER 8

WORKING WITH THE INNER SELF SYSTEM

"Everything in the universe is within you."

Rumi

Most women really take to the metaphor of the "inner cast of characters." As they embrace this way of looking at themselves, they will begin to speak of their Work Self versus their Home Self or their Home Self versus their Vacation Self. All of us have had the experience of leaving our regular lives and going away. As we unwind, we begin to feel like an entirely different person. It's one of the reasons we long to get away.

CHARTING THE INNER CAST OF CHARACTERS

As a woman begins to name her inner characters, you can "chart" them. This is a way of analyzing "who" supports their emerging sexuality and "who" does not. For example, my client Maureen came to realize that she could not go to bed, let alone have sex, until the whole house was picked up. She named this domineering inner character "Molly the Maid." Having personified this character, she also knew what her body felt like when Molly was center stage. This allowed Maureen to "direct" Molly to take the rest of the night off. Another client could not stop worrying about her children while she was making love. Her Hovering Mother was continually listening for the children, distracting her from sensation and personal pleasure. We will talk more about various Eros-inhibiting archetypes in Chapter 15. For most women, it has never occurred to them that they might be able to set limits on these domineering inner characters that carry them off in directions they do not want to go. That is the benefit of developing an Inner Director.

If a woman wants to chart her inner cast, it can be done in a variety of ways. I like to draw circles around a "table" with a name in each circle. Sometimes I draw the circles in differing sizes to show how much space they take up in someone's inner system, sometimes I cluster them to see who gangs up with whom. I sometimes draw the Vulnerable Children hiding behind whoever protects them in the inner self system. Some of my clients have artistic talent (which I do not). They have brought in drawings of their inner characters. Some women create collages on poster boards. Selecting pieces of music that match various inner self states is a great way of getting to know one's "inner cast" better. I had a client who created a group of felted dolls. This process allowed her to meditate on how each one felt when activated in her psyche, and focus on the function and history of each. You can draw a pie chart showing how much space each of these inner characters takes up. Does she like this allotment of time and energy? Would she like to change the ratio? In charting the inner cast of characters you can ask which ones support a woman's Aphrodite Self (and which ones undermine her, and why? What might this woman add to the mix that would support her in expanding her sexual essence?

VOICE DIALOGUE—GETTING TO KNOW YOU

One of the fastest and most effective ways of exploring the inner cast of characters and increasing client awareness is through a process called Voice Dialogue (Dyak, 1999; Stone & Stone, 1989; Wakefield, 2012). This system of interview will be familiar to those who have trained in Internal Family Systems (Schwartz, 1995) or Gestalt (Perls, 1969/1992) "two chair" technique, which are also effective ways of doing dialogue work.

In Voice Dialogue, the facilitator interviews a person's inner cast, character by character, allowing them to come forward and speak from their unique point of view. Each of these inner characters carries a particular archetypal resonance and has a history and a way of seeing the world. They each have a unique set of needs and an agenda. The material that emerges by interviewing each of these inner characters can solve many mysteries in the client's life. In the process, you will discover additional sexual history that wasn't previously mentioned, early decisions that were long forgotten, contradictory scripts and characters in conflict, and vulnerable children hiding behind the curtain of awareness, stirring up great anxiety. Once known, we can address the needs and goals of these parts of self, and "negotiate inner peace treaties" (Wakefield, 2012).

While the Sexual Essence Wheels suggests a number of archetypal manifestations, I like to allow my clients to come up with their own names for their inner cast. We may discuss this before the "interview," or a name may emerge during the interview. Sometimes I begin with a generic name like the Vulnerable Child, but that child may want to differentiate herself from other Vulnerable Children. I may be speaking to "Sissy," a woman's inner four-year-old on one occasion, and her thirteen-year-old "Shari" on another. The adult woman may be "Sharon." We delineate differing stages of development in this way and capture a deeper feel for each time period.

To make it clear that we are "separating out" this inner self, I ask clients to move their chairs over, or to shift to a different location on my couch. This indicates to the body that we are speaking from a specific part of the psyche. We will return to the client's original spot after the interview to signify that they are reintegrating, and to allow them to reflect on what transpired during the interview. Returning to the original position also allows the client to feel the internal shift in the quality of the energy, out and away from that specific "character." She has now experienced that she can separate out from this inner material, observe it, understand it, and direct it. In the process, she is developing her Observing Self and her Inner Director, that part of the client that can make conscious choices about which archetypal energy to lead with in various situations. Hal Stone and Sidra Stone (1989) call the process of becoming aware of what lives in us, and gaining sufficient conscious separation to direct these inner selves, the Aware Ego Process.

In conducting a Voice Dialogue session, we select the inner characters that seem to be related to the current situation. I like to begin with the archetypes the woman is most identified with, so that when she separates out from this "self," she can notice that it is possible to make space for something else. I might also talk to her Eros-inhibiting archetypes (Chapter 15) or Sexual Gatekeepers (Chapter 10), inner characters that create great difficulties for a woman's Aphrodite Self.

After moving over, the client speaks in the first person, *from* that distinct part of the psyche. For example, "I am Sharon's Good Girl Self."

Another important aspect of Voice Dialogue is that the facilitator should attempt to match the energetic state of the character being interviewed. This creates a sense of attunement and affinity. For example, if the inner character being interviewed is highly animated, the facilitator responds in a lively fashion. If the character is shy or quiet, the facilitator would slow down and proceed more quietly and gently. Some of your client's inner characters will be very reticent to speak at all. If this is the case, just sit in silence and BE WITH the client. Silence is highly underrated in therapy, and is an aspect of holding space!

The client may move to several positions and speak as several inner characters in one Voice Dialogue session, but I talk to one at a time. Often while a client is speaking from one inner character, others want to chime in to explain, disagree, or reinterpret what is being said. I assure them that we can talk to them later, but for now, we are just speaking to "so and so."[1]

If the client gets overwhelmed or flooded by emotion during one of these sessions, I will assess their level of distress and determine if we want to continue, or move back to their "center" and employ some grounding and calming interventions. I try to keep a client's emotional state within a "window of tolerance" (Levine, 2009, 2010).

Healthy people are aware of their shifting internal states and can self-regulate and operate as the organizing director of this inner self system. The more aware a woman becomes of "who" lives in her, the more able she becomes to make wise life choices, to resolve internal conflicts and negotiate between warring parts of self (Wakefield, 2012). I assure the client that we will "put them back together" before they leave, and *I always check very carefully to make sure that they are reintegrated and oriented in present time and space before they leave the treatment room.* If I assess that a client is having problems with dissociation or reintegration, we address this as a focus of treatment before proceeding further. Dissociation is indicative of trauma. It is my belief that all sex therapists should have some training in how to recognize trauma and work with dissociative states, or have some good referral sources.

Not all clients will do a "novel" thing like Voice Dialogue. Some are not comfortable with using their imaginations. Some say, "I'm not an actor." I assure them that this is not about acting, but learning to recognize the distinct energies of these inner forces that drive our lives, to learn more about the history of that energy system and how to direct it. Moving in and out of that "slice of the psyche" allows clients to experience that they are not confined to this way of being. They can direct this energy, turn the volume up and down, and make space for other expressions of Self. If a client does not want to engage in a Voice Dialogue, I can always ask about what this "part" or that "part" is thinking, feeling, and saying to them. It is not as powerful for the client as actually speaking from *inside* that self-state, but it still reveals a lot of valuable material.

What to Say After You Say Hello—Voice Dialogue Queries

Here I offer a list of queries that might be used during a Voice Dialogue session. These are not "must asks," or in any specific order. After a while, you will have the basic questions memorized and you won't need a list. The best interviews flow naturally, with questions that feel most relevant to the situation. Feel free to inquire in ways I haven't listed here. This is just a list to get you started. Allow each character to name him/her/itself (some might be creatures or objects).

Possible Voice Dialogue queries to an inner character:

- Tell me about yourself.
- What is your history?
- Ask, "How old are you?" if you sense you are speaking to an inner character who seems quite a bit younger or older.
- Tell me what was happening in (client's name)'s life at the time you (the inner character) came into being. (You might get an alternative history here from the perspective of the inner character).
- How did you learn to be (name capacities or qualities)?
- Who were your major teachers and role models?
- What is important to you? Do you have a motto, a philosophy?
- How are you trying to help or protect (the client's name)?
- What do you need?
- What do you fear?

Some additional questions you may ask about the sexuality work:

- How do you feel about the sexuality work that we are doing? (If you have given the client some homework, you can check on this as well.)
- Regarding sex, tell me what is OK and what is not OK.

- How did you come to feel this way? (Looking for script history)
- How do you feel about (the client)'s partner? (This is important because different inner characters may have very different feelings!)
- Is there anything you long for sexually? How might that be fulfilled?
- Do you have any concerns? What kind of assurance do you need related to this?
- Is there anything else you would like to say to (client's name)?

We are learning how this inner character shapes the client's world view and functioning. We are also learning to recognize how this energy is carried in the body. It is important to ask them about the "felt sense" of this archetypal energy when it is activated in her system. As our understanding of the inner self system builds, we can begin to recognize the interrelationship between inner characters and how this has an impact on the client. Resolving conflicts between inner characters is similar to any kind of conflict resolution: clarifying values, needs and concerns, judgments, and misconceptions; identifying areas of commonality; seeing where one party is willing to compromise in exchange for some compensation or assurance from the other party.

POST INTERVIEW INSIGHTS

At the very end of the Voice Dialogue session, I move the client back into her original position and give her a moment to settle and separate out from the other states she was in. Sometimes I have the client practice dialing the energies of various inner characters up and down, so that she can experience control over the degree to which these energies inhabit her. This helps a woman become aware that she has the capacity to direct this energy, with conscious intention. I begin to refer to this capacity as having an Inner Director. At this point in the session, I also give the client a chance to review any significant "ahas" about how all of this has been affecting the choices and direction of her life.

Sometimes it becomes evident that a new archetypal energy is needed, which will bring balance to a system that has tipped too far into an extreme. She may need to integrate a new inner character, an inner supporter or protector, someone bold, courageous, fun loving, or sensuous.

Tracking Dreams for Missing Elements

Following a Voice Dialogue session, I ask my clients to track their dreams. Dreams following this kind of work will offer resonant images of the changes and shifts in the psyche. A dream may bring in a character that carries the archetypal energy needed to recalibrate the inner self system. Dreams act as a conduit to the Self, and the psyche at night has an innate wisdom regarding what a person is ready to face, integrate, and work through. Dreams balance the psyche and pose questions that stir us up, introduce new energies, provide pictures of where we are, and where we are going. They are a resource that many clinicians dismiss as too difficult to understand or mere wanderings of the mind at night. Simply attending to the archetypal energies stirred up by a dream can open up new pathways of learning and provide powerful energy for change. Some dreams may be so outside our waking reality that we find them disturbing. These "shadow dreams" may present themselves as nightmares, which are particularly good at getting our attention. Dream workers emphasize that *all* of our dreams come in the service of healing, growth, and wholeness (Johnson, 1986; Singer, 1972/1994; Taylor, 2009).

We all have experienced mornings where we awaken, feeling entirely different from the night before, sometimes with fresh solutions to old problems. It is as if the brain were alive at night and new neural synapses were being wired. The new brain research is teaching us that this is exactly what happens when we have a profound emotional experience. Powerful dreams can be the catalyst for creating these axial shifts (Kalsched, 2013). When this happens, we as practitioners can amplify these effects by carrying the power of the dream forward. Donald Kalsched's (1996, 2013) work is particularly enlightening on how trauma shapes the brain and how dream work can heal. To learn more about working with dreams, read the works of Wakefield (2012), Johnson (1986), Taylor (2009), and Gordon, (2007).

Marie's Lioness

My client Marie (Wakefield, 2014) began her work with me after her Straight Arrow husband revealed to her that he had become attracted to a young woman in the office. Jack had suddenly come to life, complaining that he wanted more out of life than just being a Good Husband and a Responsible Provider. Marie was almost totally dominated by the archetype of the Devoted Mother. She tended to put herself last in all things, hadn't exercised in years, and laughed about being the quintessential Frump. Totally out of touch with her body, she had decided she wanted more in life as well. We began working together, to try to awaken her slumbering libido, not just for Jack, but for her life. She was far from experiencing herself as a sexual being, and then she brought in a dream. In the dream, she was on the African tundra watching a beautiful sleek Lioness. The dream was filled with sensual energy and that Lioness became a powerful touchstone of sensual embodiment, and her emergent sexuality. We engaged in a Voice Dialogue session where Marie "tried on" the energy of that Lioness. As Marie entered into the Lioness energy, she changed dramatically. Her face dropped about fifteen years and she stretched herself out on the couch, relaxed, confident, and downright sultry. She quieted down into a kind of timeless mystery, looked confidently into my eyes and smiled a knowing smile. I began to dialogue with the Lioness, who suddenly knew exactly how she wanted to be touched. She wanted her body stroked in long strokes, with firm, slow hands. She wanted to playfully roll around in bed without regard to who was up or down or whether anyone was about to fall off. She wanted long, lingering mornings in bed with no kids around, when she and her "lover" were rested, and there was plenty of time. We ended that session reflecting on the significant differences in the energetic feel of the Lioness and her usual Devoted Mother and Dutiful Wife. Marie was becoming the director of her inner cast, and she began to pull this Lioness energy into her life. I always marvel at what dreams can bring. Stretching out and becoming unhurried was something Marie could not remember in years. Being playful was something she had *never* been. Marie began to reorder her priorities. She began to take care of herself, and in the process she transformed from Frump to fabulous Feline. She and Jack began to get away and play, and as they kindled their sensuous fire for the very first time, Jack's interest in the Sweet Young Thing faded into the African sunset.

NOTE

1 Occasionally, I get a client who is concerned that this means they have a "multiple personality disorder" like in the movie *Sybil*. I handle this by explaining that *everyone* houses multiple ego states and subpersonalities. Having an Observing Self or "inner director" who is conscious of them and can manage them is indicative of mental health.

Bibliography

Dyak, M. (1999) *The Voice Dialogue Facilitator's Handbook, Part 1*. Seattle: L.I.F.E. Energy Press.

Gordon, D. (2007) *Mindful Dreaming: A Practical Guide for Emotional Healing Through Transformative Mythic Journeys*. Franklin, NJ: Career Press.

Johnson, R. (1986) *Inner Work: Using Dreams and Active Imagination for Personal Growth*. New York: HarperCollins.

Kalsched, D. (1996) *The Inner World of Trauma: Archetypal Defenses of the Personal Spirit*. New York: Routledge.

Kalsched, D. (2013) *Trauma and the Soul: A Psycho-Spiritual Approach to Human Development and its Interruption*. New York: Routledge.

Levine, P. (2009) *Trauma, Somatic Experiencing and Peter A. Levine PhD*. www.youtube.com/watch?v=ByalBx85iC8 accessed 11/30/2014

Levine, P. (2010) *In an Unspoken Voice: How the Body Releases Trauma and Restores Goodness*. Berkeley, CA: North Atlantic.

Perls, F. (1992) *Gestalt Therapy Verbatim*. Gouldsboro, ME: Gestalt Journal Press. (Original work published 1969)

Schwartz, R. (1995) *Internal Family Systems Therapy*. New York: Guilford.

Singer, J. (1994) *Boundaries of the Soul: The Practice of Jung's Psychology*. New York: Random House. (Original work published 1972)

Stone, H., & Stone, S. (1989) *Embracing Our Selves: The Voice Dialogue Manual*. Novato, CA: Nataraj.

Taylor, J. (2009) *The Wisdom of Your Dreams: Using Dreams to Tap Into Your Unconscious and Transform Your Life*. New York: Tarcher Penguin.

Wakefield, C. (2012) *Negotiating the Inner Peace Treaty: Becoming the Person You Were Born to Be*. Bloomington, IN: Balboa.

Wakefield, C. (2014) In Search of Aphrodite: Working With Archetypes and an Inner Cast of Characters in Women with Low Sexual Desire. *The Journal of Sexual and Relationship Therapy*, 29, 1, 31–41.

CHAPTER 9

ARCHETYPAL FLUENCY— SHIFTING STATES

"I dwell in possibility."

Emily Dickinson

ARCHETYPAL FLUENCY—SHIFTING STATES

A significant amount of writing has been done on a woman's need to "transition" to the bedroom. Suggestions are made to "simmer" anticipation, prepare the space, enlist the partner in household tasks, take a hot bath, and so on. I like to call this capacity to transition "shifting states." In transitioning from a busy work day, a woman needs to move from one set of inner selves to another if she is to become interested in sensual engagement. For the woman in the low-sex marriage (Weiner Davis, 2008) who is seeking *more* sexual engagement, she needs to consider the archetypal states she inhabits and consider which is most inviting and likely to evoke a positive response from her partner. We are talking about shifting archetypal states from task-oriented selves to pleasure-oriented selves, from a pressured, thinking orientation to a feeling, sensing orientation. Women are quite serious when they state that foreplay is a man doing the dishes to give a woman time to wind down. Taking a shower or a bath does wonders for most women in helping them shift states.

Once a client begins to develop her Observing Self and an awareness of her inner cast, she can shift her inner state with consciousness and intention. We may begin this learning process by noting the "felt sense" of various inner characters in a Voice Dialogue session, and then moving in and out of them. Shifting into a *sensual* or *being state* can be very difficult for some women and requires practice! It can feel like "doing nothing" to a productive, responsible woman. You can help her become accustomed to this state by facilitating it in your office. Once there, take some time and allow her to experience the beauty of *being*. If your client is dominated by an inner Hovering Mother, time for herself will feel selfish, indulgent, even reckless. If she houses a Corporate Climbing Workaholic, downshifting will feel foolish and inefficient and she may feel intense anxiety that she is falling behind the pack. One of the ways I suggest that women navigate these distressing feelings is to ask, "Who is upset?" meaning which of her inner characters is kicking up resistance here? Does she want *that* inner character to be center stage at this time? If not, she can direct the Workaholic or Hovering Mother (or whoever else is dominating the show) off stage. That's the purpose of developing an Inner Director.

There are a lot of ways to shift states, but women who do it well begin with conscious *attention* to the archetypal states they are in and focused *intention* regarding where they want to be. Women can learn to set limits on Eros-inhibiting archetypes. Soaking in water does wonders. Music can work like magic. Yoga gets stuck energy moving and relaxes the body. An evening walk is a lovely way to wind down. Some women read erotica to connect them with their sexual psyche and get their juices flowing. Lingerie is not just for a partner's eyes. A woman will feel far more sensual when she has just bathed in Lavender bath salts and donned a silk nightgown than when she is lying in front of the TV in oversized sweat pants.

The ISIS Wheel of Sexual Integration

Gina Ogden's (2013) ISIS wheel work is an elegant, immediate way for clients to experience shifting states while learning a great deal about their sexual scripts, and how integrated or conflicted they are about their sexuality. An ISIS wheel can be set up in a flash on a practitioner's floor, with four cards that read Heart, Mind, Body, and Spirit. I add two beaded ribbons that crisscross in the middle to establish that we have four quadrants. I then invite my clients to get onto their feet, and walk in a circle around the quadrants, talking about their experience in each dimension: heart, mind, body, and spirit. Walking from one quadrant to the next, they recognize that each space is distinctly different from the others. The movement helps clients to *experience* that they are not "wedded" to one way of feeling, thinking, sensing, or perceiving. They can shift states, moving from one quadrant to the next!

EVOCATIVE MUSIC

Music helps women shift states. It is a powerful resource often underused by practitioners and is a great way for a woman to explore archetypes of sexuality. You might encourage a client to create her own collection of songs that express the range of "selves" that live in her and help her energize desired states of being. Have her create a collection of music and encourage her to make time to move to its rhythms. She can become her own Private Dancer. As she discovers who she is when no one is watching, she can bring this rich material into future sessions.

Through music, you can explore energies, anxieties, and the power of shifting states. What are the memories and associations she has with each selection? Which of them belong to the past, the present, or the possible future? Ask her about the inner shifts that take place as she frees herself to move, particularly in the ancient feminine movement of undulation, an unhinged pelvis and a snaking spine. Gabrielle Roth (2000), creator of *Ecstatic Dance*, states that dancing is a way of "sweating your prayers." Her process invites people to allow their bodies to move through a spectrum of five rhythms that pretty much cover the energies of life: Flowing, Staccato, Chaos, Lyrical, and Stillness.

There are a growing number of Internet music sites that can help a woman explore music genres and expand her awareness of music that moves her. One is named after Pandora, the mythical sexual archetype. Your clients can create collections of music for themselves or to share with a partner during lovemaking.

BEDROOM OR BOUDOIR?

While we are on the topic of shifting states, I encourage my clients to become more intentional about their bedrooms, asking themselves, "Who decorated this bedroom?" Has it become a repository for unfolded laundry and unsorted clutter that was removed from the "public" areas of the house? How might she feel differently about the bedroom, if all this clutter were cleared? Ideally, bedrooms should be for two things, sleeping and making love. What if she activated a little French Courtesan and began to treat her bedroom as a sensuous "Boudoir" or a "Temple" for the Sexual Priestess? Spaces evoke inner states of being. Ask your clients, "How would Aphrodite decorate your bedroom?"

INTEGRATING BRIGHT SHADOW PROJECTIONS

As your client becomes more adept at "shifting states," she will be able to "try on" new energies with greater ease! Have her use her power of imagination to close her eyes and "become" a character from a book or movie or a person from history, or explore what it would be like to be someone who carries the energy she would like to have more of. It can even be a friend she admires and would like to emulate.

Chapter 7 provided a list of questions that you can ask your client as she imagines being someone else, "trying on" a new archetypal energy. I sometimes encourage my clients to experiment with carrying this energy out into the world, going someplace, like a dinner party, or even the grocery store. She might buy a piece of clothing that fits this archetypal energy. She can study how other women carry it, or watch movies of women who are imbued with this energy. How do people relate to her differently when she is in this archetypal state? If she engages a partner from this space, what changes?

Exploring the energies carried by those she admires is a way of integrating "bright shadow" projections, watering those seeds of possibility that are lying uncultivated in the seedbed of her psyche. We usually think of "shadow" aspects of the personality as "dark," but not all of them are. Shadow refers to *anything* that is disowned, demonized *or idealized* and undeveloped in the personality. Some of our bright shadow material includes being beautiful, bright, dynamic, powerful, or alluring. The very act of projecting these idealized qualities onto someone else means that they exist in that woman's psyche. These qualities are awakening and asking for integration into the conscious personality. You can explore these energies using guided visualizations, rehearsal and role play, Voice Dialogue (Dyak, 1999; Stone & Stone, 1989; Wakefield, 2012), dream work, and active imagination (Johnson, 1986).

HEY THERE, SAILOR!

My client Barbara was an Empty-Nest Mother who felt lost and without identity after her last child went to college. She was in therapy for anxiety and depression. One night, she had a dream that she had become a barmaid in a seaside tavern where sailors came to port. It reminded her of the song "Brandy" that was one of her favorite songs in her senior year of high school, right before she married her high school sweetheart. When she sang along to it, she felt the power of being able to captivate a man's heart. In the dream, her hair was loose and her dress was low, and she was bantering with a bunch of sailors gathered at her tables, fully inhabiting the sexual archetype of the Saucy Wench.

The dream shocked her, but it opened up a whole new line of exploration in her therapy. Who was this brazen wench of her dreams, whom we named Brandy? Barbara noted that Brandy was so ALIVE, so unlike her! Yes, the psyche had constellated some very strong Aphrodite energy to introduce some bold wildness into Barbara's life. She downloaded the song Brandy and listened to it, reconnecting her with a youthful energy and sensual freedom she hadn't felt in a long time. She recalled what her mid-life husband had meant to her back then. We began to work with that wild, free, captivating, bold "Brandy" energy, and she rediscovered her zest for life and reignited the sexual relationship with her husband, who had become a bit of a Couch Potato . . . until he met Brandy.

DEEPENING IMPORTANT SHIFTS

When a client experiences a deep internal shift in her core Self-definition, we want to deepen this new experience so that it becomes part of her long-term *identity*, the "new normal." You can do this by asking your client how she is going to remember this experience and integrate it during the coming week. I want her to return to the "felt sense" of this new experience with regularity, so that it becomes familiar, and she gains increasing capacity to shift intentionally into this state of being. In doing so, she will build new neural pathways, so that the shift becomes easy. She might use a visual cue that she can see on a regular basis: an image from a magazine or the Internet that she can place on her bathroom mirror or near her computer. She might find a poem, quotation, or piece of music that captures the newfound feeling. She might find a little figurine to represent her "new me." This image or figurine also might represent an aspect of herself that she is exploring. If she has a meditation practice, I recommend entering into the "felt sense" of this new energy as part of her meditation. If it came in a dream, I recommend entering into the dream image.

If the client likes the experience of carrying this new energy, she can continue to integrate it by learning to recognize the feel of it, "dialing it up and down," and intentionally cultivating it. She can also pay attention to how others carry it, watching what they do and how they operate. She might buy some new clothes that represent this energy, and look through the lens of this perspective throughout the day.

Significant inner shifts don't always happen in the practitioner's office, but when they take place, a woman will instinctively gather a "relic" from that experience: a leaf, a flower, a pad of paper from the hotel, a ticket stub. I think that every woman should have an "altar space" in her home that holds *symbolic objects* that represent her hopes, dreams, questions, inspirations, personal issues she is working through, realities she wishes to manifest, and archetypal energies she is integrating. Women already instinctively use dresser tops, window ledges, or special shelves for this purpose. I want it to become an intentional place.

BIBLIOGRAPHY

Dyak, M. (1999) *The Voice Dialogue Facilitator's Handbook, Part 1*. Seattle: L.I.F.E. Energy Press.

Johnson, R. (1986) *Inner Work: Using Dreams and Active Imagination for Personal Growth*. New York: HarperCollins.

Ogden, G. (2013) *Expanding the Practice of Sex Therapy: An Integrative Model for Exploring Desire and Intimacy*. New York: Routledge.

Roth, G. (2000) *Ecstatic Dance: The Gabrielle Roth Video Collection*. [DVD Series]. Boulder, CO: Sounds True.

Stone, H., & Stone, S. (1989) *Embracing Our Selves: The Voice Dialogue Manual*. Novato, CA: Nataraj.

Wakefield, C. (2012) *Negotiating the Inner Peace Treaty: Becoming the Person You Were Born to Be*. Bloomington, IN: Balboa.

Weiner Davis. M. (2008) *The Sex-Starved Wife: What to Do When He's Lost Desire*. New York: Simon & Schuster.

CHAPTER 10

WHERE TREATMENT STALLS—SEXUAL GATEKEEPERS

"Life shrinks or expands in proportion to one's courage."

Anaïs Nin

IS IT RESISTANCE OR A DRAGON AT THE GATE?

Treatment compliance is one of the most frustrating issues for all kinds of therapists and health practitioners. The term and concept of "resistance" was originally written about by Freud (Kaplan, 1974). Since that time, clients who will not move smoothly along a therapist's treatment ideology are given the pathologizing labels of "resistant," "non-compliant," or "unmotivated."

A practitioner can create the world's most brilliant intervention strategy, but unless a client's inner self system is aligned with the treatment goals of the therapy, the treatment will stall out. I would like to lift this pathologizing frame of reference off of clients we call "non-compliant." When we begin to work with the inner self system, these seeming impasses become avenues of exploration.

In many myths and legends where a hero or heroine is in search of some treasure, they endure much travail and finally come to the location of the treasure. There, they encounter a dragon, or some other scary beast, that stands guard at the threshold, blocking their path. They must solve a riddle, slay, or bribe this beast, in order to pass. The treasure of a woman's sexual realm is guarded by Wise Guardians and Sexual Gatekeepers. Linda Savage (1999) describes the Wise Guardians as authentic protectors who help women set healthy boundaries and discern who would be a good partner. What I am calling Sexual Gatekeepers are inner figures that have developed as a result of cultural or religious messages, authority figures from the past, or in response to traumatic experiences.

Once these Gatekeepers are installed, they operate outside a woman's awareness. They generate distressing body sensations any time she attempts to move beyond their restrictive dominion. This distress is alleviated only when a client returns to her previous limitations. Gatekeepers pose as protectors, but they actually become jailors. Their presence is one of the reasons that clients get stuck and practitioners become frustrated. Change awakens the Gatekeepers. When the change involves sexuality, there is an accompanying "Greek Chorus" of voices who call out the disastrous consequences that will befall the woman if she steps into the power and pleasure of her Aphrodite Self. Now she is surrounded by these pseudoprotectors, who act as if they are helping, but in truth, they are extinguishing her light.

DIALOGUING WITH GATEKEEPERS

Voice Dialogue is one of the most effective ways of "outing" these Gatekeepers and negotiating for sexual expression rights. Although you may encounter a Dragon, most Gatekeepers take human form. Over years of doing Voice Dialogue, clients have named them. I have met my share of religious figures: Fire and Brimstone Preachers, Proper Christian Women, Nuns and Mother Superiors. Not infrequently, I hear the Voice of God. In addition, I meet Good Behavior Police, Reputation Protectors, the Sexual Shame Squad, Armored Amazons, and Militant Feminists. Let your clients name their own Gatekeepers. They know who they are.

When I am listening to my client, she will say something like, "It's like I hear the voice of the Fire and Brimstone Preacher of my youth." Here is an excellent entry point for asking if you can talk to the Fire and Brimstone Preacher and interview "him." Have her move over and begin to ask him the queries listed in Chapter 8. Let the Fire and Brimstone Preacher tell you all about his perspectives on sex. Listen carefully and respectfully and "he" will probably give you the very script that is constraining her. Now you have something to work with in moving beyond the treatment impasse. Just bringing this material into conscious awareness creates choice and freedom.

Gatekeepers always consider themselves to be "helpful," and they usually have served an important function at some point in a woman's earlier life. It's just that their function has become outdated, and they are no longer needed. Gatekeepers have often operated as valiant protectors of vulnerable and wounded inner children who hide behind the Gatekeeper's protective stance.

Ask the Gatekeeper, "How are you protecting (client's name)?" or "Who are you protecting in (the client)'s inner world?" They may not give you access to the wounded child they are shielding, but they will likely tell you why. Now you have a picture of an earlier wounding that needs to be worked through. Gatekeepers can be protecting your client from feelings or memories that would be hard to process. Gatekeepers offer up information that may be outside a woman's conscious awareness, and working with them will solve many mysteries about why your client has made certain choices. Don't resent the Gatekeepers. Engage them, and value their input.

JENNIFER'S GATEKEEPING GRANDMOTHER

Jennifer was referred to me by a local gynecologist. She was experiencing Vaginismus, a painful contraction of the muscles at the opening of her vagina, interfering with her ability to have intercourse. Jennifer had been raised in a conservative religious household where modesty was emphasized strongly. She was so shy that her husband had never even seen her fully naked. She was explaining her situation to me. "I'm trying to have sex . . . I know it's what wives are supposed to do, but I know it's going to hurt, and that makes me feel tense, and it just gets worse and worse. I don't know what to do."

We began to talk about her history, and during the third session she had a memory of her earliest sexual feelings. She said, "I recall being twelve. I was lying on the bed, reading a love story, where these star-crossed lovers were finally united, and they kissed. Suddenly I realized I was wet down there. I ran to the bathroom, concerned that maybe I had wet my pants. When I wiped myself, it tingled, so I kept touching myself. Then I felt this sensation ripple through my whole body. It felt good and it frightened me. I remember feeling terribly ashamed. I just knew that something was wrong with me."

I began to talk to her about the changes a woman's body goes through during sexual arousal. "That's exactly how your body should respond when you are aroused. Those same feelings are an early indication that your body is ready for intercourse." She looked up with sadness. "I didn't know this. I've had no one in my whole life who I could talk to about any of this." As a sex therapist, I have found that very few women had someone truly helpful to talk to about their budding sexuality. Jennifer and I began to talk about the possibility of pleasure, and she suddenly felt the presence of her stern, Amish grandmother. This shocked and frightened her. She described this woman, in her buttoned up black dress and head covering. "She certainly would not approve of what I am doing here!" We had encountered a powerful Sexual Gatekeeper.

I explained how Voice Dialogue worked and asked Jennifer if we could learn more about this inner Grandmother, who still seemed to be with her. Jennifer agreed, then raised her eyebrows and said, "Are you sure you want to meet her? She wouldn't like *you* at all." I reassured Jennifer that I could handle her grandmother's disapproval. Jennifer moved over a few inches on my couch, closed her eyes, and began to settle into her memory of that tight-laced grandmother (the clinical term for an internalized figure from the past is "introject"). Suddenly Jennifer sat up tall and stiff and looked out at me with a fierce, critical stare. A palpable feeling of cold disapproval entered the room. Here is the dialogue that took place:

CW: (facilitating therapist) to the Grandmother: "Thank you for allowing me to speak with you."

G: (Jennifer *as her inner Grandmother*): "I really am not interested in speaking with you! I do not approve of what is going on here. I think that what you are doing here is shameful and dangerous!"

(Recall that in a Voice Dialogue session, it is important to never argue or contradict what an inner character is saying. We accept whatever this inner character offers. It is their point of view, and we want to understand it!)

CW: "Would you be willing to tell me more about your concerns? . . . How do you see what we are doing as dangerous?"

G: (She looks at me with disdain.) "In my day, we did not speak of such things. It is shameful! No self-respecting woman would be interested in *pleasure* (as she says this word, her face snarls). *Pleasure* is the playground of the devil!"

CW: "Tell me more about your life back then."

G: "I worked from morning till night tending the house and raising seven decent God-fearing children."

At that moment, I was recalling how Jennifer told me that her "God-fearing" mother had suffered from a lifetime of depression. I was thinking about what Bader (2002) talks about in his book, *Arousal*. He speaks of how some women suffer from "survivor guilt" regarding pleasure. They feel uncomfortable about surpassing a level of pleasure that their mothers (or grandmothers) were denied. I continued to dialogue with Jennifer's Grandmother and listened to a terse lecture on righteous living and the grim rules around enduring sexual duty, always with a nightgown on, as you waited for a husband's sexual interest to extinguish itself altogether. It was no wonder Jennifer's body would not allow entry. We completed this interview, and I had Jennifer move back to her original spot. She was amazed. "I had no idea that all that was in me. No wonder I feel so anxious about sex. How could I possibly relax with 'her' looking on!"

CREATIVE VISUALIZATION

Creative visualization has been employed to heal a multitude of psychic wounds (Naparstek, 2004). Visualizations are effective, because the mind does not know the difference between an imagined experience and a lived experience when the experience has a strong emotional impact. We can actually go back into a memory and create an alternative story line, bringing in what was needed at that time and allowing the client to feel how that would have changed things. Now we have a healing memory that supersedes the painful one. When we change the past, the future changes as well. It is as if the dominos fall in a different direction from before and a new "possibility sphere" opens up (Ecker, Ticic, & Hulley, 2012; Pesso, 2013).

Jennifer and I continued to talk, and I suggested that what she needed back in her adolescence was someone who would have "blessed" the early emergence of her sexual feelings, someone who would have answered her questions about the changes she was going through. The thought of having someone who would have blessed her sexuality was quite profound for her, and I could feel her internal reference point shifting. I used the language of "blessing" intentionally, because of Jennifer's religious background, but all young women need their emergent sexuality acknowledged and blessed.

INSTALLING INNER HELPERS—THE SENSUOUS WISE WOMAN

I suggested that we engage in a healing visualization in which Jennifer could "install" an inner helper, a support figure who would be encouraging instead of shaming about her body and her emergent sexuality. We talked about what this support figure might have done and said to her, back when she was twelve, thirteen, fourteen, and so on. She decided to name this inner figure her Sensuous Wise Woman.

Jennifer closed her eyes, and I guided her through an induction with some deep belly breathing. We then re-entered that early scene in which she remembered herself, as that twelve-year-old girl, who had just discovered she was aroused for the first time. We had already created an imagined version of her Sensuous Wise Woman, who believed that sexuality was a good thing instead of a shameful or frightening thing. I continued to guide Jennifer more deeply into this visualization:

"So imagine that you have run to the bathroom, concerned that you wet your pants, feeling that ripple of pleasure, feeling frightened, feeling those feelings of confusion and shame. You come out of the bathroom and find your Sensuous Wise Woman sitting on your bed. Now you have someone to talk to about what has just happened. You sit beside her, and the two of you begin to talk. She answers your questions in a way that makes you feel soothed and calm, and yet excited about your future. She explains that this is the beginning of something wonderful, blessed, and good. You are entering into a time when you will discover yourself more deeply. You are becoming a woman, and that is a *good* thing. This is a time when you can learn about yourself, your amazing body, and what you want in life. Your Sensuous Wise Woman tells you that somewhere in the future, when you feel ready, there will be a partner, who you can experience these feeling with, to engage with, and to gently learn about each other. As you look into her kind eyes, you see her happiness for you. She conveys a sense of confidence, a sense of excitement for the woman you will become. As you look into her eyes, all of your shame and shyness melt away and your body relaxes. 'Your sexuality is blessed,' she says. 'Your body is blessed. It is OK for you to feel and enjoy pleasure. Now that you are an adult, it is OK for you to join with your husband to share this pleasure.' As you listen to this Sensuous Wise Woman, you can feel your whole body relax. You can feel all the muscles in your pelvic floor relax and let go. There is no need to brace any more. She has given you a blessing that you will carry with you all of your life."

I watched Jennifer, and I could see that she was taking in this experience. When she had done so, she took a very deep breath and opened her eyes.

They held a soft light. She looked very peaceful and happy. I let her be for a moment. Then I asked her, "What was that like, to have your sexuality blessed by this Wise Woman?" Jennifer replied, "That was amazing. It had never occurred to me that I could feel so relaxed and good about my sexuality, let alone have the experience that it could be 'blessed.' I feel as if I've regained a piece of my Soul. My life would have been very different from that point forward," she said. "Your life *will* be very different," I responded.

Jennifer made good progress from that session forward. We began to talk about sexual essence and inhabiting the body. She had not realized that she could feel sensations below the outer layer of her skin. She brought her husband in and I worked with them together, providing some exercises that would help them become more comfortable, sensually attuned, and present to each other. They were both shy, but they were making their way together, exploring, managing their anxiety by moving slowly, using their breath, engaging in mindful touching that was not goal directed. They began to trust each other, to feel more deeply, relax, and respond. We talked about choices for working with Jennifer's Vaginismus. By then, the couple was comfortable enough to use fingers instead of the progressive plastic dilators that are so commonly used when treating this problem. Her shyness continued to make it difficult to have her body viewed unclothed, and many women are uncomfortable with having their vulvas viewed directly. I talked to Jennifer about cultures in which the vulva is worshiped. We looked at some art, photographs and pictures of vulvas and did some somatic work around being seen, calming her nervous system, and reassuring the Shy, Vulnerable Good Girl, an inner character that was so influential in her.

Jennifer learned to listen to her body and recognize when her body felt ready to engage in intercourse. She learned that she could adjust the pace, pause, breathe, relax, and manage her anxiety. Her sensitive husband became attuned to her and within a few months, she had overcome her vaginal spasming and they were enjoying painless intercourse. They developed the personalized cues and language that intimate couples have for signaling each other about interest, and choreographing lovemaking. They were both deepening their sense of trust as well as pleasure. Jennifer's sweetness translated into the bedroom, but now she had discovered how to play. She liked the archetype of the Sexual Pixie, a far cry from the tense, shame-filled girl who first came to see me. She developed a playful, soulful, partner-engaged style of sexuality, which suited her husband just fine.

SHOULD A WOMAN ALWAYS TRUST HER FEELINGS?

Women are often encouraged to "trust their feelings," but feelings can be generated by a variety of inner characters within the psyche, and they deserve deeper inquiry. When women are not encouraged to use the feedback system of the body as a source of discernment, their inner indicators become skewed. They rely more on internalized scripts than on actual body wisdom, and the body begins to respond to the scripts rather than the authentic Self. Once a woman untangles herself from scripts written by others and writes one more suitable and empowering, she can learn to use her body, and trust her "gut" as a feedback system. Until she masters this intuitive art, she may receive a lot of "false readings," generated by Gatekeepers and Script Monitors.

The Resolution Phase—Feeling Bad or Sad . . . What Does It Really Mean?

The resolution phase of the sexual response cycle is not often discussed in sex therapy, but it is very important for women. A woman can feel a tidal wave of emotion during and after sex: love, joy, fear, anxiety, shame, grief, anger, revulsion, loss of boundaries, and feelings of intense vulnerability. Women sometimes cry after sex, and this can be a distressing and confusing experience both for her and her partner. When we open ourselves to deep sexual experiences, it opens up our inner world. The tears might be from joy, or they may indicate that a "pocket" of long-buried emotion has opened up and is spilling out. Sometimes she has been harboring so much longing that fulfillment bursts the dam. She might have difficulty tolerating that much ecstasy. She may feel intensely vulnerable that her heart has opened, her soul was touched, that she revealed that much of herself to her partner. She may have touched in on an early abuse memory that was buried from her awareness. A woman doesn't have to know *in that moment* why she is experiencing such strong emotion. She doesn't have to explain herself. Assure her that she can ponder it on her own. It is something that can be delved into in therapy. What got opened up? "Who" in her was feeling so strongly? Can she name the emotion she was feeling? She can follow it like a golden thread back into her psyche and discover something important.

Feeling bad about oneself after sex is not necessarily an indication that a woman has done something "wrong." Before she decides, "Never do that again!" it is worthwhile for her to be aware of her inner Gatekeepers and Script Monitors. Are they enforcing constraints here, encouraging her to get back into a smaller box? It is important to unpack "bad feelings" and find out "who" is feeling bad and why. She can do this on her own once she learns the process of tracing a reaction back to inner voices or sensations, and then asking herself "who" is upset here and why? She can learn to engage in the same dialogue process you conduct in your office, journaling what she discovers. She can then determine if this is Gatekeeper restriction, or if she is receiving feedback from an Inner Wise Woman who is telling her that she is engaging in something that is not in alignment with her deepest Self.

BIBLIOGRAPHY

Bader, M. (2002) *Arousal: The Secret Logic of Sexual Fantasies*. New York: Thomas Dunne.

Ecker, B., Ticic, R., & Hulley, L. (2012) *Unlocking the Emotional Brain: Eliminating Symptoms at Their Roots Using Memory Reconsolidation*. New York: Routledge.

Kaplan, H. S. (1974) *The New Sex Therapy: Active Treatment of Sexual Dysfunctions*. New York: Brunner/Mazel.

Naparstek, B. (2004) *Invisible Heroes: Survivors of Trauma and How They Heal*. New York: Bantam.

Pesso, A. (2013) *Presentations & Lectures by Albert Pesso on Pesso Boyden System Psychomotor Therapy* (1984–2012) Kindle Edition.

Savage, L. (1999) *Reclaiming Goddess Sexuality: The Power of the Feminine Way*. Carlsbad, CA: Hay House.

CHAPTER 11

FAIRY TALE SCRIPTS WE LIVE— ARCHETYPES OF INNOCENCE, UNCONSCIOUSNESS, AND VULNERABILITY

"Rapunzel, Rapunzel, let down your hair!"

The Brothers Grimm

Women are raised on fairy tales, and we deeply internalize these stories. They form the basis of our romantic scripts. While fairy tales can shape the psyche, they are also drawn *from* the psyche. Fairy tales portray archetypal "truths" about human life and human nature, and the characters in these tales represent different aspects of the psyche (Gould, 2006; Nelson, 1999; Pinkola Estés, 1992; Stein & Corbet, 1999; Von Franz, 1977/1990).[1]

MAIDENS

Fairy tales are filled with maidens, high spirited, playful, and exuberant, or shy, innocent, sweet, idealistic, and softly adoring. The Maiden is an Uninitiated Girl, full of potential. As an adolescent girl discovers her own Desire Awakening Maiden, she becomes aware that her sexuality has power. This may be frightening at first, but she may also begin to enjoy her power to enchant. A slightly older manifestation of the Maiden is the gifted young woman who works as a Protégé to a great Teacher or Sage. When her adoring gaze falls upon him, he feels vitalized, elevated, and young again. He also feels powerful in his capacity to shape her in a particular way. *My Fair Lady* (*Pygmalion*) is one such story.

In spite of all the protestations of the women's movement about "objectification," women still draw a tremendous sense of power and self-esteem from an awareness that they are "desirable," and their love narratives often center on this theme (Young-Eisendrath, 1999).

Older women are anxiously aware of losing their power to the Maidens around them. Ask the Wicked Queen in the story of Snow White. The multibillion dollar cosmetics and plastic surgery industry attest to this. Nervous Wives understand the power of a Sweet Young Thing who can "lure" a seemingly sane and intelligent man into reckless circumstances with no thought to the consequences.

THE ARCHETYPE OF THE VIRGIN

In the days of the Greek pantheon of Goddesses, the word *Virgin* meant "whole and complete unto herself." Virgin Goddesses like Athena, Artemis, and Hestia fulfilled their roles with no need of a man. They had other important reasons for living (Shinoda Bolen, 1984). The definition of "virgin" has come to mean a woman who has never had vaginal intercourse. The emphasis on the unbroken hymen began around the time that women came to be viewed as property. In a culture based on male privilege, men wanted "first rights" and "sole possession" of their women, and women with considerably less power conformed to these norms in an effort to secure their futures with men who had the power to protect and provide for them (Eisler, 1996).

McCormick (1994) notes that as women gain more power, they tend to be more relaxed about their sexuality and have a greater number of sexual partners than their less powerful sisters. Women's "purity" is still promoted in many conservative religious circles, with an emphasis on "saving oneself," for that "one special man." Many of these women find it difficult to switch "on" their sexuality after years of constrictive messages. Marriage does not free them to be sexual, because anything resembling carnal desire has become indelibly linked with prohibition and shame.

Fairy Tale Syndromes

Sleeping Beauty Syndrome—The Unawakened Girl

Iliana leaned forward and spoke in earnest, her huge, dark eyes looking deeply into mine. Married now for five years, she had never had an orgasm. She came from a strict Catholic background and was a virgin when she married. She had long anticipated passionate, rapturous experiences, like the ones portrayed in the movies. Her husband appeared to have very little sexual skill or sensitivity. The reality of her actual experience was devastating to her. Her question was, *"How long must I wait?"*

Many women suffer from what I call the *Sleeping Beauty Syndrome*, passively waiting to be awakened by a Dream Lover, who will scale her castle walls, kindle her fire, and send her into orchestra-swelling bliss. Captive to the values of a patriarchal society, ever so feminine, she waits.

Because young men receive such distorted sexual education, they often haven't the faintest idea how to arouse a woman, and a woman who has no knowledge of her own body, and has never aroused herself, is unable to offer helpful suggestions. The two partners fumble together, and very little useful information gets passed back and forth as they attempt to hide their disappointment, manage embarrassment, and shore up fragile egos. Because our sex education is so poor, and because few people possess the confidence or skill base for the kind of communication that deepens sexuality, this sad situation can go on for years, sometimes for an entire relationship.

Cinderellas and Entitled Princesses

Many women live in a Cinderella world, waiting to be rescued from their boring or miserable lives by a handsome, charming Prince, possibly even rich! Their stance is disempowered and passive as they wait to be rescued. They can become so caught up with this fantasy that they pass up "ordinary" men who might be wonderful partners. Their fairy tale can begin to resemble the Princess and the Pea as they fuss over things that are not "just right," and pick at their partner's imperfections. Add a bit more entitlement and they become full-on Spoiled Princesses. These girls want life handed to them on a silver platter without doing any real work to enrich themselves intellectually, relationally, emotionally, or sexually. Many of them spend a lot of time adorning the exterior package, but they are not women of substance and they do not attract partners of substance. As a couples therapist, I have seen these "beautiful people" marry, and then struggle tremendously, because once the thrill of the conquest wears off, there is no one "home" on either side to relate to!

Some Cinderellas link their lives to the first "prince" to come along. They move in with men before they really know them, or marry and then become lulled into a false sense of security. Remaining emotionally young, undeveloped, and passive, they are highly vulnerable if their partner goes "off script." Their marriage may disintegrate, hurt and disillusionment follow, at which point they are plunged back into the land of cinders, as Wounded Women, often as single mothers, struggling to make ends meet. With repeated cycles, the bitterness deepens and envelops them like a dark shroud, making it even more difficult to find a worthwhile partner.

The Velveteen Rabbit Syndrome

In the story of the Velveteen Rabbit, the little cloth rabbit cannot become "real" without the love of the little boy. This parallels the experience of many women who feel that they cannot be "real" unless they are in a relationship. Underlying this is the fear that they are too ordinary to be the recipient of real love. Once again we come back to the necessity for a woman to be Self-defined and have a sense of substance outside of a relationship, the feeling of being "real" in her own right. Becoming "real" takes courage and fortitude. The reward is in engaging with another "real" person (Raiten-D'Antonio, 2004).

The Rapunzel Girl—Sheltered in the Mother World

Rachel was a yoga teacher who had embraced its lofty, spiritual philosophy. She was beautiful, and every time Patrick looked at her with "lustful eyes," Rachel was turned off. Rachel was a Rapunzel girl, raised in a high tower, separated from the patriarchy as much as possible by her feminist mother, a professor at a university. Rachel had been indoctrinated from an early age that she was never to be "objectified." Rachel had tired of the thinking-oriented world of her mother. She was deeply drawn to Patrick, an earthy, woodsy kind of guy, but she could barely tolerate his appreciative eyes on her, or his Hungry Wolf energy. Rachel was repelled by anything too "base." Ogden (1990) once classified this type of woman as a Shrinking Violet, delicate, easily upset by anything too earthy or instinctual. Rachel wanted a spiritual sexuality that was lofty and pure and didn't stir her up too much. The couple came to me in a sexual impasse.

In the fairy tale, Rapunzel draws the young prince to her when he hears her angelic singing. Rapunzel represents the Unawakened Maiden. She is innocent, has never had her feet on the earth, or fully engaged with life. She loves her protected, idealized, interior world. The dark side of the Mother world (the Witch) keeps her captive. The Witch offers "protection," but separates her from the fullness of life. She is untouched by real human experience. In the fairy tale, she doesn't even realize that she has been imprisoned by loftiness and overprotection until she meets the young prince. Love draws her into the forest, the instinctual world, and her journey of individuation.[2]

Rachel was drawn to the yoga studio because it was a quiet, gentle environment. Things never got too "alive." She could be embodied there, but in a controlled kind of way. She was terrified of things being out of control, and even more of her instinctual self.

What had originally drawn her to Patrick was his grounded earthiness. He had a kind of dauntless strength to him. "I feel so protected by him, but his intensity overwhelms me!" Patrick was drawn to Rachel's ethereal Muse-like beauty, and idealized her lofty, spiritual view of the world. In many ways they were opposites, which made their relationship a perfect container in which to integrate the "shadow" characteristics carried by the other.

In working with Rachel, I discovered that accessing her Aphrodite Self felt like a betrayal of her feminist mother. Her mother had struggled to raise her alone, always promoting the life of the mind and denigrating being controlled by desire. Rachel was surprised to discover that she had an inner Gatekeeper, which she named the Feminist Warrior, who held deep fears about being disrespected, and blocked the path of passion. This Gatekeeper also filled her with feelings of shame and anxiety when she imagined herself activating anything instinctual, like an inner Wild Woman. In a Voice Dialogue, we were able to negotiate the right to enter a "protected passion zone."

Because Rachel identified so deeply with the Sexual Essence Quadrant of the Mystic/Muse, I brought out a book of old paintings in order to explore the archetype of the artist's Muse more deeply. We looked at these beautiful women, and I asked her to imagine the artist who was painting them. How was he looking at them? She answered, "With great appreciation for their beauty." This opened a door for her, and she began to consider that Patrick might be doing the same when he gazed in appreciation upon her own beautiful body. In one session she shared her realization that "appreciation is different than objectification." I encouraged Patrick, the Hungry Wolf, to integrate a bit more lofty Prince, with which to meet the High Towered Rapunzel Angel. One day he covered the bed with rose petals. "Good Princely move," I affirmed.

Reading Rianne Eisler's (1996) *Sacred Pleasure* and learning about the history of women's power in Sacred Sexuality was profoundly helpful for Rachel and helped her to become curious about the archetype of the Sexual Priestess. Patrick was willing to attend a Tantra workshop with her, and with her growing sense of sexual power, Rachel was able to encounter Patrick's more instinctual energy, and to "let her hair down." After wandering in the brambled forest for many years, they found a safe place where they could meet and love.

Waifs and Poor Little Match Girls

My client Wendy was a sweet Waif who reminded me of the Poor Little Match Girl. A highly neglected child, she had such low self-esteem that she didn't believe she had enough flame to warm anyone's heart. Filled with self-loathing, she believed all she had to offer was sex. What she ended up being was Prey to a string of Predators who picked her out as an easy target. Lacking any sense of real value, longing to be loved, she would fall in bed with anyone who offered her the slightest bit of attention. She was often heartbroken. We began working with her vulnerable Little Match Girl, and her inner cohort, the Hopeless Romantic, who longed to be "swept away," but more often was "swept downstream." Wendy began to understand that casual sex doesn't fill the emptiness inside, that the wounding at the core had to be healed first.

As she began to realize that she had strengths and gifts to offer the world, she developed a core of self-esteem, and she came to believe in her value. She began to really look at her potential partners with eyes wide open. As her archetypal energy continued to strengthen and shift from Waif to Wonder Woman (her chosen heroine), the Predators began to shy away and she began to attract quality partners.

The Problem of the Dream (Demon) Lover

Part of growing up is accepting that partners are human beings, not Gods and Goddesses. Girls want to live in fairy tales. Women can visit the heights of Mount Olympus, but we can't live in the realm of the Gods. We need to be able to walk on earth, embracing human life and love. Certain women become "addicted to love." What they are actually addicted to is the neurochemistry of early romance (Fisher, 2004). The settled feelings of a long-term relationship are too mundane to them. This is a woman who can fall prey to engaging in an endless string of seductions by Players and Charmers who harbor corresponding addictions, or partners who can begin a relationship with great panache, but not remain in one. The Dream Lover often turns into the Demon Lover (Woodman, 1982). He enchants and offers intense sexual experiences, but can't stick around or work through the inevitable difficulties of building a life with someone. Tennov (1999) calls that early stage of romance "limerance," the sparkly, exhilarating feeling driven by neurochemicals like dopamine and PEA (phenylethylamine), which is a brain chemical that creates feelings of elation, exhilaration, and euphoria (Fisher, 1992). Women who are "addicted to love" wander in the land of idealized projections, seeing their lovers through a neurochemical haze. The "love potion" that often accompanies these dreamy escapades is alcohol or drugs. Even legitimately appropriate partners eventually demonstrate their humanity, the fairy tale crumbles, and they go off again in search of the Perfect Man.

Notes

1 I highly recommend Joan Gould's (2006) book *Spinning Straw Into Gold*. She has done a wonderful job of outlining how fairy tale themes weave through women's fantasy longings and shape their lives and how we can transcend their limitations.

2 Donald Kalsched (1996) offers some remarkable clinical insights and suggestions regarding the complexity of working with a "Rapunzel" client.

Bibliography

Eisler, R. (1996) *Sacred Pleasure: Sex, Myth, and the Politics of the Body—New Paths to Power and Love*. San Francisco: HarperCollins.

Fisher, H. (1992) *Anatomy of Love*. New York: Fawcett Columbine.

Fisher, H. (2004) *Why We Love: The Nature and Chemistry of Romantic Love*. New York: Henry Holt.

Gould, J. (2006) *Spinning Straw Into Gold: What Fairy Tales Reveal About the Transformations in a Woman's Life*. New York: Random House.

Kalsched, D. (1996) *The Inner World of Trauma: Archetypal Defenses of the Personal Spirit*. New York: Routledge.

McCormick, N. (1994) *Sexual Salvation: Affirming Women's Sexual Rights and Pleasures*. Westport, CT: Praeger.

Nelson, G. (1999) *Here All Dwell Free: Stories to Heal the Wounded Feminine*. Mahwah, NJ: Paulist.

Ogden, G. (1990) *Everywoman's Guide to Sexual Style and Creating Intimacy*. Deerfield, FL: Health Communications.

Pinkola Estés, C. (1992) *Women Who Run With the Wolves: Myths and Stories of the Wild Woman Archetype*. New York: Ballentine.

Raiten-D'Antonio, T. (2004) *The Velveteen Principles*. Deerfield, FL, Health Communications.

Shinoda Bolen, J. (1984) *Goddesses in Every Woman: A New Psychology of Women*. New York: Harper Perennial.

Stein, M., & Corbet, L. (Eds.) (1999) *Psyche's Stories: Modern Jungian Interpretations of Fairy Tales*. Willmette, IL: Chiron.

Tennov, D. (1999) *Love & Limerance: The Experience of Being in Love*. Lanham, MD: Scarborough House.

Von Franz, M. (1990) *Individuation in Fairy Tales*. Boston: Shambhala. (Original work published 1977)

Woodman, M. (1982) *Addiction to Perfection: The Still Unravished Bride*. Toronto, ON: Inner City.

Young-Eisendrath, P. (1999) *Women and Desire: Beyond Wanting to Be Wanted*. New York: Three Rivers.

CHAPTER 12

FROM DAUGHTER TO WOMAN

"And the day came when the risk to remain tight in a bud was more painful than the risk it took to blossom."

Anaïs Nin

How Does a Girl Become a Woman?

Fairy tales are filled with stories of undifferentiated, idealistic girls passing through trials and adversities on the journey to becoming a woman (Gould, 2006; Stein & Corbet, 1999). What does it mean to be a woman, not just a female, but a Woman? How does a woman know when she has "arrived?" When I ask my clients about this, their answer are highly revealing. Some of them are dumbstruck, having never considered the question. Some will tell you straight out that they still feel like dependent girls, constantly referencing others to see what they should think, feel, and do. A woman can live as a "daughter" for her entire life, unless something propels her into a growth cycle.

Ann Ulanov and Barry Ulanov (1994) write of women who come into analysis, stalled out at an early stage of development, living largely unconscious roles with little relationship to the deep feminine. They are identified with scripts given to them by their mothers and operating as obedient daughters of a patriarchal value system. They are unhappy but cannot say why. They consider themselves Good Women, but what they are is Good Girls, virtuous and faithful. They have abdicated their growth into full personhood, abandoned their inner life, and in so doing, betrayed themselves.

The Anima Woman

Women become highly intuitive regarding what others want from them. Some are particularly good at morphing into a man's Dream Woman. The anima is a psychological term within Jung's thinking that refers to the projected ideal that originates from a man's psyche, which represents aspects of the undeveloped feminine within *him*. Certain women are particularly talented in intuiting this projection and morphing into who the man wants her to be. In this way, she becomes an Anima Woman. Such women can be *very* attractive to men, as many men long for a woman who will carry the feminine for them, tending them, feeling for them, and in doing so, relieve them of the hard work of integrating their own feeling, relating, and receptive dimensions. The traditional marriage is based on this model. The man carries the masculine and the woman carries the feminine and the two (incomplete) halves make a whole.

A man's anima projection will differ from man to man, which is why one can never really predict what type of woman a (heterosexual) man will be attracted to. Although he may be superficially drawn to a "type," there will always be an unconscious pull to a set of qualities, corresponding with longings that come from deeper in his psyche. When a man meets a woman who matches his anima projection, he will feel mysteriously drawn to her. Sometimes he may feel like he has been "struck by lightning," suddenly overwhelmed by attraction for someone who has crossed his path. This is the mystery of these idealized projections, that sense that you have met "the one" you have been looking for your entire life.

Polly Young-Eisendrath (1999) writes of the exorbitant amounts of time, energy, and money that women spend hoping to become, or remain, one of these "objects of desire." American woman have led the race in the pursuit of the perfect body and perpetual youth. They seem to be less concerned that underneath, they are suffering from a sense of emptiness, disconnected from deep resources, dependent on the whims of others to define their value. Such women are continually anxious. Although their exteriors may be lovely, they live in fear that they will be discarded for someone younger, more beautiful, and more captivating.

Women who are grounded in the Self do not live with such fears. Their beauty is substantive and enduring. They live by an inner light that emanates from the core of their being and shines from their eyes. They are luminous women.

The Woman on the Pedestal—The Femme Inspiritrice

Women long to be adored, but the woman on a pedestal leads a lonely life. The more familiar word is *Muse*. I actually prefer the term "Femme Inspiritrice," French for "inspirational woman" (Leonard, 1993). She differs from the Seductress in that she is worshiped from a distance. She has an otherworldly quality, ineffable, ethereal, able to inspire great works of art, literature, and music. She has "the face that launched a thousand ships."

Women for whom the archetype of the Muse is "home base" are often mystified by the worship they inspire. They are also faced with a terrible quandary, because the Muse must remain an ideal. Because she is admired from a distance, to let someone close, would allow familiarity, and the admission of ordinary aspects. To do so would destroy the mystique. Living in this arms-length archetype, she runs the danger of becoming nothing more than a "projection screen" for the fantasies of others. Integrating archetypes like Wife or Mother may feel like a demotion, stepping off the idealized pedestal, opening herself to be known as a mere human being, and thus, vulnerable.

The Handless Maiden

Here is one more fairy tale that deserves attention. It tells the story of a girl's struggle to come out of passive submission in an abusive, devaluing situation, and to grow back her "severed hands," her creative instrumentality (Lindley, 1995; Nelson, 1999).[1] The story begins with a careless, foolish father, who inadvertently sold his daughter to the Devil. Although the girl's "goodness" initially protects her, eventually it is the occasion by which she loses her hands. The story exemplifies what can happen when the feminine is devalued and used as an instrument to promote patriarchal interests. One dilemma after another befalls the passive "girl," whose identity is defined by others. As she begins to work her way out of her dilemma, she mobilizes her inner resources, becomes a self-activating woman, and as a result, grows new hands.

Corporate Wives, Politician's Wives, and Clergy Wives can easily fall into the syndrome of the Handless Maiden, becoming an extension of their husband's identity but having no real power or identity of their own. They truncate their own development to be what their husband needs them to be, and thereby remain dependent girls. If such a woman should become "discarded," she is likely to be devastated and rageful. Now she is a Scorned Woman. If she can recover from having vested her life into the identity of another, move beyond the betrayal, and do her inner work, she will be on the way to becoming a Luminous Wise Woman, rather than a Bitter Dark Queen.

Dark Queens and Fading Beauties

There is no pathology in wanting to be attractive or desirable, but the woman who bases her self-worth on being "the fairest in the land" is destined to become an envious Dark Queen, or an insecure Fading Beauty. Linda Leonard (1993) and Arlene Landau (2011) write about the difficult time that Muses have with aging. Fading Beauties do not go easily into their elder years. Women who are accustomed to captivating men's attention and enchanting with superficial physical beauty often find it hard to relinquish this particular power as they age. The solution is for her to turn to the rich reservoirs of beauty that reside in a woman's depths. Aphrodite is not linked to age. A woman can retain her sparkle across the lifespan when it is fed from her depths. If she cannot embrace elder Goddess, she will likely become a bitter Dark Queen, filled with envy and resentment for the younger women around her.

Beyond Objectification

Philosopher Ann Cahill (2001) makes the argument that what women are really complaining about in the fight against "objectification" is being treated *only* as a body, to the exclusion of minds, hearts, and souls! After two generations of feminists having campaigned that women should not be viewed as sex objects, some women are coming forward to assert that they *want* to be experienced as an "object of desire!" If they have *never* experienced being the focus of someone's desire, they may have lived feeling overlooked, unattractive, and unchosen. Cahill argues that "objecting to objectification" *separates* a woman from an identification with her own body. Our bodies are central to our process of becoming. They are not peripheral or less important than other aspects of us. Women need to claim their bodies, and some enjoy being admired. To be treated as a body is not inherently degrading or dehumanizing. It's that we don't want to be treated *only* as a body, with no *subjectivity*, and no internal experience apart from being derivative of someone else's desires.

FATHER'S DAUGHTERS AND THEIR UNINHABITED BODIES

Marion Woodman (1982, 1985) talks about the uninhabited bodies of many women in analysis, particularly those in quest of extreme thinness. These women restrict nourishment on many levels of their lives. It is difficult for a woman to claim her sexuality when she is overidentified with being pleasing and non-threatening. Woodman refers to these women as Father's Daughters because they have gone into unconscious compliance with their father's needs and idealized view of them. They form an idealized "love affair" with the father and split off from their instinctual sexuality. Murdock (1994) talks about how the difficulty that Father's Daughters have breaking free from this possessive psychic hold and actualizing their adult sexuality in a relationship apart from the father. An adult love relationship can feel like an abandonment and betrayal of the deeply embedded father-daughter bond.

As women reach mid-life, the bleakness of their unlived lives becomes increasingly evident. If such a woman responds to this by engaging in a process of inner work and individuation, her growth may seriously destabilize her marriage. A woman who is in touch with her deep feminine consciousness becomes embodied, connected to her instinctual self, and inherently sexual. If she has been an Anima Woman, relating to a husband as either a providing, protective "father," or nurturing and comforting him as a "little boy," he may find her newly empowered sexuality overwhelming.

DEPENDENCE AND THE BALANCE OF POWER

Dependence shuts down a woman's sexual voice (Hite, 1993; Stone, 1997). Although a woman may be well past her teenage years, any significant form of dependence, where she does not determine her own life, places a woman in the archetypal position of Daughter. Some women react to the sense of entrapped dependence by moving from Dependent Daughter into Rebel Daughter, but *this is still Daughter*, as it is *in rebellion against*, rather than a true "graduation" into luminous womanhood. To graduate, a woman must move *beyond* rebellion into Self-definition and Self-determination.

The balance of power in a relationship and the divisions of labor in the home are particularly treacherous areas for women who are seeking to become more empowered, and this relates directly to her sexuality. Although it is possible for a man and woman to decide consciously that he will be the Provider and she will be the Homemaker and Nurturer of Children, it will take a continuing conscious effort for her not to slide into the unconscious role of Daughter, dependent on the Parental Provider. This is because in our Western cultural we value competition and production over nurture and cooperation. Who gets the "final say" is often weighted towards the wage earner. Dependency inevitably leads to desexualization, because it leads to resentment and triggers an unconscious, but strongly felt, incest taboo (Pinkola Estés, 1992; Stone, 1997; Woodman, 1985; Young-Eisendrath, 1984, 1993).

There is an old saying that when a woman finds her voice in the boardroom she finds it in the bedroom. I have not found this to be true. However, I *have* found that when a woman finds her voice in the bedroom, she *will* find her voice in the living room, as well as the boardroom. It is fascinating to watch the shift in power that occurs when a woman begins to connect with her instinctual sexuality and discovers her sexual "voice." Over the years, men have brought women into my clinical practice, because the woman lacks desire. As we begin to search for her inner flame, she begins to learn about what lights her up and pleases her. As she comes to life, her partner may get more than he bargained for, because full-blooded women begin to say what they want, in *all* areas of their lives.

DEVELOPMENTAL PASSAGES

The Meaning of Menarche

Asking about first menstruation is a common question for sex therapists. Why? We want to understand a woman's relationship to her body, and the stories women tell about first menstruation give us a lot of insight. Beginning one's menses is an important rite of passage. I know so many women whose mothers handed them a box of pads or tampons and told them to read the instructions, as if this was something the mother did not want to become involved with. What a communication! Menstruation is one of the great mysteries of womanhood. It ties us in with the cycles of the moon. Women who work and live together begin to synchronize their cycles. Menstruation creates a cyclical awareness in a woman's consciousness that underlies all of life. Women who are in tune with their bodies recognize that their bodies are in a different energetic, intuitional, and sensual state every day of the month.

Here is an opportunity to have a meaningful discussion about what it means to be a woman, what it means to have the capacity to conceive a child. So many of our girls struggle alone with how to handle adolescent feelings of loneliness, longing, confusion, and anxiety. Does she have an embodied Wise Women around her who can help her navigate these vulnerable times? Will she succumb to sexual pressure before she feels ready, in a search for love or acceptance? Where will she turn for answers and support? Most mothers had poor examples in their own mothers, and they passed down their own ambivalence about their bodies to their daughters. Very few women had good sexual role models.

Sexual Initiation

The archetype of Sexual Initiation is itself a significant developmental passage. A girl's first sexual experience can establish a trajectory for how she feels about her sexuality from that point forward. If her first experience is physically or emotionally painful, or humiliating, she may enter into her adult sexuality with a tentative or self-protective attitude about sex. If the experience was predatory, especially at a young age, she may think of herself as little more than an object, for the use and pleasure of others.

The Individuation Affair

The Self is always seeking to awaken us and an unexpected infatuation can shake a woman up and take her out of a suspended state. Love breaks through the dry-hardened earth of a woman's life and begins to move the stagnant waters of her depths. A woman whose flame has gone out will sometimes come ablaze with the entrance of a forbidden love affair. In these relationships, she feels the energies of boldness, daring, adventure, inspiration, even transformation and transcendence. She begins to revel in being embodied and coming to life (Heyn, 1992).

Affairs can be tremendously destructive to relationships, but sometimes what is being destroyed is a condemned building that should have been renovated or vacated a long time ago. Suddenly this woman is breaking out of a life that has become too small for the requirements of her soul, which is why I call these affairs, which seem so reckless, *individuation affairs*. Suddenly she is with someone who is meeting her, engaging with her, seeing her as appealing, beautiful, and full of potential. In this reflected light, she begins to feel passionate about herself and her life. Might some of this awakening have occurred by less dramatic means? Perhaps. Might she have begun to grow, mature, and become more differentiated on her own? Perhaps. But women who are sleepwalking rarely embark on personal-growth projects. Women on "automatic" rarely come into therapy. They may get shocked awake by a *husband's* affair or desire to leave the marriage, but if that doesn't happen, it might be *their own* love affair that shakes them up, causing them to see how devitalized their lives have become. Some women manage to navigate these strong attractions and begin to renegotiate their lives and their existing relationships. If they cannot renegotiate the marriage, they may decide to leave it. What is clear to me is that the Self seeks any means it can to awaken us.

Menopause and Beyond

We will talk more about women in later life in Chapter 19, entitled "Women of a Certain Age."

THE SACRED PROSTITUTE IN WOMEN'S DREAMS

Qualls-Corbett (1988) writes of the dream content of women struggling with their disowned and devalued sexuality. Their dreams reflect how much female sexuality has been demonized, feared, and repressed by male religious authorities. Into their dreams, a figure from the prepatriarchal past begins to surface, the Sacred Prostitute. Woodman (1985) writes of how these dreams surface in women who have no historical knowledge of this archaic figure. A female client, trapped in an idealistic perfectionism, who had little knowledge of the history of women's sexuality, dreamt of becoming a "sacred whore," a servant of Aphrodite. She was shocked and disturbed initially by this "shadowy" dream, but the dream led her to integrate Aphrodite's energy into her life, which was ultimately the solution for her troubles. Aphrodite has often been vilified by patriarchal culture as a "whore," precisely because of her refusal to be subjugated, her Self-determination, her love of pleasure and play, and her powerful alchemical energy. Women need her in their process of moving out of "daughter," valuing embodiment, and embracing the full expression of conscious womanhood.

Moving From the Object of Another's Life to the Subject of One's Own

Becoming a woman means that the woman has moved beyond being the *object* of someone else's script into becoming the *subject* of her own script. She has graduated from Father's Daughter (the devoted "good girl" who trades personhood for provision and protection) and Mother's Daughter (the protected and undifferentiated feminine who never becomes too independent, but remains loyal to her mother and her mother's values) into becoming her own person. Women know that they will pay a price for this (Gould, 2006; Murdock, 1994; Woodman, 1982, 1985, 1993). A conscious woman must make well-considered choices, take responsibility for her life, and invest herself into enterprises and relationships that have depth and meaning for her. She may love and care for others deeply, even sacrificially, but this will be a conscious choice, rather than fulfilling the requirement to meet the needs of others. As a conscious woman, attuned to her depths, she takes her own needs and desires seriously, and her sexuality takes on a whole new meaning.

Note

1 Gertrude Nelson's examination of the tale of the Handless Maiden is marvelous and a "must read" for individuating women. In the same book she also looks at the story of Briar Rose (Sleeping Beauty).

Bibliography

Cahill, A. (2011) *Overcoming Objectification: A Carnal Ethics*. New York: Routledge.
Gould, J. (2006) *Spinning Straw Into Gold: What Fairy Tales Reveal About the Transformations in a Woman's Life*. New York: Random House.
Heyn, D. (1992) *The Erotic Silence of the American Wife*. New York: Random House.
Hite, S. (1993) *Women as Revolutionary Agents of Change: The Hite Reports and Beyond*. Madison: University of Wisconsin Press.

Landau, A. (2011) *Tragic Beauty: The Dark Side of Venus Aphrodite and the Loss and Regeneration of Soul*. New Orleans, LA: Spring Journal.

Leonard, L. S. (1993) *Meeting the Madwoman: Empowering the Feminine Spirit*. New York: Bantam.

Lindley, D. (1995) The Girl Without Hands. In M. Stein & L. Corbett, L. (Eds.) *Psyche's Stories: Modern Jungian Interpretations of Fairy Tales* (pp. 51–64). Wilmette, IL: Chiron.

Murdock, M. (1994) *Father's Daughters: Breaking the Ties That Bind*. New Orleans, LA: Spring Journal.

Nelson, G. (1999) *Here All Dwell Free: Stories to Heal the Wounded Feminine*. Mahwah, NJ: Paulist.

Pinkola Estés, C. (1992) *Women Who Run With the Wolves: Myths and Stories of the Wild Woman Archetype*. New York: Ballentine.

Qualls-Corbett, N. (1988) *The Sacred Prostitute: Eternal Aspect of the Feminine*. Toronto, ON: Inner City.

Stein, M., & Corbet, L. (Eds.) (1999) *Psyche's Stories: Modern Jungian Interpretations of Fairy Tales* (Vol. 1). Wilmette, IL: Chiron.

Stone, S. (1997) *The Shadow King: The Invisible Force That Holds Women Back*. Lincoln, NE: iUniverse.

Ulanov, A., & Ulanov, B. (1994) *Transforming Sexuality: The Archetypal World of Anima and Animus*. Boston: Shambhala.

Woodman, M. (1982) *Addiction to Perfection: The Still Unravished Bride*. Toronto, ON: Inner City.

Woodman, M. (1985) *The Pregnant Virgin: A Process of Psychological Transformation*. Toronto, ON: Inner City.

Woodman, M. (1993) *Conscious Femininity: Interviews With Marion Woodman*. Toronto, ON: Inner City.

Young-Eisendrath, P. (1984) *Hags and Heroes: A Feminist Approach to Jungian Psychotherapy With Couples*. Toronto, ON: Inner City.

Young-Eisendrath, P. (1993) *You're Not What I Expected: Learning to Love the Opposite Sex*. New York: Morrow.

Young-Eisendrath, P. (1999) *Women and Desire: Beyond Wanting to Be Wanted*. New York: Three Rivers Press.

Chapter 13

THE REALM OF DESIRE

"Desire for what?"

Gina Ogden

SEXUAL DESIRE DISORDERS

Sexual desire disorders are one of the most common reasons that women come for sex therapy today, and this diagnosis is considered one of the most difficult disorders to treat (Leiblum, 2010). The diagnostic term for this continues to change, but regardless of what the *DSM* calls it, treating low sexual desire has become a focus of strong interest in sexology, with lots of books having been written on the topic (Cervenka, 2003; Hall, 2004; Leiblum, 2010; McCarthy & McCarthy, 2003; Mintz, 2009; Ogden, 2008; Resnick, 2012; Schnarch, 2009; Weiner Davis, 2003, 2008; Watson, 2013; Young-Eisendrath, 1999). Helen Singer Kaplan (1979) was the first sexologist to emphasize that desire was an essential element in the sexual response cycle.

Women often speak of desire as if it were a commodity that comes and goes mysteriously. In the absence of a "discourse of desire" they are accustomed to suppressing their own desires, and then either controlling or responding to the desires of others. They are sensitive to the dangers of being labeled as a Sexual Woman and their disconnection with their innate eroticism leads to sex without arousal, a lack of adequate lubrication, which leads to sexual discomfort, loss of interest, bracing, avoidance, inability to achieve orgasm, and sometimes chronic pelvic pain. It is ironic to have clients say, "I have desire, just not for my partner!" It's no wonder that women struggle with desire.

RECONCEPTUALIZING DESIRE

In October of 2000, twelve clinicians and social scientists met to formulate a New View of Women's Sexual Problems (Kaschak & Tiefer, 2001), which challenged the basis by which the *DSM* characterizes women as sexually dysfunctional. They outlined many ways in which the *DSM* does not adequately acknowledge the realities of most women's lives and is inherently sexist. For example, the string of *DSM* descriptions of what is currently called Female Sexual Interest/Arousal Disorder all fail to note that women who lack "desire" are often not interested in having sex that is not pleasing to them (APA, 2013).

Kleinplatz (2012) and Schnarch (2000) suggest that a lack of desire might be an indication of "good judgment." Perhaps the sex that is being had is not worth wanting. Women are not encouraged to ask themselves what kind of sex might be meaningful or pleasurable in the first place. Ogden (2008) emphasizes that we need to begin to ask clients, "Desire for what?" Fine (1992) argues that a key part of the problem is that there is no "discourse of desire" in the sex education we provide to our girls. McCormick (1994) emphasizes that our entire frame for what constitutes "normal" sexual desire is centered on a masculine model of sexuality. Historically, sexologists have counted the number of times that intercourse takes place, as if that measures a successful sex life. We also count the occurrence and intensity of a woman's orgasms, as if that measures sexual function or sexual satisfaction.

Returning to problems with the *DSM*, it fails to note that women are often subject to role overload and family and work obligations that fill every waking hour of the day. This creates a relentless workload that leads to overwhelming, chronic fatigue (Basson et al., 2003; Ogden, 2008; Tiefer, 2012). Part of this is caused by the inequitable divisions of household duties and a lack of participatory support by spouses. Cartoons portraying a man doing the dishes as "foreplay" speaks to most women.

Social construction of roles and scripts contributes to women's exhaustion, but another aspect, which is rarely in the feminist conversation, is that women get hijacked by powerful archetypal energies. These are part of a woman's psyche, and once activated, the culture encourages and amplifies them until they carry her away into a largely unconscious, imbalanced compulsion to sacrifice herself in the caretaking of others.

Psychiatric disorders also contribute to women's lack of desire, and we do not always acknowledge the prevalence of anxiety, mood disorders, personality disorders, and the general difficulty that women have with emotional dysregulation. Early negative attachment experiences create anxious, ambivalent, or avoidant attachment patterns (Poole Heller, 2008), which also foreclose upon a woman's capacity to be present and enjoyably connected. Many women dissociate during sex because they have unresolved emotional or sexual trauma in their history. Women who have been abused or betrayed find it difficult to open their hearts, let alone stay in their bodies.

Basson and Loulan

In response to the New View perspective, Basson (2000) created a circular model that incorporates relational factors into a woman's sense of desire, acknowledging that how a woman feels about her partner is important in determining her interest or willingness to engage in sexual activity. Basson emphasizes that women often engage in intercourse for the "spin-offs" they receive as a result: emotional closeness, bonding, love, affection, commitment, acceptance, even toleration. The sense of desire occurs for many women *after they begin* to engage in sexual activity.

Loulan's (1984) conceptualization of the sexual response cycle places the concept of "willingness" at the first stage. This means that a woman is willing to open herself to desire, to show up and engage and see if desire appears. Circling back to Basson, a woman needs to feel good enough about her partner to want to be willing!

The Madonna-Whore Split

Because the Madonna-Whore split is so embedded in the modern psyche, I always look for this in my clients. Women have been raised with an ongoing series of double-binds and confusing messages around their sexuality (Hite, 1994; Young-Eisendrath, 1999). Does my client believe that these are the only two possible categories and she has to choose one to the exclusion of the other? Might this paradigm be coming from her partner, who wants her a bit hotter, but not too hot? I recall a couple who came in after ten years of a low-sex marriage. He complained that she had no sexual desire. What surfaced was that during their first few months of marriage, he had commented that it wasn't proper for a woman to be so hungry for sex. She felt shamed, blew out her flame, and hadn't relit it since.

DESIRE AND IDENTITY—MAKING A PLACE FOR APHRODITE

We have already established that there is a blizzard of factors that ice out women's sexual desire: exhaustion, role overload, lack of privacy, intrapsychic conflict, partner conflict, negative sexual scripts, sexual pain, health factors, unrewarding sexual experiences, and unresolved trauma. Resolve all of these factors and a woman still needs an erotic, pleasure-oriented identity. If there is not an honored place and a protected space for Aphrodite in her life, she will not value her sexuality. A woman can engage in sex, but in order for her to *desire* sex, and to appreciate it as a pleasurable, connective, creative expression of the Self, she has to house an Aphrodite Self. She has to revel in her Sexual Essence. The Aphrodite woman is in touch with her inner flame. She nurtures and protects that flame.

MEETING THE KEEPER OF THE FLAME

On the second evening of Gina Ogden's ISIS sexuality weekend, women gather in a circle around the altar they created on the opening night. This altar is filled with objects they brought, one to represent something about their sexual story they want to let go of, and one to represent something about their sexual story that they want to keep or develop. The altar is surrounded by a ring of burning candles. It is night and Ogden drums the group into an inner journey where we each meet our Keeper of the Flame (Ogden, 2006, 2013). Being in a circle of women who are all entering into the same experience makes it particularly powerful. As each woman enters her interior world and encounters her own Keeper of the Flame, she receives a message about her sexual journey and how she will carry the gifts of the weekend forward into her life.

Once a woman has found her inner flame, it will illuminate her world. Now she has choices. Making choices that are increasingly in alignment with the Self and being responsible for those choices is what differentiates a girl from a Woman.

Bibliography

American Psychiatric Association (2013) *Diagnostic and Statistical Manual of Mental Disorders, 5th Ed., DSM-V*. Washington, DC: American Psychiatric Association.

Basson, R. (2000) The Female Sexual Response: A Different Model. *The Journal of Sex and Marital Therapy, 26*, 51–65.

Basson, R., Leiblum, S., Brotto, L., Derogatis, L., Fourcroy, J., Fugl-Meyer, K., . . . Weijmar Schultz, W. (2003) Definitions of Women's Sexual Dysfunction Reconsidered: Advocating Expansion and Revision. *Journal of Psychosomatic Obstetrics and Gynecology, 24*, 221–229.

Cervenka, K. (2003) *In the Mood Again: A Couple's Guide to Reawakening Sexual Desire*. Oakland, CA: New Harbinger.

Fine, M. (1992) Sexuality, Schooling, and Adolescent Females: The Missing Discourse of Desire. In M. Fine (Ed.) *Disruptive Voices: The Possibilities of Feminist Research* (pp. 31–59). Ann Arbor: University of Michigan Press.

Hall, K. (2004) *Reclaiming Your Sexual Self: How You Can Bring Desire Back Into Your Life*. Hoboken, NJ: Wiley & Sons.

Hite, S. (1994) *The Hite Report on the Family: Growing Up Under Patriarchy*. New York: Grove.

Kaplan, H. S. (1979) *Disorders of Sexual Desire*. New York: Brunner/Mazel.

Kaschak E., & Tiefer, L. (Eds.) (2001) *The New View of Women's Sexual Problems*. New York: Haworth.

Kleinplatz, P. (2012) Is That All There Is? A New Critique of the Goals of Sex Therapy. In P. Kleinplatz (Ed.) *New Directions in Sex Therapy: Innovations and Alternatives*. (2nd ed., pp. 101–117). New York: Routledge.

Leiblum, S. (Ed.) (2010) *Treating Sexual Desire Disorders: A Clinical Casebook*. New York: Guilford.

Loulan, J. (1984) *Lesbian Sex*. Duluth, MN: Spinsters Ink.

McCarthy, B., & McCarthy, E. (2003) *Rekindling Desire: A Step-by-Step Program to Help Low-Sex and No-Sex Marriages*. New York: Brunner-Routledge.

McCormick, N. (1994) *Sexual Salvation: Affirming Women's Sexual Rights and Pleasures*. Westport, CT: Praeger.

Mintz, L. (2009). *A Tired Woman's Guide to Passionate Sex: Reclaim Your Desire and Reignite Your Relationship*. Avon: MA: Adams Media.

Ogden, G. (2006) *The Heart and Soul of Sex: Making the ISIS Connection*. Boston: Trumpeter.

Ogden, G. (2008) *Return of Desire: A Guide to Rediscovering Your Sexual Passion*. Boston: Trumpeter.

Ogden, G. (2013) *Expanding the Practice of Sex Therapy: An Integrative Model for Exploring Desire and Intimacy*. New York: Routledge.

Poole Heller, D. (2008) *Healing Early Attachment Wounds: The Dynamic Attachment Re-patterning Experience- Module 1* [manual]. Louisville, CO: Diane Poole Heller.

Resnick, S. (2012) *The Heart of Desire: Keys to the Pleasures of Love*. Hoboken, NJ: Wiley and Sons.

Schnarch, D. (2000) Desire Problems: A Systemic Perspective. In S. Leiblum & R. Rosen (Eds.) *Principles and Practices of Sex Therapy* (3rd ed., pp. 17–56). New York: Guilford.

Schnarch, D. (2009) *Intimacy & Desire: Awaken the Passion in Your Relationship*. New York: Beaufort.

Tiefer, L. (2012) The "New View" Campaign: A Feminist Critique of Sex Therapy and an Alternative Vision. In P. Kleinplatz (Ed.) *New Directions in Sex Therapy: Innovations and Alternatives* (pp. 21–36). New York: Routledge.

Watson, L. (2013) *Wanting Sex Again: How to Rediscover Desire and Heal a Sexless Marriage*. New York: Berkeley.

Weiner Davis, M. (2003) *The Sex-Starved Marriage: A Couple's Guide to Boosting Their Marriage Libido*. New York: Simon & Shuster.

Weiner Davis, M. (2008) *The Sex-Starved Wife: What to Do When He's Lost Desire*. New York: Simon & Schuster.

Young-Eisendrath, P. (1999) *Women and Desire: Beyond Wanting to Be Wanted*. New York: Three Rivers.

CHAPTER 14

THE BIG "O"

"The pleasure of living and the pleasure of the orgasm are identical."

Wilhelm Reich

MYSTERY . . . MEANING . . . MECHANICS

In 1991, The Kinsey Institute (Reinisch, 1991) estimated that one of every ten women had never experienced an orgasm. According to Cass (2007), being orgasmic continues to be an elusive experience for many women. Women who have never had an orgasm often feel like they have not yet become "real women." They find it difficult to talk about, and it may become a shameful secret. They wonder what makes them different and experience feelings of sadness, disappointment, anger, frustration, embarrassment, and intense longing. They may continue having sex, enjoying the closeness or affection, but feel cheated of this mysterious, elusive experience. Women fake orgasmic response to reassure their partners, or live with the criticism that they are "hung up" or "too inhibited." Their partners can easily internalize inadequacy as "bad lovers." This is one of the tender problems that brings couples into sex therapy.

On the other hand, some women feel deficient if they do not have an orgasm every time. Apfelbaum (1995) cites this as a new performance anxiety in women. We also need to guard against creating a new hierarchy of "superior" orgasm: "multiple" orgasms, "extended" orgasms or "female ejaculatory" orgasms. Most women express that although orgasm is important, it is only part of their sexual experience and not the be-all, end-all of sex. Ogden's (1994/2007, 2006, 2013) research encourages us to move beyond "counting and measuring" as a benchmark of sexual "function" or satisfaction.

Unfortunately, there are many women who still labor under the myth that the only "legitimate" way to reach orgasm is through intercourse alone, and if they require additional stimulation, they are somehow defective or "sexually immature." Here we see the lingering legacy of Freud, who insisted that a "mature woman" would abandon her interest in the clitoris and focus on the vagina, the "proper receptive organ for the penis" (Berman, Berman, & Bumiller, 2005). What is abundantly clear is that intercourse is the most inefficient way for a woman to reach orgasm. Most American women still seem unaware that less than 30% of women are able to reach orgasm through intercourse alone (Cass, 2007; Foley, Kope, & Sugrue, 2012; Hite, 1976).

Women who are "vaginally" orgasmic have figured out how to create clitoral stimulation in other ways, for example, angling the penis along the frontal wall, or situating their pelvis for maximal clitoral contact. Sheri Winston's (2010) *Women's Anatomy of Arousal* provides some wonderful diagrams of female anatomy, showing the legs of the clitoris traveling behind the frontal wall of the vagina. Most women are not aware that the highly sensitive head of the clitoris is only the beginning of its structure, with legs that fork back like a wishbone into the pelvic region. The urethral sponge (also known as the G-spot), is also located on that frontal wall and becomes highly sensitive when a woman is aroused and engorged. It too can be stimulated with fingers or a well-angled penis.

THE INTERFERENCE LIST

The host of things that interfere with a woman getting "over the top" into orgasmic release are many. She may be experiencing anxiety over her weight or the post-childbearing stretch marks on her belly; she might be concerned about how she looks in the throes of passion; she may fear the state of ecstasy itself, feeling like she is coming to pieces, or about to die; she may not feel entitled to pleasure; she may feel insecure about her sexual "performance" or worried about work, kids, aging parents, or finances; she may not have enough sex education to understand how orgasms come about; she may not have enough sexual agency to give her partner feedback; she may be concerned that if she does suggest something, she may look like a "whore," or evoke anger, defensiveness, or rejection. Women close down their responsiveness when they are afraid that they are being used or lied to, or when they fear abandonment. Women's hormones play a role in orgasm and certain medications inhibit responsiveness without a woman's awareness. The advice given blithely on talk shows, to "just let go and enjoy yourself," is inadequate, unfair, and outright infuriating to sex therapists who understand that an inhibited orgasmic response is a complex issue!

SHIFTING PARADIGMS FROM DOING TO BEING

Distraction is the number one enemy to desire, arousal, and orgasm (Basson, 2000). Because most people think of sex as something they *do*, rather than an expression of who they are, or a pathway to connection and pleasure, it often becomes a task. Moving from *doing to being* is difficult in a culture that emphasizes productivity. When many women attempt to do this, the internal pressure to get back to the task list is so intense that they find a state of *being* difficult to sustain. Women who have not made space for Aphrodite in their world are highly distractible. During sex, they drift off to other issues in their lives and their lengthy to-do list. Attending to oneself, and doing the inner work to create a space for *being* and for *sharing pleasure*, feels like a criminal self-indulgence to some women, and evokes a challenging, "Who do you think you are?" from the task-oriented, responsible selves inside.

SEX STIRS UP INTENSE EMOTIONS

Sex can take us through the full spectrum of human emotions. In the positive spectrum, we find joy, delight, peace, gratitude, ecstasy, and bliss, but sex can also stir up difficult emotions like vulnerability, rage, and shame.

Sometimes, amazing sexual experiences stir up strong feelings of *hostile dependence* (Young-Eisendrath, 1993). In these cases, a woman begins to feel very defensive and angry towards the person she is becoming deeply attached to. She begins to revisit old abandonment or engulfment issues and this makes her feel very vulnerable. Vulnerability can be difficult, but aggression is even more distressing for women. Esther Perel (2007, 2010) writes of how some women do not let go into their eroticism because they fear their aggressive impulses. Being in the throes of passion can move a woman into selfish desires for pleasure and instinctual aggression to get her there.

Rage and Shame

Harriet Lerner (1985) wrote a famous book called the *Dance of Anger*. More recently, Ruth King (2007) has given us *Healing Rage*. King's work provides us with more helpful steps for moving beyond this overwhelming emotion, along with explanations of how rage can disguise itself, split us in two, and force us to control or withdraw from life. Behind our rage is pain and a deep need for comfort.

Levine (2010) suggests that we move through highly aggressive states like rage (fight) when we come out of fear and immobilization. Women have a lot of things they can be angry about, having endured a lot of injustice, with their life energy suppressed or harnessed for the needs and purposes of others. Women are extremely fearful of the intensity of their rage, and they will often shut down and return to immobilization rather than take the risk that they might be compelled to act out the violence inside them (Leonard, 1982). They intuitively sense that a sexual release might also release their rage (Levine, 2010).

Women's sexuality has been exploited and shamed in numerous ways. Shame is one of the most debilitating emotions that stops women in their tracks and blocks the path to sexual empowerment. Shame is a huge topic for women, especially around their sexuality. Brene Brown's (2007, 2012) research on shame is unsurpassed.

Fear, aggression, rage, and shame are all overwhelming emotions that shut women down. Many women will walk away from what they really want in life rather than face these emotions. An empowered woman does the inner work she needs to do to move through and beyond. She develops emotional regulation skills and does the healing work to re-empower herself. She begins to focus on what she wants to create, rather than the injustices that have been perpetrated on her. As she moves down the path, she gains confidence, because she can see her goal.

Regina's Rage

Regina explained that she knew exactly why she never had an orgasm. "In order to get there, I know I will have to go through my rage, and I have these brief impulses to kill my partner. I don't want to feel that kind of rage, so I'm not going there."

Regina and I began to work with her rage, which she had been carrying since she was twenty two and had her heart broken by a young "prince" who was supposed to be the answer to her life, rescuing her from an emotionally deprived lonely existence of home. She had opened her heart for the first time to this partner, and the pain of his rejection had almost killed her.

Helping women to release their rage requires providing a protected, grounding, containing environment for the process. Regina's rage went way back into the neglect of childhood. We employed some of King's (2007) work around Rage Reflections, and we began to process small rages, progressing as she gained the sense that she would not hurt herself, me, or anyone else with a firestorm. On some days, we sent her rage into the center of the earth, on others she wrapped herself in the blanket on my couch so that she wouldn't "destroy the universe," a fear of many women who have suppressed their rage for a long time. She took up kickboxing. She wrote letters to "the Prince," expressing what had never been said, and letters to her neglectful mother, and to the father she had never known. When she was ready for a ritual of release, we burnt the letters and let the smoke rise to the heavens. After this, she began to dream of nurturing figures, and I recognized the appearance of the Great Mother. We used the manifesting dream figures of the Great Mother to conduct some active imagination work in which she was held by this figure, who infused her with the loving nurturance she had needed her whole life. She talked about this process with her lover, who encouraged her to do whatever she needed to do to feel more in bed, even if this meant becoming furious. In the safe container of this permission, Regina began to move through her emotional states rather than repressing them. As she moved through anger, grief and shame, she began to experience wonderful states of joy where once there had been only despair and rage.

SELF-PLEASURING—SELF DISCOVERY AND EMBODIED MEDITATION

All books on becoming orgasmic recommend "self-pleasuring" or "solo practice" as a way of getting to know your body. I recall the first time I ever heard someone say the word *masturbation* in public. It was 1976, and Betty Dodson's first book, *Liberating Masturbation* was required reading for my Introduction to Women's Studies class. As I opened the book, I was stunned to see the portrayal of vulvas, sketched in pencil, each so unique, so beautiful, resembling flowers and velvet draperies, and doorways into the sacred feminine mysteries. That women's studies class opened up my world, inviting me to explore my own sexuality, and empowering me to throw off many of the sexually crippling scripts that I had internalized during my early years in a fundamentalist church.

Self-pleasuring is still a "touchy subject" for many women, who harbor scripts from early religious training on the "evils" of masturbation or feel dependent on a man to "give them" an orgasm. I have had clients who would prefer to go through a string of terrible partner choices rather than to buy themselves a good vibrator.

Dodson (1996) emphasizes that self-pleasuring is an important part of the developmental journey and learning how your body responds is essential to sexual communication with a partner. For the preorgasmic woman, it is one of the most powerful ways of awakening out of the Sleeping Beauty Syndrome, where she is passively waiting for *someone else* to give her this pleasure. Although partnered sex has many wonderful aspects, not all women can secure partners and obtaining a sexual partner is not a priority for all women.

Dodson emphasizes that masturbation is not just for kids, or for the woman in between love affairs, or for old women who can't find a partner. She advocates masturbation as a legitimate form of sexual expression for all women. Self-pleasuring can be a way of slowing down and tuning into oneself. It can become a form of embodied mindfulness for women and is the sexually empowered woman's way of staying in connection with herself and enjoying sexual pleasure throughout her whole life.

BIBLIOGRAPHY

Apfelbaum, B. (1995) Masters and Johnson Revisited: A Case of Desire Disparity. In R. Rosen& S. Leiblum (Eds.) *Case Studies in Sex Therapy.* (pp. 23–45) New York: Guilford.

Basson, R. (2000) The Female Sexual Response: A Different Model. *The Journal of Sex and Marital Therapy, 26,* 51–65.

Berman, J., Berman, L., & Bumiller, E. (2005) *For Women Only: A Revolutionary Guide to Reclaiming Your Sex Life*(2nd ed.) New York: Henry Holt.

Brown, B.(2007) *I Thought It Was Just Me (But It Isn't).* New York: Gotham.

Brown, B. (2012) *Daring Greatly.* New York: Gotham.

Cass, V. (2007) *The Elusive Orgasm.* Cambridge, MA: Da Capo.

Dodson, B. (1996) *Sex for One: The Joy of Selfloving*. New York: Three Rivers.

Foley, S., Kope, S., & Sugrue, D. (2012) *Sex Matters for Women: A Complete Guide to Taking Care of Your Sexual Self*. New York: Guilford.

Hite, S. (1976) *The Hite Report: A Nationwide Study of Female Sexuality*. New York: Seven Stories.

King, R. (2007) *Healing Rage: Women Making Inner Peace Possible*. New York: Gotham.

Leonard, L. S. (1982) *The Wounded Woman: Healing the Father-Daughter Relationship*. Boston: Shambala.

Lerner, H. (1985) *The Dance of Anger: A Woman's Guide to Changing the Patterns of Intimate Relationships*. New York: Harper & Row.

Levine, P. (2010) *In an Unspoken Voice: How the Body Releases Trauma and Restores Goodness*. Berkeley, CA: North Atlantic.

Ogden, G. (2006) *The Heart and Soul of Sex: Making the ISIS Connection*. Boston: Trumpeter.

Ogden, G. (2007) *Women Who Love Sex: Ordinary Women Describe Their Paths to Pleasure, Intimacy, and Ecstasy*. Boston: Trumpeter. (Original work published 1994)

Ogden, G. (2013) *Expanding the Practice of Sex Therapy: An Integrative Model for Exploring Desire and Intimacy*. New York: Routledge.

Perel, E. (2007) *Mating in Captivity*. New York: Harper.

Perel, E. (2010) The Double Flame: Reconciling Intimacy and Sexuality, Reviving Desire. In S. Leiblum (Ed.) *Treating Sexual Desire Disorders*. New York: Guilford.

Reinisch, J. M. (1991) *The Kinsey Institute New Report on Sex: What You Must Know to Be Sexually Literate*. New York: St. Martin's Press.

Winston, S. (2010) *Women's Anatomy of Arousal: Secret Maps to Buried Pleasure*. Kingston, NY: Mango Garden.

Young-Eisendrath, P. (1993) *You're Not What I Expected: Learning to Love the Opposite Sex*. New York: Morrow.

Chapter 15

EROS-INHIBITING ARCHETYPES

"The body-unconscious is where life bubbles up in us. It is how we know that we are alive, alive to the depths of our souls and in touch somewhere with the vivid reaches of the cosmos."

D. H. Lawrence

Sometimes there is a territorial war inside a woman for "who" will run her life. Powerful archetypes compete for space and can crowd out a woman's Aphrodite Self. I call these inner characters Eros-inhibiting archetypes.

THE GREEK GOD EROS

In Greek mythology, Eros was the masculine God of love in all its forms: erotic, sexual, romantic, brotherly, and spiritual. As the son of Aphrodite, he energized connection, joining, relatedness, and renewal. He activated libidinal energies to forward a person's development into their unique human potential (Harris, 2007). *Eros* is the root of the word *erotic*.

In my work with women who are seeking to embody more Aphrodite energy, there are particular archetypes that dominate a woman's life, crowding out her Sensuous, Erotic, and Pleasure-Oriented Selves. These Eros-inhibiting archetypes may help a woman fulfill certain roles and responsibilities, but if they begin to dominate her life, they will drain her, desexualize her, and disconnect her from her lust for life, her inner flame.

Eros-Inhibiting Archetypes

The Pleaser

This inner character shows up in almost every woman's life because women are raised to be pleasing and accommodating. The problem with the Pleaser is that she is so *other* oriented. The Pleaser is terrified that if she does not please, she will be abandoned or replaced by someone more pleasing. When a woman is dominated by this archetype, she will not "rock the boat" by bringing up her personal needs and desires (she likely doesn't know them). It is such a bitter irony that being what others want you to be becomes one of the main sources of female sexual malaise. Although women find pleasure in pleasing someone they love, *when the woman herself is not being related to, she vanishes.* Women who provide "service sex" as a Pleasing Partner tend to reach their limit on "serving it up."

In talking about his wife, one of my clients said, "I want to please her. I ask her what she wants, but she doesn't seem to know." This happens. When a woman has a domineering Pleaser or Accommodator in her inner cast, she can begin to drift along, ignoring the signals from her inner world. She becomes disconnected from her own experience and may have a difficult time finding the pathway back without help. When asked what she wants, she may not know. What she does know is that her inner light has faded along with her sexual desire.

The Good Girl

Closely related to the Pleaser is the Good Girl. Developmentally, Good Girls and Pleasers are always "daughters." When they were young, they looked around to see if they were getting in trouble with the big people, the authority figures in their lives. They are still looking around, only now the authority figures are inside. You can refer back to Chapter 10, for a long list of Gatekeepers that stand watch to make sure Good Girls are not getting out of line. With the host of Gatekeepers looking on, it is difficult for a Good Girl to access her instinctual self, let alone her inner Wild Woman.

The Inner Patriarch

Sidra Stone (1997) wrote an important book called *The Shadow King*. It describes a powerful inner character she calls the Inner Patriarch. Here is a notorious Gatekeeper, who lurks in the psyches of women, directing their actions and putting guardrails on their behavior. It is all in the name of protection, so that the woman will not get herself into the kind of "trouble" that "he" believes will befall a sexually empowered woman. Mothers in a patriarchal society oversee the installation of the Inner Patriarch in their daughters, transmitting the same inner policing that the mother herself has lived with.

Sidra Stone recounts a story of Nan, who was distressed because she was unable to feel pleasurable sensations, particularly below the waist. In a Voice Dialogue session, Sidra encountered her Inner Patriarch (a Gatekeeper), who explained that in order to keep Nan safe after she reached adolescence, he put a protective band around her body that functioned like a medieval chastity belt. Outside of her awareness, this band of protection was still operating every time she tried to open herself to sexual pleasure. During the session, Sidra "negotiated" with Nan's Inner Patriarch and he came to understand that she could take care of herself now, and so he could release the protective band around Nan's body. After being freed from this psychic "chastity belt," Nan was able to access her adult Aphrodite Self and explore her sexuality.

The Good and Proper (Dutiful) Wife

In Hite's (1994) work on archetypes of family life, she describes how the archetype of Wife and Mother severely inhibit a woman's sense of sexual empowerment. We underestimate the whitewashing power of the archetype of the Wife on flesh-and-blood women. In *Marriage Shock: The Transformation of Women Into Wives*, Heyn (1997) outlines the gradual erosion of a woman's erotic edge as she is turned into a virtuous, self-sacrificing, proper "wife." Heyn asserts that if we ever bothered to really see female sexuality through the eyes of women, rather than through the eyes of men, we would see a far more erotically charged and richly textured landscape. She encourages women to be conscious of the gravitational pull that the archetype of the Good Wife has on her Erotic Self and to write a new script for marriage.

The Hovering, Responsible Mother

The Mother is one of our most revered archetypes because we truly understand how essential nurture is to the formation of little people. It is not just the demands and responsibilities of the role that erode a woman's erotic edge, the pull of this powerful archetype draws her energy away from her partner and toward the children in selfless devotion. She may continue to have sex, but now it becomes a responsibility, part of her role as a Good Wife. She feels she needs to nurture the relationship, and respond to complaints from her partner, who likely feels abandoned on a deeper level, as her energy flows increasingly to the children. In deference to their needs, she abandons anything that feels selfish or indulgent. Pleasure is indulgent. Out it goes.

In paying less attention to herself, she may begin to feel fat and dowdy, less desirable, frisky, or playful (Reibstein & Richards, 1993). Perel (2007, 2010) talks about how eroticism involves a certain degree of aggression and selfishness, both of which are antithetical to the selfless, soft orientation of the Nurturing Mother.

Aphrodite Has Left the Building

Sidra Stone (1997) also writes about how deadly the archetype of the Mother is to a woman's "Aphrodite Self." Men are often mystified by the shift that occurs when a woman becomes a Mother. He may long for the Lover he once knew. While the Good Father in a man may appreciate his wife's caring devotion to the children, the Lover in him becomes hungry and begins to behave increasingly like a Vulnerable, Needy Child. This archetypal shift is felt by her, and she begins to experience him as one more drain on her already overtaxed energy (Stone, 1997). In response to his sense of "abandonment," a man may give up trying to re-engage a woman's Aphrodite Self, invest himself more heavily in his career, and move more deeply into his role as Father and Provider. He may submerge his own erotic energies, or take his eroticism away from the Wife and Mother, fulfilling his needs online, or with an erotic partner outside of the home.

As the couple begins to devote themselves to the family, they often become too tired and preoccupied to be sexual with one another. The Lovers get subverted under Responsible Parental archetypes such as Provider, Nurturer, Household Administrator, Chauffeur, Disciplinarian, and Soccer Dad and Mom. None of these parental archetypes carries sexual energy. Viewing relationships from this perspective, it is easy to see why so many modern relationships drift into a sexless malaise.

Reclaiming the Lost Erotic—Running Away From Home

One of the ways that a woman can reawaken her Aphrodite Self is to "run away from home." Women who are Mothers almost have to leave the home before they can escape the entrainment of that archetype, but women who have worked with me have been able to get their Aphrodite energy going by "trying on" a variety of sexual archetypes. The mere entrance into these energies breaks up the energy of Eros-inhibiting archetypes. Some of the archetypes that have explored are French Courtesan, Pampered Mistress, Call Girl, Vamp, Blond Bombshell, Sex Kitten, Sexual Priestess, Medieval Tavern Wench, Stripper, Harem Girl, Gypsy, Geisha, Erotic Masseuse, and Bohemian. A woman doesn't have to dress the part to inhabit these energies, but some women who favor the "sexual path preference" (Mosher, 1980) of Role Enactment, enjoy dressing up. When women learn to shift states, they learn to carry archetypal energies on their own. The important point is that she is giving all of her caregiving, responsible, serious selves the night off.

These evenings do require some time and intention, but the playfulness they activate is highly energizing and well worth it. We get very serious as adults, with our many responsibilities and anxieties. We forget how to play, and playfulness is an important component of a satisfying, intimate relationship, essential for great sex (Kleinplatz et al., 2009; Metz & Lutz, 1990).

For women with kids, I suggest forming a babysitting co-op where there can be a circling Responsible Mother, while giving one of the members a child-free evening. Scheduling strategic sleepovers works well. Pick up the bedroom, and have yummy food on hand, or just "run away" to a nearby hotel.

The Spectator (The Sexual Critic)

Masters and Johnson (1970) named spectatoring as the greatest enemy to sexual enjoyment. We can personify the Spectator as an inner character, and dialogue with him, her, or it. The Spectator could also be called the Sexual Critic, because she or he is constantly judging and evaluating a woman's sexual "performance" to see if she measures up. The Spectator can team up with the Shame Squad, the Inner Patriarch, or the Pleaser, distracting a woman from sensations, self-awareness, and an authentic engagement with her partner. Conducting a Voice Dialogue session with the Spectator will help a woman to recognize this Eros-extinguishing presence and direct him or her out of the bedroom.

The Athena Woman

When you are a woman, you don't complete a PhD dissertation, climb a corporate ladder, or build your own business without a fierce kind of focus. In the Greek Pantheon of Goddesses, Athena was the goddess of war, strategy, knowledge, purity, arts & crafts, learning, justice and wisdom, intelligence, consciousness, education, eloquence, and power. Her energy is tough, clever, and independent. Athena is a Virgin Goddess, whole and complete unto herself, and an important archetype in the fight for women's rights (Shinoda Bolen, 1984). Athena women climb the ladders of success by operating strategically within patriarchal parameters. Universities and professions are filled with Athena women, who worked twice as hard as the men around them to excel in a man's world. When you are sitting in the presence of an Athena woman, you can feel her sharp mind, but you may not be able to feel her heart, and she may be very disembodied. She may treat her body like a machine, something to be exercised and fed so that it will support her work.

Cynthia's Island Girl

My client Cynthia was an attractive, intelligent Athena Woman who went to the Bahamas with her boyfriend and discovered her Aphrodite Island Girl. She had never felt so happy and relaxed and vowed that she was going to make time for her sensual self when she got home! But when she returned home, she was faced with an onslaught of responsibilities and work deadlines. Her furrowed brow returned, along with the stress and irritability. Over time, her Island Girl was forgotten, crowded out by her Thinking-Oriented Career Woman. Her stress was compounded by her boyfriend's complaints about her withdrawn moodiness. I helped Cynthia "install" her Island Girl as a permanent member of her inner cast, so that her priorities could include time for replenishment and pleasure. This recalibration helped in every area of her life, including the surprise she felt when she realized that rest, relaxation, and the endorphins of romance actually improved her productivity.

ARCHETYPES OF ARMOR

We all have protective defenses, born of painful past experiences. The Armored Amazon, Warrior Queen, Brilliant Skeptic, Psychology Professor, Ice Princess, Porcupine, Anxious Avoider, Willful Withholder, and the Protective Distance-Keeper are all inner characters I have encountered who protect Vulnerable Children inside. A woman may not be consciously aware that these adversarial or impenetrable archetypes are present in her inner cast. They become accustomed to this habitual way of defending themselves and think of it as "who I am."

WORKING WITH PROTECTIVE DEFENSES

This breed of Gatekeeper is born as a result of experiences where the client felt overwhelming vulnerability or hurt. When this happens, people make important decisions about how they will be in the future. Depending on the intensity of the resolution, those decisions can stick, and become part of the unconscious operating system of the client, out of awareness, but powerfully influential. As a woman begins to feel more of a sense of personal power, these defenses can be surfaced, examined, and potentially retired.

When you sense one of these Strategic Protectors in a woman's inner self system, get them out from behind the curtain and interview them. Ask them about their history. Find out the circumstances in which they came into being and how they are trying to protect her now. What calls them into action at the present time? These protective defenses served an important purpose at one time, but that time may be long gone. These inner defenders may be standing like angry guards between the woman and the intimacy and pleasure she is seeking.

Women want to relate and to love, but women also want to be *related to* as unique persons, with *subjective experiences of their own*. Although they may not be able to voice it in just this way, women are not inspired to love by being made into "objects" who play parts in other people's scripts, and they will set up protective defenses. Check to see if this is what your client is experiencing.

The Protective Underachiever

The Protective Underachiever uses a passive defense. This inner self simply refuses to try. It is not surprising to meet this inner self in a woman who is living with a critical, demanding partner, with whom she has a history of never being enough. This woman knows she has much more sexual potential available in her, but she is exhausted with keeping up as it is. She feels she is being measured by an escalating performance standard. As a practitioner, you need to check to see if this is actually happening, or if the pressure is coming from *inside her* and being *projected out* onto her partner!

Behind the Underachiever, you will find *Vulnerable Children*. When you interview these inner selves, they will tell you that no matter how hard they try, nothing is ever enough. They may have had parents who were relentlessly raising the bar of achievement on them. You may encounter a Pleaser who ran out of steam. Check and see if your client picked a partner like her parents. It happens. If so, there is even more work to be done to get a Self-defining, Self-affirming core in place.

Eros-Inhibiting Expectations

Any time a sexual partner has a preconceived performance expectation, they will miss out on the gifts of the experience that is currently available to them *in the present*. The pressure to have every sexual experience be a "10" creates problems for both partners and activates inner protectors in women. If she is operating under a *performance script*, have her rewrite it into a *pleasure script* or a *connection script*. Have her expand her sexual menu to include a variety of pleasure oriented activities. She does not have to order the same meal twice (Iasenza, 2001). A sexuality based on matching or topping the last experience is not sexual relating, it is performing. Yes, we want to continue to open into amazing experiences, but let's also not denigrate the importance of simple, "feel good" sex in the menu of possibilities. It serves to maintain the bond of connection and mediate marital stress in long-term couples (McCarthy & McCarthy, 2004).

The Withholder

When women withhold sex, it is one of the ways they communicate displeasure. Women also shut down sexually because they feel hurt, anxious, and overwhelmed. Women are not raised to address issues directly; therefore, they have very poor conflict resolution skills. Add power inequities, and partners with their own inability to resolve conflict and you have a recipe for sexual shutdown. Passive undermining is a strategy of powerless people. If you interview the Protective Withholder, this is likely to be the kind of material you hear, and there will be valid reasons for all of it.

As a practitioner you must take into account the larger picture of this client's life. All of it is related to her sexual expression. Is she in a place to determine her own life? Where is her sense of agency? The woman who has no voice and is economically dependent cannot be sexually free. She needs good negotiation and communication skills like the ones taught in *Difficult Conversations* (Stone, Patton, & Heen, 1999), but women also need the right "archetypal stance" from which to communicate.

Women often give up on negotiating for what they want far too early! They attempt to get their point across, try once or twice using the same approach, and when they don't get the result they want, they give up, or write their partner off as "hopeless." They may resort to the tactics of oppressed people, going through the motions without caring, quietly undermining, going underground with her own agendas, pulling in third parties (complaining to their mother or their friends), and so on. Every archetypal stance that a woman holds will evoke a different response from her partner. More on this in Chapter 21, on becoming a Sexually Empowered Woman.

The Protective Distance-Keeper

Many therapists are unaware that some people have a limited tolerance for positive experiences. It seems unimaginable to many therapists! The reality is that people with difficult histories can become very uncomfortable when things go "right." They can become overwhelmed by closeness, positive touch, or hearing words of love from a partner. Eye contact can be particularly difficult for some people (Poole Heller, 2008; Siegel, 1999).

In Peter Levine's (2009, 2010) somatic experiencing work, he proposes that we can help people increase their capacity for love and pleasure by "titrating," or giving small doses of something that would overwhelm the client's nervous system if given in a larger dose. In this way, a person could learn to "tolerate" love, support, acceptance, and pleasure and trust that these things don't lead to loss, hurt, or danger.

Creative visualization can be useful because the client can visualize an experience and exit it if they become overwhelmed. The practitioner can watch the client carefully to make sure that they do not go beyond a tolerable range of nervous system arousal. If the client becomes frozen or agitated, pause, slow down, and work with her right there to help build her skills in self-regulating, calming herself down, and staying in the body. You can use breath, body scanning with a description of sensations, and soothing memories that help her shift states and de-escalate the nervous system. You can anchor the past in the past, and ask her about sights, sounds, and sensations in the here and now.

Sex is filled with potential triggers for women. If a woman has a history of trauma, the practitioner can help her develop some verbal and non-verbal signals so that when she gets overwhelmed, she can pause, calm herself down, or redirect what she is doing, rather than pressing forward, no longer engaged and possibly dissociated. The idea is to reteach the nervous system through healing experiences, so that the body learns that closeness and sex can be safe with a safe partner.

BIBLIOGRAPHY

Harris, B. (2007) *The Fire and the Rose: The Wedding of Spirituality and Sexuality*. Wilmette, IL: Chiron.

Heyn, D. (1997) *Marriage Shock: The Transformation of Women Into Wives*. New York: Villard.

Hite, S. (1994) *The Hite Report on the Family: Growing Up Under Patriarchy*. New York: Grove.

Iasenza, S. (2001) Sex Therapy With "A New View." In E. Kaschak & L. Tiefer (Eds.) *A New View of Women's Sexual Problems* (pp. 43–46). Birmingham, NY: Haworth.

Kleinplatz, P., Menard, A. D., Paquet, M., Paradis, N., Campblee, M., Zuccarino, D., & Mehak, L. (2009) The Components of Optimal Sexuality: A Portrait of 'Great Sex.' *Canadian Journal of Human Sexuality, 18*, 1–2, 1–13.

Levine, P. (2009) *Trauma, Somatic Experiencing and Peter A. Levine PhD* www.youtube.com/watch?v=ByalBx85iC8 accessed 11/30/2014.

Levine, P. (2010) *In an Unspoken Voice: How the Body Releases Trauma and Restores Goodness*. Berkeley, CA: North Atlantic.

Masters, W., & Johnson, V. (1970) *Human Sexual Inadequacy*. Boston: Little, Brown.

McCarthy, B., & McCarthy, E. (2004) *Getting It Right the First Time: Creating a Healthy Marriage*. New York: Brunner-Routledge.

Metz, M., & Lutz, G. (1990) Dyadic Playfulness Differences Between Sexual and Marital Therapy Couples. *Journal of Psychology and Human Sexuality, 3*, 1, 167–182.

Mosher, D. L. (1980) Three Dimensions of Depth of Involvement in Human Sexual Response. *The Journal of Sex Research, 30*, 1, 1–42.

Perel, E. (2007) *Mating in Captivity*. New York: Harper.

Perel, E. (2010) The Double Flame: Reconciling Intimacy and Sexuality, Reviving Desire. In S. Leiblum (Ed.) *Treating Sexual Desire Disorders: A Clinical Casebook* (pp. 23–43). New York: Guilford.

Poole Heller, D. (2008) *Healing Early Attachment Wounds: The Dynamic Attachment Re-patterning Experience- Module 1* [manual]. Louisville, CO: Diane Poole Heller.

Reibstein, J., & Richards, M. (1993) *Sexual Arrangements: Marriage and the Temptation of Infidelity*. New York: Charles Scribner's Sons.

Shinoda Bolen, J. (1984) *Goddesses in Every Woman: A New Psychology of Women*. New York: Harper Perennial.

Siegel, D. (1999) *The Developing Mind: How Relationships and the Brain Interact to Shape Who We Are*. New York: Guilford.

Stone, S. (1997) *The Shadow King: The Invisible Force That Holds Women Back*. Lincoln, NE: iUniverse.

Stone, D., Patton, B., & Heen, S. (1999) *Difficult Conversations: How to Discuss What Matters Most*. New York: Penguin.

CHAPTER 16

TRAUMA AND THE SOUL OF APHRODITE

"A wise woman refuses to be anyone's Victim."

Maya Angelou

TRAUMA, ABUSE, AND SHAME

One of the major factors that separate women from their innate eroticism is a history of trauma and abuse. A history of sexual abuse and rape can cause women to overidentify with being a sexual object (high percentages of prostitutes were sexually abused as children), and it can also lead to a perpetual stance of sexual avoidance. Research indicates that one in three women in this culture have experienced unwanted or traumatic sexual experiences, often at a young age, often at the hands of someone they should have been be able to trust (Bass & Davis, 1988; Maltz, 1991).

Sexual violation deeply affects identity and script formation. Victims of childhood sexual abuse have arrested or distorted sexual development, and clinicians need to inquire into this history. When you are asking about a woman's sexual story, keep in mind "who" is responding. Depending on which of a woman's inner selves is reporting the history, you may get a dismissive report, "Oh, it happened a long time ago, I don't think about it anymore." Meanwhile, the younger "self" who experienced the abuse is nested in her psyche, filled with overwhelming feeling.

Depending on the degree of trauma, the sexually abused "self" may be significantly walled off, surrounded by a psychic membrane that protects her from revisiting overwhelming memories and states of emotion. That membrane gets challenged when the client becomes sexually intimate. Orgasm, emotional merging, and close physical proximity challenge the ego integrity of each sexual partner. The fear of a loss of control can make it too threatening to open up to pleasure (Phillips & Frederick, 1995).

THE BODY REMEMBERS

Keeping emotional reactivity at bay takes a lot of energy and can interfere with a woman's capacity to be present or to feel deep sensation, because traumatic memories live in the body (Rothschild, 2000, 2003). Women with this history often dissociate during sex and partners can easily "personalize" this emotional absence and lack of responsiveness. Not understanding the degree of internal disruption the woman is dealing with, the partner can become defensive, insecure, or critical. The cocktail of brain chemicals that cascade during the early blush of romance helps a woman override her emotional avoidance, but once in the stability of a long-term relationship, her brain chemicals settle down, and old triggers resurface. When these couples sit in my office, they are confounded by their current sexual malaise. "What happened? We were so great together in the early relationship," they say. In my opinion, it is a necessity for every clinician who works with sexuality to be trained in some form of intervention shown to be effective in treating trauma.

In working with clients with trauma, you may discover that your client has a Sexual Self who is quite young, frozen in the time period the trauma occurred, and unable to engage in adult activities. In cases of severe abuse, these young inner selves can be completely split off from the waking personality, and highly reactive when exposed. This client may be suffering from a full-blown Dissociative Identity Disorder or Borderline Personality Disorder. Assessing and treating these highly fragile clients requires specialized clinical training (Phillips & Frederick, 1995).

HELPING THE KIDS BEHIND THE CURTAIN

As women heal from sexual trauma, they often describe the experience as reclaiming a lost part of themselves, even "reclaiming a lost part of my soul." The abused children that live in clients hide in the background of the psyche, like "kids behind the curtain" (Wakefield, 2012). To them, even being in a body may be too dangerous, and a joyfully embodied sexuality is out of the question. In order to shield them from further harm, the psyche creates a wall of Protective Gatekeepers that stand out in front like powerful sentries. This set of Gatekeepers may not even allow you access to the Inner Child. As a practitioner, if you invite this client into an exploratory exercise, the answer may be a resounding, "No! We do not explore." Breaking the silence and telling secrets they promised they would never tell is a big deal for these Inner Children. Never force the child out, as this mimics the violation of the original event. We clinicians tend to think of this as resistance, but it is an invitation to dialogue with the *Gatekeepers* who are protecting these Vulnerable Children. In time, the child may emerge, but in the meantime, the Protective Gatekeeper knows all about the Child and can provide crucial information for that Child's restoration and healing.

The Power of the Pause

If a woman knows she has the power to press the "pause button" in sexual interactions, she is more likely to feel more confident to engage. The "power of the pause" means she can slow down, calm down, breathe, get in her body, regroup, use inner resources, and perhaps stop for now. Over time, if her partner works with her, the positive experience of safe engagement will rewire the previous reactivity that was etched into her brain by previous hurt or trauma. By utilizing these healing strategies, people who have been avoiding closeness their whole lives have learned to be close and securely attached (Poole Heller, 2008).

We can employ Voice Dialogue with the Wounded Child, asking what she needs and how much closeness and good stuff she can handle right now. How much is "just right?" We can use creative visualization to imaginatively reconstruct what was needed at crucial developmental junctures in her life, and allowing that experience to sink into the body's memory as a new reality (Pesso, 2013). With the power to say "yes," "no," and "pause," a woman can venture forward. With this sense of agency, she can redirect what is happening. With a sense of agency, the self-protective patterns of complete avoidance or habitual dissociation will transform into a growing sense of presence and engagement, and become the "new norm."

Affirmation for the Traumatized Inner Child

Here is a wonderful affirmation from Diane Poole Heller (2011), for the woman recovering from violation, forced to be a sexual object for another. She can say to herself, "Your sexual energy is yours, to do with what you want. It does not belong to anyone else. You can choose how to express it, with whom and when. You can set a boundary, and you can invite people in. You have the right to say yes, and you can say no."

Sexual Abuse and the High Achiever

A history of sexual abuse can lead a woman into careers that are heavily thinking oriented. Many women with damaging histories become high achievers, as this helps to compensate for the feeling that they are fundamentally damaged. These highly polished adult women may fall to pieces in intimate relationships, reverting to a much younger ego state.

It could be said that every woman raised in this culture has some degree of sexual trauma, because we internalize such toxic messages about what sex is and what it means, along with the shaming and constricting scripts regarding who, when, where, how, and why we are to have sex.

THE ARCHETYPE OF DAMAGED GOODS

There are any number of ways that a woman can begin to think of herself as Damaged Goods and dialoguing with "Damaged Goods" in a Voice Dialogue session can be a profound experience for the woman who was not conscious that she held this identity. In Chapter 11, we talked about Waifs and Poor Little Match Girls. Part of this identity is the belief that no one could possibly want them. Women who have the identity of Damaged Goods often block or dismiss gestures of real interest that come their way. They don't believe in the possibility that anyone could love them. Stuck in their own rejecting vicious cycle, they confirm the "truth" that they are unlovable.

Having a history of childhood sexual abuse is one way in which a woman can view herself as Damaged Goods, but there are others. Adult rape victims can become deeply traumatized, feeling so vulnerable and damaged they can no longer relate to a loving partner. The woman with genital herpes or human papillomavirus (HPV) can internalize judgment and rejection, now believing that she is out of the running for a meaningful relationship or a fulfilling sex life. Until a woman resolves questions about her sexual identity or gender identity, she can spend years of her life feeling that "something is wrong with me." Women with physical disabilities can internalize the unfair projections that many place on them as "non-sexual women." If they internalize this, they may begin to see themselves as unappealing, which creates an archetypal stance that affects their ability to find a partner. Damaged Goods can become a dark character in the story of a woman's life.

Sexual Pain Disorders

Women who suffer from sexual pain disorders like Vaginismus (spasming at the opening of the vagina), Dyspareunia (painful intercourse), or other health issues that have an impact on a woman's ability to be sexual, may despair of ever feeling like they can offer a partner a "normal," satisfying sex life. They feel like Damaged Goods. These conditions can be related to unresolved sexual trauma, but they can also be related to underlying medical issues, or from a lack of understanding regarding the changes a woman's body goes through during the sexual response cycle, which allow for comfortable, potentially pleasurable intercourse.

This spring I was invited to present at a "getting your groove back" event for new moms. I had a follow-up conversation with pelvic physical therapists, Tracy Sher and Heather Edwards, in which we continued to discuss women's sexual pain issues. Many of their patients are distressingly uneducated about the sexual response cycle. Some of the women these physical therapists see have chronic pelvic floor issues that began with them tightening in anticipation of the discomfort they would feel when they allowed sexual penetration before they were sufficiently aroused, relaxed, or lubricated. This tightening led to a syndrome in which *chronic* pelvic tension *prevented* arousal and lubrication, which escalated the woman's sexual difficulty. Edwards commented that when these women talk about sex, it is as if they experience themselves as no more than "holes" into which a partner's penis is inserted . . . for his pleasure. Basic sexual education changes their whole sexual experience and transforms the lives of these women who have been in long-standing sexual distress.

The Survivor

Some women become overidentified with having overcome some wound, until this becomes an encompassing identity, a way of being darkly heroic. Carolyn Myss (2003) calls it "woundology." These are women who will inform you within five minutes of knowing them that they are "survivors" of something. The Survivor is an archetype. When it becomes a woman's core identity, it crowds out more vitalizing possibilities.

DIALOGUING WITH "DAMAGED GOODS"

Voice Dialogue (Stone & Stone, 1989, Wakefield, 2012) and Internal Family Systems (Schwartz, 1995) are effective interventions for accessing and healing the traumatized inner selves that reside, often split off, in a client's psyche. Frozen in time, many of these inner selves have never told their story, certainly not from the state they were in when the trauma happened. I cannot emphasize how different it is to let *the inner child* tell the story of her abuse, *rather than the adult tell the story of the child's abuse*. I allow my clients to name their own inner characters, but I always talk about the archetype of Damaged Goods.

For women who have been abused, most of them had nowhere to go with these experiences. Being in the presence of a calm facilitator who will listen to her and believe her is in itself profoundly healing. She may hold contradictory versions of the story. A major part of the healing process is to allow all her inner selves to talk as she weaves together a cohesive narrative of what happened. Her inner children will carry fear and shame, needing affirmation that what they did to survive was what they needed to do at that time. Some experiences had a mixture of pain and pleasure. The *adult woman* may feel guilty and ashamed at the realization that she traded sexual involvement for attention or connection, but *the child* had no awareness that she was being manipulated.

In working with trauma, you want to watch the client's level of distress. In earlier days, therapists believed in allowing clients to "get it all out" and become flooded with emotion. Most of the current somatically oriented therapists (Levine, 2005, 2009, 2010; Ogden, 2006; Poole Heller, 2008; Siegel, 1999) believe that it is important to keep the process work within a "window of tolerance," to prevent overwhelm and further reinforcement of the trauma circuits of the brain. We can work with clients to help them access inner resources to downshift arousal states in the body. One way of doing this is to have your client locate a vivid positive memory that activates a bodily sense of calm. This is a memory they can return to if they become distressed to help them settle and self-soothe. It is important to teach a woman that she has these resources available to her and that she can access them any time she becomes significantly distressed. She can learn to tune into her body and down-shift her nervous system, drawing upon positive memories that help her to shift states, anchoring herself in the here and now. The ultimate goal is to fade the vividness of the negative memory by rerouting the trauma tracks of the brain (Ecker, Ticic, & Hulley, 2012). Traumatic memories may be part of her story, but they do not have to define her.

You don't want to open this material up late in a session, as you need time to unpack it, process it, and allow the client to pull herself together. If you know that you are going to be entering into this material, you might want to schedule an extra-long session to create some buffer time. It is not within the scope of this book to cover all the important aspects of working with trauma. I highly recommend reading the work of the somatic psychotherapists listed in the previous paragraph, along with the work of Al Pesso (2013). Better yet, go train with one of them to gain greater mastery in working with trauma.

Over the years, I have listened to numerous women talk about their childhood sexual traumas. They are often not aware of the extent to which these wounded inner child influence their lives, choices, and sexuality. Her Vulnerable Child may have kept her away from *all* life experiences that cause anxiety (not just relationships). She may have been continually numb during sexual experiences. Conversely, she may have become highly sexualized. She may be re-enacting the abuse, to try to make sense of it, or change the outcome. She may only experience herself as worthwhile or powerful when she is seducing, or acting as an *object of other people's pleasure*. When we are working with women who have these histories, we are helping them to reclaim their sexual *subjectivity* and to move beyond being other people's "objects."

Experiences That Heal

We are formed and reformed by experiences that carry intense emotional "charge." Corrective emotional experiences heal the past and displace entrenched paradigms (Hartman & Zimberoff, 2004). The brain's neural circuits related to early learning can be unlocked and rewired when we raise the original negatively charged learning experience to consciousness, and then juxtapose an emotionally positive experience that counteracts the original learning. The synapses in the brain actually disconnect at these times and reconsolidate into new neural pathways (Ecker et al., 2012). Powerful dreams can also create profound healing experiences. Jungian analysts have understood this for a long time, but recent brain research shows how this neuropsychic process actually happens.

THE DEFENSIVE SELF-CARE SYSTEM RELEASES ITS PRISONERS

Jungian analyst and trauma expert Donald Kalsched once believed that the deeply embedded negative forces of self-protection that resulted from extreme trauma were almost immutable (Kalsched, 1996). This is because many of them were formed in the client's early life, and they became entangled with the formation of personality. The thinking was that a client could become more conscious of when and how these defenses were activated, but the defenses could never truly be eliminated. In his most recent book, Kalsched (2013) states that he no longer holds such a pessimistic view. With further clinical experience and in incorporating the perspectives of *attachment theory, neuroscience*, and *body-centered psychotherapy*, he now believes that these seemingly intractable defensive self-care systems (what I call Protective Gatekeepers) can be transformed. Working with affect, reparative attachment experiences, and body-centered psychotherapies, these inner protectors will release their "prisoners," these "inner children" and allow the client to move forward into a life of greater freedom and wholeness.

WHAT THE NEW BRAIN SCIENCE IS TELLING US

Patterns of neural connectivity underlie all perception and thought. In thinking about this from a Jungian perspective, our "complexes" are patterns of neural connectivity. Particular pathways become strengthened as they are repeatedly travelled, and we begin to think of these responses as "who we are and what we do." Our personalities are far more changeable than we once thought, because neurological synapses can be strengthened, retrained, and redirected. New experiences alter patterns of connectivity. Whenever we have a deeply upsetting or intensely satisfying new experience (including powerful dreams!) we create new paths through the brain (Cozolino, 2006; Siegel, 1999).

Introducing Ideal Protectors

One of the great gifts of Al Pesso's (2013) work is the symbolic reconstruction work he does, in which he takes clients back into an early scene, and through an imaginal process he introduces what was needed at that time: protection, nurture, support, comfort, encouragement, acknowledgment, acceptance, and so on. By entering into the creative visualization, and really *feeling* the emotional impact of receiving what was needed "back there then," the patterns of the brain are remapped, leading to a permanent shift in the client's sense of self. Sometimes, when a woman realizes that her life would have been very different, it creates sadness, but the experience also opens a "possibility sphere" and allows her to make different choices from that point forward.

Secondary Trauma—Doing Your Own Work

As a clinician, you must do your own work and *continue* to do so over the course of your career as a sexual healer. Some of the stories you hear are very tragic, very terrifying, and very enraging. You will feel these experiences in your body because you are in the field of the client's energy. It will move through your body, and some of it will lodge there. Develop your own clearing practices and processing resources to move that energy out, so that you are not storing it, or becoming depleted, or physically ill.

Bibliography

Bass, E., & Davis, L. (1988) *The Courage to Heal: A Guide for Women Survivors of Child Sexual Abuse*. New York: Harper Perennial.

Cozolino, L. (2006) *The Neuroscience of Human Relationships: Attachment and the Developing Social Brain*. New York: Norton.

Ecker, B., Ticic, R., & Hulley, L. (2012) *Unlocking the Emotional Brain: Eliminating Symptoms at Their Roots Using Memory Reconsolidation*. New York: Routledge.

Hartman, D., & Zimberoff, D. (2004) Corrective Emotional Experiences in the Therapeutic Process. *Journal of Heart-Centered Therapies, 7*, 2, 3–84.

Kalsched, D. (1996) *The Inner World of Trauma: Archetypal Defenses of the Personal Spirit*. New York: Routledge.

Kalsched, D. (2013) *Trauma and the Soul: A Psycho-Spiritual Approach to Human Development and Its Interruption*. New York: Routledge.

Levine, P. (2005) *Healing Trauma: A Pioneering Program for Restoring the Wisdom of Your Body*. Boulder, CO: Sounds True.

Levine, P. (2009) *Trauma, Somatic Experiencing and Peter A. Levine PhD* www.youtube. com/watch?v=ByalBx85iC8 accessed 11/30/2014.

Levine, P. (2010) *In an Unspoken Voice: How the Body Releases Trauma and Restores Goodness*. Berkeley, CA: North Atlantic.

Maltz, W. (1991) *The Sexual Healing Journey: A Guide for Survivors of Sexual Abuse*. New York: HarperCollins.

Myss, C. (2003). *Sacred Contracts: Awakening Your Divine Potential*. Carlsbad, CA: Hay House.

Ogden, P. (2006) *Trauma and the Body: A Sensorimotor Approach to Psychotherapy*. New York: Norton.

Pesso, A. (2013) *Presentations & Lectures by Albert Pesso on Pesso Boyden System Psychomotor Therapy* (1984–2012). Kindle edition.

Phillips, M., & Frederick, C. (1995) *Healing the Divided Self: Clinical and Ericksonian Hypnotherapy for Post-Traumatic and Dissociative Conditions*. New York: Norton.

Poole Heller, D. (2008) *Healing Early Attachment Wounds: The Dynamic Attachment Re-patterning Experience- Module 1* [manual]. Louisville, CO: Diane Poole Heller.

Poole Heller, D. (2011) *Enlivening Intimacy, Sensuality, and Sexuality*. DARe Module3 Demo-Gun. DAR B9. Louisville, CO: Diane Poole Heller.

Rothschild, B. (2000) *The Body Remembers: The Psychophysiology of Trauma and Trauma Treatment*. New York: Norton.

Rothschild, B. (2003) *The Body Remembers: Casebook*. New York: Norton.

Schwartz, R. (1995) *Internal Family Systems Therapy*. New York: Guilford.

Siegel, D. (1999) *The Developing Mind: How Relationships and the Brain Interact to Shape Who We Are*. New York: Guilford.

Stone, H., & Stone, S. (1989) *Embracing Our Selves: The Voice Dialogue Manual*. Novato, CA: Nataraj.

Wakefield, C. (2012) *Negotiating the Inner Peace Treaty: Becoming the Person You Were Born to Be*. Bloomington, IN: Balboa.

CHAPTER 17

POWERFUL PANDORAS— ARCHETYPES OF INFAMY

"I used to be Snow White . . . but I drifted."

Mae West

In acknowledging the spectrum of sexual archetypes that women inhabit, we must include some archetypes of "infamy." A woman does well to have at least a whiff of these archetypes in her perfume mix, just to serve as a shadow remedy. She doesn't have to "act them out," but a tiny dose of these energies will shift her archetypal mix, to give her enough "danger" to go after what she wants in her life. It will also protect her from being bullied or intimidated by her Inner Patriarch, Eros-inhibiting archetypes or other Gatekeepers. Women tend to err on the side of being sensitive to other people's feelings and concerned about how their decisions will have an impact on others. Archetypes of infamy are more *impersonal*, which is a quality that most women can use more of. They are located in the dark portions of the Sexual Essence Wheels, as they are generally judged as "selfish," but these power archetypes are what a woman often needs to forward her *own* passionate interests, and free her to go after what *she* wants.

THE SEDUCTRESS, THE SIREN, AND THE FEMME FATALE

In mythology she is compelling but dangerous, crafty and deceitful. She captures men and will not let them go. The Sirens of the Odyssey were capable of pulling sailors off their course and luring them onto the rocks.

The legend of Pandora tells us that her beauty loosed trouble upon the world. As the Femme Fatale, the Fatal Attraction, she is both dangerous and irresistible. She will use you for her own purposes, be it promotion or pleasure. She cares nothing for your feelings. She is a Predator, a Man Eater. When she is done with you, she will spit you out and move on. She is hated and disparaged by less enchanting women, particularly Wives, when they fear that their husbands have lost interest in them.

Seductresses sometimes marry, but other women instinctively distrust them. A Seductress is likely to be flirting with your husband when you are not looking. She may be arranging a secret dalliance. She is not interested in the approval of other women. She plays for fun and to experience her power to captivate.

Ellen White's (2007) book *Simply Irresistible* reframes the dangerous Siren in a positive light and creates a typology by which a woman can locate herself, and potentially model herself after some of the great Sirens of history.

THE ADULTERESS

Although many men express the desire for an attractive woman who can "let her hair down" behind closed doors, men want a Devoted Woman. Adultery in the male world has been tolerated throughout history, but the archetype of the Adulteress is still held with considerable contempt in our patriarchal society.

Do women have sex outside of their committed relationships? They do. The numbers are hard to determine, because women are reticent to admit to affairs. They understand that public opinion and sanctions for their unfaithfulness is far harsher than for errant husbands. Opportunity has a lot to do with having an affair, and as women have entered the workforce, and begun to travel, their opportunities have increased.

When Dalma Heyn (1992) published *The Erotic Silence of the American Wife*, it unsettled a lot of people. Many of the women that Heyn interviewed for the book were not traveling business women, but women just beginning to unawaken to themselves, moving out of the archetypes of Good Girl, Self-Sacrificing Servant, Devoted or Perfect Wife. They met someone who was willing to *see them in a new way* and with that person they were able to expand beyond their previous erotic identity. Prior to these sexual awakenings, they described their lives as muted, desiccated, half alive, on ice, under wraps. Although the women in these interviews did not use the term "individuation," these affairs marked intense growth experiences.

The Mistress

She has been vilified as a selfish Home-Wrecker or a Predator; pathologized as a Masochist, or a woman in search of a Father Figure; objectified as a Sex Object and Fantasy Woman; envied as a Free Agent; and admired as the Femme Inspiritrice of a great man's life. Her myth, magic, and mystery have been romanticized in the writings of Drury (1968/1993) and Griffin (1999).

Ann Ulanov and Barry Ulanov (1994) describe how men long for the tending, holding maternal in their lives, a place to find love, comfort, and security (the Wife). However, at some point, men also need the exciting and transforming feminine, found in a woman with whom they can be instinctual and erotic (the Seductress). Finding one woman who can carry both of these archetypes and integrating the split in their own psyches is no small task for men. The historical resolution, which many men have resorted to, is to enjoy the stable comforts of a marriage and a home, while seeking their inspiration and erotic fulfillment outside.

Part of the intrigue of the Mistress is that she shows herself only at her best and she often gets the best of the man (Drury, 1968/1993). Wives carry their own power in social acceptability and the currency of longevity. The wife may get the security and social esteem, but she is relegated to the mundane, the details of managing a house, and it is difficult to match the mystique of a woman who doesn't bother herself with the mundane. In the protected setting of stolen moments, the Mistress comforts, entices, and enchants. With the power of attention, she can cause her object of affection to feel like the most powerful, wonderful, appealing person in the world. With her power of intuition, she can discover the hidden fantasies of her lovers and make them a reality. Eroticism is her special currency and she lives in the world of intrigue. No wonder she is despised and envied by the traditional wives of the world, who have been cast in such droll roles.

If a Mistress succeeds in displacing the standing Wife, which is rare (Subotnik, 2005), she will move into the archetype of the Home-Wrecker. The ex-Mistress will never be fully welcomed into her new world, as the Faithful Wives of her husband's old friends will despise her. In entering into the territory of house holding, she loses her mystique. With the ex-wife now in the archetype of Scorned or Betrayed Woman, the ex-Mistress may find herself in the crossfire of ongoing retaliation, particularly if children are involved.

POWER PLAY—THE DOMINATRIX AND THE SUBMISSIVE

In Jack Morin's (1995) research on "core erotic themes," over half the women interviewed had obvious references to dominance and submission. They found mild power play in sexual dynamics very exciting. Of key importance was finding a partner with whom they felt safe to explore.

At this publication, the *Fifty Shades of Grey* (James, 2012) series has sold over one hundred million copies worldwide, indicating a curiosity in women about an edgier eroticism, including BDSM. Eisler (1996) suggests that women would not be turned on by domination if they were not socialized in a world that links sexuality *with* domination and eroticizes violence. Being trapped in a situation where you are forced into *unwanted* sex acts is *never* OK for a woman, and should be considered abusive. Because of the fuzzy line and concerns regarding power inequities and violence towards women, many feminists have strong objections to all BDSM or "kink" practices that involve Bondage, Discipline or Domination, Sadomasochism or Submission.

On the other side of the argument, McCormick (1994) lists a number of feminist sexologists who challenge "politically correct" sexuality that constrains women's sexual autonomy. McCormick emphasizes that women should be free to explore their sexuality in any way they wish and no dimension of sexuality should be excluded. Thomas Moore (1990) looks into the writings of the Marquis de Sade and offers us a depth psychology perspective on the shadow aspects of the human psyche that lurk behind our sentimentalized views of "loving." Margaret Nichols (2006) argues that there are many misconceptions regarding the BDSM culture and we would do well to understand it better before judging. Sexologists Kleinplatz & Moser (2006) have edited a scholarly work on sadomasochism, which invites clinicians to reconsider their uninformed assumptions about playing with power, and what it is really about, before judging it so harshly. Their work debunks many of the myths held by outsiders of the "kink" culture.

In my opinion, the "vanilla" culture would do well to learn something from the sophisticated communication, consent, and detailed contracting procedures that are normative within the BDSM culture. Participants have extensive conversations and clear agreements regarding symbolic and sexual activities: what is allowed and desired, what is strictly off limits, what they might be willing to do under certain circumstances, and what the signals are to communicate one's wishes.

Although some women enjoy symbolic submission, others enjoy being on "top." The archetype of the Dominatrix is a powerful archetype of sexuality. Mistress Lorelei (2000) provides a detailed instruction manual with scripts, talk, safe words, sets and props, costumes, and instructions for enacting scenes as a Dominatrix. She details "power play" for five specific archetypes: Nursemaid, Governess, Queen, Amazon, and Goddess.

Amazons, Rebels, and Bad Girls

In *Meeting the Madwoman*, Linda Leonard (1993) lists the Armored Amazon and the Revolutionary as two archetypes in rebellion against the patriarchal forces that would constrain them. Sidra Stone (1997) writes about Rebel Daughter energy, which is the flip side of the Good Girl. She is still a "daughter," because she is rebelling *against* the Inner and Outer Patriarchs in her world. Tough Girls and Bad-Ass Broads are proud, strong, and challenging, dancing out on the skinny branches, refusing to comply with "the rules."

In recent years, there has been a glorification of Bad Girls. We see them idealized in music videos and advertisements. The Bad Girl struts her stuff, wearing black leather and spiked heels, looking like a young Dominatrix. The college Hook-up Queen is purported to be able to have sex like a man: Find 'em, Fuck 'em, and Forget 'em. Reality shows based on the archetype of Girl Gone Wild have become popular, and the Porn Star has been elevated to an icon. Although I am an advocate of a woman's right to sexual Self-determination, the archetypal expressions of many of these Rebels and Bad Girls feel deeply cynical, angry, and reactionary to me. I wonder if the underlying motivation is not to "show them," rather than sourcing this eroticism from their own creative depths.

To my way of thinking, these rebellious expressions of female sexuality represent an explosion of Dionysian energies in an overly Apollonian culture. Dionysus was the god of wine, chaos, madness, and ecstasy, Apollo was the God of order, linear thinking, and power. When we consider that sexuality and the instincts have been denigrated, suppressed, and controlled for so long, we know that these energies have become "shadow," and a Dionysian rebellion would be inevitable. The "dark" sexuality we now find openly displayed on the Internet is an illustration of what happens when instincts go underground, turn feral, and re-emerge in a parade of shadow material. We seem to be engaged in a struggle to bridge the deep divides that exist between instinct and consciousness, body and soul, sexuality and spirituality. When we look at the chaos that Internet sexuality is causing, it is clear that consciousness and integration have yet to follow.

The Slut

I sometimes hear clients referring to a time in their past as their "Slut period," and I do not let this go by without pressing the pause button. I want to know how many partners and activities she was involved in to earn this denigrating label (which we do not give to men who do the same thing). The responses vary considerably.

What was driving this "behavior?" We talk about women's many motivations for being sexual (Meston & Buss, 2009). Was she lonely and trying to get someone to love her? Was she sexually curious and learning about herself? Was she angry or feeling rebellious and expressing this through sex? Was she pressured into sex because she didn't know how to say no? Was she soothing feelings of sadness and anxiety, filling some emotional emptiness? Was she enjoying the sense of power she found in her capacity to seduce? Did she simply love the pleasures of sharing eroticism with another human being? I point out to her that there are other ways of viewing this time in her life, and that we do not have the same level of judgment for men who do the same thing. I invite her to reframe this as a time of learning and seeking. She was working through vulnerability, rebellion, loneliness, anxiety, emptiness, and confusion in the best way she knew how at that time. It was a time of curiosity, freedom, and self-discovery.

Cassie, the Hookup Queen

College life has managed to redefine what might have been called a "Slut" twenty years ago. Now we have the college Hookup Queen, a new archetype of today's youth culture (Paul, McManus, & Hayes, 2000).

My client Cassie wanted to change her exhaustive "hooking up" practices, and we began to delve into what this was really about. She concluded that it was a way for her to feel valued and powerful for a night. I asked her how she felt the next day. She usually felt hung over and depressed. We began to investigate other ways of her feeling valued and experiencing her power. As she integrated some Virgin Goddess energy from the Athena realm, she began to get focused and serious about her career path, and saved the Sex Kitten for a boyfriend who would appreciate her bright mind in addition to her powerful seductiveness.

WOUNDED APHRODITE

Deanne, the Scorned Woman

Deanne had married Dave, who was on the fast track to partner at a big law firm. She focused her life on him and supported his career from the home front, maintained her appearance, raised three kids, and gave charming dinner parties. They operated as a very traditional couple and built a life together. After twenty-two years of devotion as a Corporate Wife, he dumped her for a younger woman. Deanne's whole sense of identity and value crumbled as her position and lifestyle fell away. She was now an aging Anima Woman who had never really defined herself as anything other than Dave's Wife. After the divorce, she became possessed by the archetype of the Scorned Woman. She decided she was going to "show him!" She stretched the divorce proceedings out for several years, argued aggressively over the settlement, and managed to freeze some of the assets during the process, which encumbered Dave's freedom to create a new life. In addition, she decided to seduce a series of his closest friends and made sure that Dave heard about it. Did all of this help to ease her pain? Not really. Sure, she had proven she could be powerful, and that she could still seduce a man, but the rage was subsiding, and the sadness was now flooding in. She was empty and lonely and realizing that her life now revolved around hating her ex-husband. It was time to discover Deanne, to find a new archetypal stance, re-story her life, and explore what her sexuality might mean apart from being a duty or an instrument of revenge.

THE SEX ADDICT

Women used to come into my practice announcing themselves as Love Addicts. In recent years, an increasing number of women are identifying themselves as Sex Addicts. They feel out of control about their sexual behavior. There is a lot of controversy today about whether "sexual addiction" exists. A highly profitable treatment industry has grown up around the diagnosis, and there is a complaint that the label gives people an irresponsible "easy out" . . . "I can't help my behavior. I'm a Sex Addict." Some sexologists argue that the label is a product of a sex-negative society that is moralistic and judgmental (Joannides, 2012).

Patrick Carnes (1983) was the early pioneer in the sexual addiction treatment world. He created an assessment instrument for determining if one is a Sex Addict. Joannides (2012) and Meston & Buss (2009) point out that many of his "criteria" are true for "non-addicts" as well. This includes various motivations for having sex that most people act on at some time in their life, but which are not considered pathological in "traditional," coupled sexuality. These motivations include: to assuage loneliness, relieve anxiety, experience being wanted, find love, mood alter, forget some inner pain, express rage, boost self-esteem, experience the power to seduce, or grab the attention of some prized person.

Carnes asserts that Sex Addicts are more obsessed than the average person with sexual things, and they will pursue dangerous or high-risk sex, and have sex when they do not intend to do so. The Sex Addict begins to experience highly negative consequences to their work life, health, finances, and important personal and family relationships. This seems to be the most valid criteria for treatment. The debate continues as to whether we should consider this a compulsive disorder, or an "addiction;" in any event, it has become a new archetype.

When a woman comes in diagnosing herself as a Sex Addict, I want to understand who lives in her inner cast. "Who" is behaving in this out of control fashion, and what need they are trying to fill? What are the triggering events and "who" is getting triggered? "Who" is doing the judging, and by what criteria? What other resources does she have to draw on to soothe herself rather than using sex to quell the pain or make her feel more alive?

Carnes (1997) has created a corresponding diagnosis, the Sexual Anorexic. Here we have the Sex Addict who has swung to the opposite extreme and in their terror and revulsion at their previous behavior, they have now formed an *aversion* to sex. This side of the continuum is equally distorted and extreme, with underlying pathology that needs to be addressed. Being a Sexual Anorexic is very different than being a Celibate, as the Anorexic's choice to be sexless is driven by aversion, rather than a choice to redirect their passionate energies into other creative outlets.

Do I believe we have a growing problem with sexual compulsivity? I do, and I agree that the Internet has put jet fuel on the fire. At the bottom of all of this, I think *people are seeking connection* . . . what Diane Poole Heller (2011) calls *"contact nutrition."* In an increasingly depersonalized world, we have a *ravenous touch hunger.* In a high-pressured, "get ahead," thinking-oriented world, people are seeking some *instinctual release.* We are too imbalanced toward the life of the mind and toward production. The old saying goes that you can never get enough of what you don't really need, and in my opinion, that is what is fueling our "sex addiction."

Tammy Kent (2011) says a good assessment tool for any addiction is the following:

> If you discover a desire that when fed, only results in a bigger appetite or greater feeling of emptiness, then your energy field and your feminine nature need care. Instead of filling a void, remember the deeper flow that—when restored—will sustain you. (p. 287)

The only way to truly achieve freedom from any "addiction" is to trace it back to its source and heal the disruptions and imbalances that led to the insatiable hunger.

Sexual Anorexic or Celibate?

Is an attractive woman who voluntarily chooses not to have a sexual partner necessarily pathological? Is she a Sexual Anorexic, secretly wounded, and in retreat? Or has she made a legitimate choice to direct her passionate energies into something other than a sexual relationship (Cline, 1993)? In my view, the true Celibate woman is not asexual. She may be filled with creative juice, love being embodied, have sexual feelings, and may enjoy her sexuality through self-pleasuring, but she remains single and often sexually uncoupled because she is directing her passionate involvement into something other than a sexual relationship.

Over the years, I have met quite a few religious sisters. Of the Nuns I have known, many have described states of ecstasy during prayer. If you look at Bernini's sculpture *The Ecstasy of St. Teresa of Avila* you will see one of the most erotic statues in the world, with Teresa in the throes of a deep religious ecstasy. Imposed celibacy in religious life has greatly confused us about the archetype of the true Celibate. What the church has done is to vilify the body and all things sexual, and to reinforce the split between body and soul. This has driven sexuality into the underworld and the church is reaping the whirlwind, with a shadow outcropping of horrific proportion.

BIBLIOGRAPHY

Carnes, P. (1983) *Out of the Shadows: Understanding Sexual Addiction.* Minneapolis, MN: Compcare.

Carnes, P. (1997) *Sexual Anorexia: Overcoming Sexual Self-Hatred.* Center City, MN: Hazelden.

Cline, S. (1993) *Women, Passion & Celibacy.* New York: Carol Southern.

Drury, M. (1993) *Advice to a Young Wife From an Old Mistress.* New York: Random House. (Original work published 1968)

Eisler, R. (1996) *Sacred Pleasure: Sex, Myth, and the Politics of the Body—New Paths to Power and Love.* San Francisco: HarperCollins.

Griffin, V. (1999) *The Mistress: Histories, Myths, and Interpretations of the "Other Woman."* London: Bloomsbury.

Heyn, D. (1992) *The Erotic Silence of the American Wife.* New York: Random House.

James, E. (2012) *Fifty Shades of Grey.* New York: Vintage.

Joannides, P. (2012) The Challenging Landscape of Problematic Sexual Behaviors, Including "Sexual Addiction" and "Hypersexuality." In P. Kleinplatz (ed.) *New Directions in Sex Therapy* (2nd ed., pp. 69-84). New York: Routledge.

Kent, T. L. (2011) *Wild Feminine: Finding Power, Spirit & Joy in the Female Body.* New York: Atria.

Kleinplatz, P., & Moser, C. (2006) *Sadomasochism: Powerful Pleasures.* Binghamton, NY: Harrington Park.

Leonard, L. S. (1993) *Meeting the Madwoman: Empowering the Feminine Spirit.* New York: Bantam.

McCormick, N. (1994) *Sexual Salvation: Affirming Women's Sexual Rights and Pleasures.* Westport, CT: Praeger.

Meston, C., & Buss, D. (2009) *Why Women Have Sex: Understanding Sexual Motivations—From Adventure to Revenge (and Everything in Between).* New York: Times Books.

Mistress Lorelei. (2000) *The Mistress Manual: The Good Girls' Guide to Female Dominance.* Eugene, OR: Greenery.

Moore, T. (1990) *Dark Eros: The Imagination of Sadism.* Woodstock, CT: Spring.

Morin, J. (1995) *The Erotic Mind: Unlocking the Inner Sources of Sexual Passion and Fulfillment.* New York: Harper Perennial.

Nichols, M. (2006) Psychotherapeutic Issues With "Kinky" Clients: Clinical Problems, Yours and Theirs. In P. Kleinplatz & C. Moser (Eds.) *Sadomasochism: Powerful Pleasures* (pp. 281-300). Binghamton, NY: Harrington Park.

Paul, E., McManus, B., & Hayes, A. (2000) "Hookups:" Characteristics and correlates of college students' spontaneous and anonymous sexual experiences. *The Journal of Sex Research, 37,* 1, 76–88.

Poole Heller, D. (2011) *Enlivening Intimacy, Sensuality, and Sexuality.* DARe Module3 Demo-Gun. DAR B9. Louisville, CO: Diane Poole Heller.

Stone, S. (1997) *The Shadow King: The Invisible Force That Holds Women Back.* Lincoln, NE: iUniverse.com.

Subotnik, R. (2005) *Will He Really Leave Her for Me?* Avon, MA: Adams Media.

Ulanov, A., & Ulanov, B. (1994) *Transforming Sexuality: The Archetypal World of Anima and Animus.* Boston: Shambhala.

White, E. (2007) *Simply Irresistible.* Philadelphia, PA: Running Press.

CHAPTER 18

BODY DRAMA

"In freeing the body, we free the heart to experience the power of love."

Gabrielle Roth

OUR STRUGGLE TO LOVE OUR BODIES

A woman's relationship with her body, and particularly her body image, has a significant impact on her sexuality. What are the factors that stand in the way of a woman's embracing her own body? Kilbourne (1999, 2010), Hite (1993), and Wolf (1991), all write about the impact that the media and fashion industry have on women's self-esteem. Most adult women know this intellectually, but the impact is largely unconscious. We struggle to escape the relentless comparisons and judgments we heap upon ourselves for not measuring up to movie-star bodies, and those airbrushed, photoshopped images in magazines. Preoccupation with a negative body image is one of the major impediments to women enjoying their sexuality or even seeking a relationship (Daniluk, 1998). Many women do not want to be seen naked and avoid certain sexual activities because they do not feel good about how their bodies look.

Anne Katz (2009) writes about women who have cancer, who often experience their bodies as having turned on them. Cancer treatments and surgeries disfigure them and make sex painful. The whole experience drains them of energy and libido, and it is not uncommon for women to push away even the most loving partner.

Because women dislike their bodies, they are often not *in* them, which is absolutely necessary in order to have a full experience of one's sexuality. Although a woman may work out at the gym or do yoga, her relationship to her body may be more like relating to an object that can be manipulated with muscles that can be sculpted.

When you are in your body, you can respond to others from your Sensate Self. Becoming embodied is a process and it usually involves facing some emotional or physical pain. Intelligent women are notoriously disembodied and our thinking-oriented culture exacerbates this. Spiritual women can become highly disembodied because their orientation is about *ascending* rather than *descending* into the dark, fertile earth. Judith Blackstone (2012) teaches a series of embodiment exercises for spiritual people who are barely on this earth. In Pinkola Estés's (1992) classic work, *Women Who Run With the Wolves*, she emphasizes the importance of women remaining connected to their instinctual life, rather than floating off into a rigid, perfectionistic, idealized, and disembodied world.

Being embodied means that you are tuned in to the deep sensations of the body, the "felt sense" of life experiences (Gendlin, 1978). This refers to being aware of how your physical body is responding to an image, situation, person, or event. Risa Kaparo (2012) writes about the difference between the word *soma* and the word *body*. *Soma* has to do with how life senses itself in the here and now, whereas the *body* is an object that can be shaped and moved around. We mistreat out bodies when we consider them objects to be manipulated. They are extensions of the body of the Goddess, living, breathing, and wanting to be engaged.

It's Not Just a "Feeling," It's Also a Sensation

Practitioners often ask clients what they are feeling and clients often respond, "I feel happy or sad," and so on. Begin to take your client deeper into the body. "Sad" is really a concept. Ask your client where she feels sad in her body? What is the sensation . . . particularly from the neck down that tells her she is sad? You are looking for descriptions like, "tightness in my abdomen, a knot in my stomach, heavy pressure in my chest, weakness," and so on.

Tuning Into the Body as a Mindfulness Practice

I encourage my clients to develop a practice of tuning into their bodies many times throughout the day . . . to see if they are still *in* their bodies. This is a powerful mindfulness practice. We tend to live in our heads, out of touch with the sensations in the body. Our bodies become "things" that we drag around all day. We push the body, we ignore its signals, we occasionally throw food into it (and often not very nourishing food).

When a woman checks in with her body, I also want her to check to see if she is *bracing* or *holding* anywhere. Women do a lot of protective bracing without even realizing it. This can become habitual. In sessions, I ask her to see if she can let that go and still feel safe. Being able to move through the world in a more relaxed state helps us to be more open to life. This is also something worth checking in on while a woman is making love. Is she bracing herself for something? If so . . . what . . . why? Has one of her inner characters become anxious or concerned? Is the body sending her an important signal? If so, what is it?

How the Body Speaks

Metaphoric concepts can be translated into physical actions. With a client who would cave in under the pressure of her husband's intensity, Macnaughton (2004) asked her to stand up and sense her feet on the ground. After doing so, the client could suddenly feel her legs and this embodied awareness strengthened her to withstand her husband's pressure. I utilize this when I am working with women who are just coming into their own self-awareness and sense of agency. I have them stand up on their own two feet, feel their legs underneath them, and imagine growing roots deep into the earth. I can visibly see them becoming more grounded and solid as they do this.

Our bodies are full of inhibited gestures. In the process of growing up and learning how to behave, we stop ourselves from doing what we really want. "Impulse control" they call it. Many of these impulses get stored in the muscle memory of our bodies and we can become *over*-inhibited. It can be very helpful for clients to be able to move their bodies in ways they would not out in the world, in response to what they are feeling. For example, many a woman wants to experience having space to be herself, space to think, feel, and live her life. I may ask her to take her hands and push them out, and trace a space bubble that feels just right. How does it feel to map out a circle of space for herself? What can she do now, that she couldn't before? Certain motions can be very significant for women. What happens if she arches back and opens her arms to the sky? What happens if she straightens her spine and begins to walk tall and proud? What if she unlocks her pelvis and begins to move like a snake? What is the difference between curling up in a fetal ball or pushing out her arms and yelling "stop!"? What happens when a woman completes a motion she wanted to make in the past, but dared not, out of fear of loss or punishment?

Change can feel extremely threatening. When you have clients who feel like they are "coming apart," have a blanket handy so they can wrap themselves up in it and feel more contained. Some of my colleagues have weighted blankets. The weight calms and soothes a woman who feels ungrounded or out of control. Sometimes women don't move because the very act of moving mobilizes a cascade of stored emotions.

Guided Imagery—What If I Were Desirable?

One of the interventions I have found to be effective with women who feel too old to matter or who dislike their bodies is a Guided Imagery exercise where I have them imagine being in a body that is truly desirable. If the woman is able to do this, I ask her to notice how she is experiencing her body. What does it stir up for her? I ask her to imagine engaging with a partner from this place, knowing she is desirable. If she cannot possibly imagine herself as such, we work with *that* material. Confidence is so immensely attractive in a woman, and women who are not "attractive" by "cultural standards" of beauty become beautiful when they are in their Aphrodite energy.

Linda Savage (1999) has written a series of healing rituals that can support women in loving and accepting their bodies as vessels of expression for their sexuality across the lifespan. When a woman is able to see herself as attractive and desirable, she carries herself differently, and she *cares* for herself differently. It is amazing to note the transformative changes in a woman's appearance when she begins to inhabit this inner space. Is it her physical package? No. It is the *archetypal energy* she is carrying that becomes magnetic. For many women, an invitation into this imaginal exercise will raise a tidal wave of vulnerable feelings. This becomes the work of the hour, dialoguing with all the Voices of Denigration, Shame, Warning, and Despair, all the Gatekeepers that block her way to her connection with the possibility of being the *positive* object of someone's desire, in this body, at this age and stage of her life.

HELEN, THE ZAFTIG TEMPTRESS

Helen was a beautiful, big woman: 5'11" tall, flawless olive skin, dark eyes, thick wavy hair, and a lot of curves. She sat, unsmiling, in the circle of women during a Luminous Woman® Weekend, slowly opening up during mealtimes, as the other women began to draw her out. On the last day, she volunteered for some "wheel work" (see Ogden, 2013) on the large altar the women had co-created on Friday evening. The altar was laden with objects brought by each woman, one to represent something she wanted to let go of, and one to represent something she wanted to embrace or claim.

Helen and I walked around the large altar, through the quadrants of Mother, Warrior, Lover, and Mystic. She had placed a picture of a man in the mother/heart section. She wanted to let go of the grief and anger she still felt for trusting him, for conceiving a child, which she had raised alone, unmarried, for many years. She had also placed a picture of herself as the young woman she had been when she met him. She wanted those years back and the possibility of college that had been interrupted by her pregnancy.

As we walked the circle, she entered the quadrant of the Mystic, the realm of the spirit. She looked down at the figures representing a woman's mystical self and spoke of the shame and condemnation she had experienced from her very orthodox family. An Unwed Mother was the equivalent to a Whore. When we got to the quadrant that represented the Embodied Lover, she began to cry. The women around the circle held the space quietly and patiently. We all continued to breathe. "Tell me what's happening for you," I said after a while. She replied, "I'm lonely . . . and nobody would want me. I squandered my chances. Now I'm just old and fat, with no education, and no future."

I looked at her, standing there, with her beautiful skin, her thick, wavy hair, and her dark, angry eyes. I could see the faint silhouette of full-bodied curves hiding underneath an oversized shirt. "You mean you're zaftig," I commented. She looked up and laughed. Her father was Jewish, and she knew the meaning of the word. "What's that?" said one of the women in the circle. I replied, "Zaftig is a wonderful Yiddish word, meaning full bodied, curvaceous, and quite luscious." "I want to be zaftig!" said Sue, who was Helen's opposite, a size 4, thin and straight, with almost no breasts or hips. Helen turned to her, "I'll gladly give you half of me." The women laughed.

"How many women in this room are happy with their bodies?" No one raised a hand. This is typical of women. Even the most beautiful women I know have issues with their bodies. After some further exchanges, I asked Helen who she admired as a really attractive woman in the movies. "An older woman?" she asked. I replied, "Yes, that would be fine, but she needs to be full figured." Helen thought, "OK. How about Sophia Loren?" "Great!" I thought. We had already been "trying on" other archetypes in this workshop, so Helen was familiar with the process of imagining being someone else. She closed her eyes to imagine that she was Sophia Loren and then opened her eyes again. With a hand on her hip, she took a pose like Sophia on the red carpet. Her head was held tall and she looked me straight on with a relaxed, seductive gaze that would melt anyone who fell under it. I asked Helen to walk in this new energy and she began to cross the room. Her stunning, sensual presence filled the room and I could not imagine her walking by any man with blood in his veins who would not stop to take in this voluptuous, captivating woman.

I continued to work with her in this energy and the women in the circle began to laugh with delight, whoop, and applaud. Helen, woman of legend, who could launch a thousand ships. "Do you understand that it's not about the shape of the body you are inhabiting . . . It's the energy inhabiting it." Helen began to cry. "Yes," she replied. I continued, "So what do *you* want to do with your life now?" "I want to go back to school . . . and I want a lover," she said. "Great," I replied, "I think from where you are standing you can probably have both of those."

We talked about the determination and endurance it would take to begin and complete the long process of a college education. Helen decided that she needed an archetypal energy that was cooler and more focused for this goal. She decided that she needed a bit of an inner Judi Dench for that, and immediately she shifted states into a more warrior-like mode. Helen was getting the hang of using actresses to activate archetypal energies. We worked on anchoring these states in her body, and memorizing their "felt sense." To reinforce this memory, she decided to get pictures of Sophia and Judi to post on her bathroom mirror. They would be her inner support team.

Helen returned home and enrolled in school. Six months later she sent me a picture of herself on a recent date. She had layered her hair around her face, and was dressed in a soft wrap-around dress that showed off her beautiful curves . . . Aphrodite incarnate. She wrote that she had met someone who loved her, and her body, exactly as it was. Ironically, in the throes of new love, she had lost her appetite and the weight was dropping off with little effort. The caption read, "Zaftig and lovin it!"

BIBLIOGRAPHY

Blackstone, J. (2012) *Belonging Here: A Guide for the Spiritually Sensitive Person*. Boulder, CO: Sounds True.

Daniluk, J. (1998) *Women's Sexuality Across the Life Span: Challenging Myths, Creating Meanings*. New York: Guilford.

Gendlin, E. (1978) *Focusing*. New York: Bantam.

Hite, S. (1993) *Women as Revolutionary Agents of Change: The Hite Reports and Beyond*. Madison: University of Wisconsin Press.

Kaparo, R. (2012). *Awakening Somatic Intelligence: The Art and Practice of Embodied Mindfulness*. Berkeley, CA: North Atlantic.

Katz, A. (2009) *Woman, Cancer, Sex*. Pittsburgh, PA: Hygeia Media.

Kilbourne, J. (1999) *Can't Buy My Love: How Advertising Changes the Way We Think and Feel*. New York: Touchstone.

Kilbourne, J. (2010) *Killing Us Softly 4: Advertising's Image of Women* [documentary film]. US: Media Education Foundation.

Macnaughton, I. (2004) The Narrative of the Body-Mind—Minding the Body. In I. Macnaughton (Ed.) *Body, Breath, & Consciousness: A Somatics Anthology* (pp. 33–47). Berkeley, CA: North Atlantic.

Ogden, G. (2013) *Expanding the Practice of Sex Therapy: An Integrative Model for Exploring Desire and Intimacy*. New York: Routledge.

Pinkola Estés, C. (1992) *Women Who Run With the Wolves: Myths and Stories of the Wild Woman Archetype*. New York: Ballentine.

Savage, L. (1999) *Reclaiming Goddess Sexuality: The Power of the Feminine Way*. Carlsbad, CA: Hay House.

Wolf, N. (1991) *The Beauty Myth: How Images of Beauty Are Used Against Women*. New York: William Morrow.

CHAPTER 19

WOMEN OF A CERTAIN AGE

"Life really does begin at forty. Up until then, you are just doing research."

Carl Jung

WOMEN AT MIDLIFE AND BEYOND

The average life expectancy for a woman in 1900 was around forty; most never even reached menopause. Today the life expectancy for a woman is eighty four. That means that a woman will live well over a third of her life beyond menopause (Northrup, 2012). Our youth-oriented society continues to treat older women as if they were sexually "expired." This represents a lingering, antiquated worldview where sex is seen as primarily for procreation and post-menopausal women should be done with it. Research supports the fact that women of all ages are sexual creatures (Daniluk, 1998; Foley, Kope, & Sugrue, 2012). Unfortunately, the attitude that postmenopausal women are also "postsexual" has led to a distressing lack of information regarding how an older woman can maintain her sexual health. In research conducted by AARP (2005), 88% of women 45 years of age and beyond faced some sort of sexual problem for which they did not seek help. Most of these difficulties are a result of hormonal changes and are *easily addressed* (Northrup, 2012). The time restrictions placed on physicians often discourages them from providing necessary information about postmenopausal dryness, tissue changes, and urogenital atrophy, but time limitations are not the only problem. Kingsberg, Wysocki, Magnus, and Krychman (2013) surveyed

3,016 postmenopausal women suffering from vulvar and vaginal atrophy symptoms: dryness, painful intercourse, and irritation. She found that only 56% of them had discussed their symptoms with their health care providers. In another study, fewer than 9% of doctors asked women about any sexual problems (National Women's Health Resource Center, 2009). This disconnect has resulted in the unnecessary loss of sexual pleasure and function for a lot of women (Kingberg, 2002). The postmenopausal vagina *does* require special care, but sex in later life can be deeply pleasurable (Price, 2006).

PLEASURE IN THE GOLDEN YEARS

For some women, getting older means becoming more confident and self-aware and thus developing more capacity for a body-centered sexuality (Bonheim, 1997; Daniluk, 1998; Goldman, 2006; Hite, 1976, 1993; McCormick, 1994; Ogden, 1999, 2006, 2008; Price, 2006). Contrary to stereotypes of loneliness, women in their later years are finding pleasure and someone to love them. Although men's and women's motivations for sex may be different in their younger years, by midlife, their expectations and interests become more similar. Women become more interested in bodily pleasure and as men's sexual functioning changes, it gives them a chance to slow down, experience more sensual pleasure, and engage in sex to express love (Burgess, 2004; Meston & Buss, 2009).

Women over sixty are beginning to openly describe the pleasures and fun of sex in the "golden years," with the sense of agency that comes from knowing what they want and having the confidence to ask for it, no longer having concerns with pregnancy, and having released much of their preoccupation with body image (Price, 2006). Women in the boomer generation are *not* going into their elder years as faded, asexual beings.

Prioleau (2003) has a special area of interest in the archetype of the Seductress. She writes of the Silver Foxes who continue to enchant. A woman can remain sensually alive, romantically interested, and sexually active her entire life in a variety of ways that may or may not include intercourse (McCormick, 1994; Price, 2006). DeLamater and Hyde (2004) have emphasized that we need more sexuality models that take into account life stage development and the stages of a relationship. Shinoda Bolen (2001) describes the secret of the sparkle that continues on in older Aphrodite women.

Women do not have "expiration dates" stamped on their foreheads. If we look at women's sexual development around the archetypal Sexual Essence Wheel, we find that the shy Shrinking Violet at age eighteen can become a self-assured Seductress at age forty, a Grey Goddess at sixty five and a Rocking Chair Soul-Mate at eighty. The secret to a lifetime of sensuous delight is not counting the number of candles flickering on the cake; it is caring for the inner flame.

The Grey Goddess Vs. Dark Queen

A woman who is connected to her Aphrodite Self does not become less appealing with age. She need not become an envious Dark Queen or an insecure Fading Beauty. As she relinquishes the outer trappings of youth, her depth of personhood and delight in living deepens her beauty. It shines in her eyes and in her appreciation for the wonders of being alive. Philosophers refer to a quality that certain people possess as a "plenitude of absolute being." It develops from a life well lived and leads to a sense of fullness, depth, and generosity of spirit. This is the true allure of the woman who moves with grace and gratitude into her elder years.

Some of the women and men in Kleinplatz et al.'s (2009) study of "great sexuality" in long-term relationships, were over sixty. They were still sexually engaged, able to be present, attuned, in the moment, practicing extraordinary communication, being genuine, transparent, and playful, and sometimes transported to realms of bliss and peace.

The Cougar

The recent trend of older women with younger men has generated a new archetype, the Cougar. She challenges old stereotypes in which men prefer younger women. It seems that some younger men appreciate a woman with life experience, confidence, and sexual expertise.

Old Maid, Grieving Widow, or Free Spirit?

In days past, the single older woman was thought of in a negative light, as an Old Maid or a Spinster. The assumption was that she was "unchosen." This, of course, may have been an entirely misbegotten assumption. She may have chosen not to marry, turning down a number of proposals.

She may have had numerous meaningful love affairs. As an aging Femme Inspiritrice, Muse, or Mistress, she may have had a rich sexual history that she could look back on with fondness. She may have channeled her erotic energy into an art form, a cause, or an intellectual pursuit. She may have been a lesbian flying under the radar of public disapproval.

Society tends to project loneliness and vulnerability onto the Widow, but she may be experiencing a newfound freedom. Once the heavy weight of being a Caregiver is over, she may throw off the shroud, ditch the Good Wife and the Well-Behaved Woman, and let her hair go long and grey. She might become a Bohemian Artist or kick up her heels and become a traveling Adventuress.

Paula's Predicament

Paula was a "woman of a certain age." She had married an alcoholic, and for many years she redirected her life energy into a successful career in business. At sixty five, she retired, got divorced, and started a life of her own. She came to see me, because she wanted help with the "dating scene." She had joined an online dating site, gone out on several dates, and was highly disillusioned. She had discovered that people were not what they promoted themselves to be. The one person she did like hadn't called her back. She proclaimed, "I guess men aren't interested in a sixty-five-year-old Divorcée. They want some Sweet Young Thing. I guess it's either time for some plastic surgery, or I should just hang it up and become one of those eccentric gardeners. I don't even want to get married again. I'd just like someone I can go out with occasionally. It's been so long since I've had sex, I'm not sure I even remember how. But some days, I think about how it might be nice to have somebody in my bed . . . somebody who actually wanted to be there."

I suggested to Paula that we work together for a while before she wrote a check to her surgeon or cashed it in on men. I felt the strong armor she had cultivated, being married to an alcoholic, and what it took for her to become a successful business woman in a man's world. She was Nobody's Fool, but I wondered if those "savvy eyes" might have stirred up some vulnerability when she was out on a date. Over time, I discovered that she came from down to earth, Nebraska farm people. She had a quick, wry sense of humor, and could banter with the best of them. When she accessed this part of herself, she transformed into a relaxed, earthy woman. Paula got involved with the community garden and also began to cultivate her backyard. She was finding her own resonance, now that she was out from under the pressure of work and the shadow of being married to a numbed-out alcoholic. Paula also had a big, generous heart, which she had covered over to survive in the business world. As she began to settle into herself, I could see her essence emerging: earthy, hearty, easygoing, a Good Time Gal. She began to date a fellow she met in her community, and I put her in contact with a gynecologist . . . just in case, as I suspected that she might be suffering from postmenopausal vaginal atrophy. The doctor confirmed this and prescribed a program of vaginal rehabilitation. Paula bought a vibrator that had lots of bells and whistles and managed to turn her rehab program into a comedy skit, but she followed through on it religiously. She had the realization that she really didn't care for stuffy, overeducated men. She really wanted to be around men who were handy, earthy, and knew how to laugh. They reminded her of the men she grew up with, before she got all educated and sophisticated. At last report, she had settled into a warm, easy relationship with a retired contractor who loved her cooking and was building raised beds for her garden. She reported that she had retired the bells and whistles and everything was working fine. Neither she nor her lover wanted to get married again. She was enjoying the freedom and fullness of her life.

Good Time Gals

There is a particular kind of woman who is appealing because of her warm, friendly, earthy nature. She is usually a bit older, and isn't the slightest bit interested in being an "object of desire." Her good humor and generous nature make her a community well-being resource, loved by many people. She has her feet on the ground, and carries a relaxed confidence. She might be an Aging Hippy, an Earth Mother, an Artist, a Free Spirit, or a Shop Owner. You will see her as the Friendly Neighborhood Waitress, or the local Tavern Wench. She is always glad to see you, calls you "honey," knows your order, and asks if it will be "the regular." You feel welcomed, nurtured, and relaxed in her presence. She's a Good Time Gal.

Raising a Glass to Baubo

This section would not be complete without a nod to Baubo. I visited my cousin, Susan, in June of this year. We were in the kitchen cooking together, sipping a glass of wine, and she was introducing me to some of her favorite music. She twinkled at me and said, "I bet you'll like this one." It was a young singer who is not exactly known for good behavior. I had never heard the song before, but as soon as the chorus began, we started to laugh. It was the kind of laughter that women do when no one is looking, with really good friends, where you can drop all pretenses or need to "behave." In that moment we were young and wild and laughing outrageously at this cut-loose raunchy lyric. The spirit of Baubo was in the room, that shocking, outrageous little Goddess who heals and energizes and reminds us not to take ourselves too seriously. Her presence is marked by this kind of rip-snorting belly laughter.

Baubo is a little known "trickster" Goddess. You will find her playing a minor, but highly crucial part in the myth of Demeter and Persephone. She witnessed Persephone's abduction and tells desperate Demeter where to find her daughter. This ends Demeter's grief and leads to a reflowering of the earth. Baubo is an important aspect of women's psyche. She is irreverent and ribald, generally depicted with her skirts hiked up, exposing her genitals, not to be lewd, but because she is just outrageous and can't be tamed. She defies our calcified seriousness about life. She awakens women and reminds them of their animal nature and is continually trying to get women to loosen up and let go of the well-behaved veneer.

A cousin to Baubo are the Sheila-na-gigs and the double-tailed mermaids that can be found in various medieval churches and cathedrals throughout Europe (Lubell, 1994). These can be interesting to look for, and there is some rather boring scholarly conjecture regarding the meaning of these figures. My own opinion is that the image of the spread vulva is an ancient symbolic invitation into the raw, uncivilized, transformational energies of the deep, sacred feminine.

BIBLIOGRAPHY

AARP: The American Association of Retired Persons.(2005) *Sexuality at Midlife and Beyond: 2004 Update of Attitudes and Behaviors.* http://www.aarp.org/relationships/love-sex/info-05-2005/2004_sexuality.htm

Bonheim, J. (1997) *Aphrodite's Daughters: Women's Sexual Stories and the Journey of the Soul.* New York: A Fireside Book/Simon & Schuster.

Burgess, E. (2004) Sexuality in Midlife and Later Life Couples. In J. Harvey, A. Wenzel, & S. Sprecher (Eds.) *Handbook of Sexuality in Close Relationships.* Mahwah, NJ: Lawrence Erlbaum.

Daniluk, J. (1998) *Women's Sexuality Across the Life Span: Challenging Myths, Creating Meanings*. New York: Guilford.

DeLamater, J., & Hyde, J. S. (2004) Conceptual and Theoretical Issues in Studying Sexuality in Close Relationships. In J. Harvey, A. Wenzel, & S. Sprecher (Eds.) *Handbook of Sexuality in Close Relationships*. Mahwah, NJ: Lawrence Erlbaum.

Foley, S., Kope, S., & Sugrue, D. (2012) *Sex Matters for Women: A Complete Guide to Taking Care of Your Sexual Self*. New York: Guilford.

Goldman, C. (2006) *Late Life Love: Romance and New Relationships in Later Years*. Minneapolis, MN: Fairview.

Hite, S. (1976) *The Hite Report: A Nationwide Study of Female Sexuality*. New York: Seven Stories.

Hite, S. (1993) *Women as Revolutionary Agents of Change: The Hite Reports and Beyond*. Madison: University of Wisconsin Press.

Kinsberg, S. (2002) The Impact of Aging on Sexual Function in Women and Their Partners. *Archives of Sexual Behavior, 31*, 5, 431–437.

Kingsberg, S., Wysocki, S., Magnus, L., & Krychman, M. (2013) Vulvar and Vaginal Atrophy in Postmenopausal Woman: Findings from the REVIVE (REal Women's VIews of Treatment Options for Menopausal Vaginal ChangEs) Survey. *The Journal of Sexual Medicine, 10*, 7, 1790–1799.

Kleinplatz, P., Menard, A. D., Paquet, M., Paradis, N., Campblee, M., Zuccarino, D., & Mehak, L. (2009) The Components of Optimal Sexuality: A Portrait of 'Great Sex.' *Canadian Journal of Human Sexuality, 18*, 1–2, 1–13.

Lubell, W. (1994) *The Metamorphosis of Baubo: Myths of Women's Sexual Energy*. Nashville, TN: Vanderbilt University Press.

McCormick, N. (1994) *Sexual Salvation: Affirming Women's Sexual Rights and Pleasures*. Westport, CT: Praeger.

Meston, C., & Buss, D. (2009) *Why Women Have Sex: Understanding Sexual Motivations—from Adventure to Revenge (and Everything in Between)*. New York: Times Books.

National Women's Health Resource Center. (2009) *Sex & Intimacy After Menopause*. http://www.healthywomen.org/sites/default/files/FF_SexAftMeno.pdf

Northrup, C. (2012) *The Wisdom of Menopause: Creating Physical, Emotional Health During the Change*. New York: Bantam.

Ogden, G. (1999) *Women Who Love Sex: Ordinary Women Describe Their Paths to Pleasure, Intimacy, and Ecstasy*. Boston: Trumpeter.

Ogden, G. (2006) *The Heart and Soul of Sex: Making the ISIS Connection*. Boston: Trumpeter.

Ogden, G. (2008) *Return of Desire: A Guide to Rediscovering Your Sexual Passion*. Boston: Trumpeter.

Price, J. (2006) *Better Than I Ever Expected: Straight Talk About Sex After Sixty*. Berkeley, CA: Seal.

Prioleau, B. (2003) *Seductress: Women Who Ravished the World and Their Lost Art of Love*. New York: Penguin.

Shinoda Bolen, J. (2001) *Goddesses in Older Women: Archetypes in Women Over Fifty*. New York: HarperCollins.

CHAPTER 20

THE PORN STAR AND THE SEXUAL PRIESTESS

"Rescuing the sacred priestess from the remote recesses of the collective unconscious is a via regia (royal road) to the redemption of the feminine erotic soul."

Rachel Hillel

THE PORN STAR

There has been a recent ascendancy of the archetype of the Porn Star, and an increasing number of men and women are coming into sex therapy, feeling hurt, betrayed, angry, or demoralized by the impact of pornography on their relationships and their sexuality. Many young women have expressed intense insecurity and performance anxiety because they cannot compete with the behaviors or the bodies of women in pornography or the sexual expectations of the young men they meet. Many women feel betrayed when they discover their partner's involvement with porn (Maltz & Maltz, 2010). It is beyond the scope of this book to cover the debates around free speech, freedom of expression, "female-friendly" porn, the difference between erotica and pornography, and to what degree pornography is destructive and debasing to women.

What is problematic is the script conveyed by much of pornography in which women are happy with anything that men do to them, require nothing, derive satisfaction by giving satisfaction, are easily pleased, ready responders, and expert performers in sexual acts oriented around male sexual fantasies and desires. This portrayal sets the stage for disappointment and frustration with "real women" who have needs and desires of their own (Dines, 2010).

The central thesis of this book is that women are naturally erotic when they are in touch with their sexual essence, and that a woman's sexuality is most expressive when it is sourced from the inside out, and met by a partner who is present, attuned, and able to engage.

Ian Kerner (2004, 2008) is the author of *She Comes First*, the best book on the art of cunnilingus I have ever read. He is considered one of the hippest young sex therapists in the country and considers pornography "junk food" compared with the potential nourishment found in the satisfying sexual relationship with a real human partner. He asserts that the images and expectations promoted by pornography can "toxify" the sexual field.

In previous generations, a man's first introduction to a woman's body may have taken place with still photographs. The first introduction to partnered sexuality usually took place between two fumbling, awkward human beings, with little useful information about what to do. Today, pornography is becoming a primary vehicle of sexual education for our young people, *before* any real human interaction takes place. This exposure is imprinting sexual expectations and *performance* scripts, and the importance of presence, attunement, authentic expression, communication, and a real encounter between two human beings isn't in the equation.

Although a woman has the freedom to explore all forms of sexuality and to be any kind of sexual being she desires, this choice should originate from her, from her own subjective desire or curiosity, not in response to scripts and standards set by the pornography industry, or in capitulation to partner pressure. It is also OK for a woman to want to please a partner, but the woman who lives only to please or placate a partner is not operating out of a place of sexual empowerment. This kind of sexual placating cannot be sustained over time without extracting a high price on a woman's body, psyche, and soul.

Polly Young-Eisendrath (1999) believes that the pornography industry is driven by the Pandora archetype, loosed from her box. I agree. When we denigrate the body and disown and suppress something as powerful and instinctual as human sexuality, these unintegrated energies will move into the shadowlands and become something dark and feral.

Thomas Moore (1998) suggests that one reason that pornography has become so inescapable in our culture is that we take less and less time for the soul-deepening aspects of the sensual and sexual life. The images of pornography become a sort of dark counterbalance in a culture that is obsessed with the mind and pursuing an increasingly technological future.

I join Young-Eisendrath and Moore in the belief that we are reaping the whirlwind of eons of repression with the dark upsurgence of pornography. It has become a Dionysian outbreak (the God of wine, sensuality, chaos, lust, and ecstasy) in an overly Apollonian (detached, power-driven, orderly, controlled, thinking oriented) culture. I believe that those who are caught up in the destructive aspects of pornography are actually in search of the bright, restorative aspects of Aphrodite, but don't know where to find her.

THE SEXUAL PRIESTESS

In recent years, while presenting to groups of women, I have begun to refer increasingly to the archetype of the Sexual Priestess, and her power to draw men into the sexual mysteries. Hillel (1997), Qualls-Corbett (1988), Woodman (1982, 1985) and Eisler (1996) have all written about her. She comes from that early time in history, when the power of the sacred feminine was revered and sexuality was viewed as one of the ways in which women healed the world. We have so many relationships today that suffer from an empty "performance" of sex, with little that is life giving or inspiring for the souls of the two participants, who are rarely in communion with each other. As women begin to re-anchor in their depths and experience the life-giving energies of Aphrodite, they are becoming revolutionary agents of change. They are interested in sexual experiences that are filled with pleasure, encounter, playfulness, adventure, depth, and meaning.

We are seeing a resurgence of images of sacred vulvas, the energies of Aphrodite and the ancient Sexual Priestess/Sacred Prostitute surfacing in women's dreams and sexual imagination (Hillel, 1997; Qualls-Corbett, 1988; Woodman,1985). In my travels and presentations, I meet an increasing number of women who are training in sacred and esoteric sexuality. We are at a turning point in history, where Aphrodite's energy is being felt everywhere, sometimes in her darker form, split off from relationship, but increasingly in ordinary women who want their sexuality to have meaning, and to be imbued by the power of its transformative energy. Women want to bring sexuality out of the shadowland. They want to "make love, not war."

The Sexual Priestess is the antidote to the soulless aspects of pornography. Carrying this archetype, a woman is capable of bringing her partner into a place of union and communion, with herself, and with the universe. In ancient days, union with a Sexual Priestesses was considered an opportunity for cleansing, healing, blessing, and restoring soul. As women begin to embody this archetypal energy, they too can heal, humanize, and open up transformational states. The Sexual Priestess changes the script of performance-oriented sexuality. The Sexual Priestess is about Pleasure, Connection, Depth, Mystery, and more. Her power originates initially from the Mystic realm of the Sexual Essence Wheels, but she draws from the full circle, Nurturing, Romancing, and Seducing partners into her essential gift for weaving together sexuality and spirituality, body and soul.

BIBLIOGRAPHY

Dines, G. (2010) *Pornland: How Porn Has Hijacked Our Sexuality*. Boston: Beacon Press.

Eisler, R. (1996) *Sacred Pleasure: Sex, Myth, and the Politics of the Body—New Paths to Power and Love*. San Francisco: HarperCollins.

Hillel, R. (1997) *The Redemption of the Feminine Erotic Soul*. York Beach, ME: Nicolas-Hays.

Kerner, I. (2004) *She Comes First: The Thinking Man's Guide to Pleasuring a Woman*. New York: HarperCollins.

Kerner, I. (2008) *Sex Detox: Recharge Desire, Revitalize Intimacy. Rejuvenate Your Love Life*. New York: HarperCollins.

Maltz, W., & Maltz, L. (2010) *The Porn Trap: The Essential Guide to Overcoming Problems Caused by Pornography*. New York: HarperCollins.

Moore, T. (1998) *The Soul of Sex*. New York: HarperCollins.

Qualls-Corbett, N. (1988) *The Sacred Prostitute: Eternal Aspect of the Feminine*. Toronto, ON: Inner City.

Woodman, M. (1982) *Addiction to Perfection: The Still Unravished Bride*. Toronto, ON: Inner City.

Woodman, M. (1985) *The Pregnant Virgin: A Process of Psychological Transformation*. Toronto, ON: Inner City.

Young-Eisendrath, P. (1999) *Women and Desire: Beyond Wanting to Be Wanted*. New York: Three Rivers.

CHAPTER 21

BECOMING A SEXUALLY EMPOWERED WOMAN

"Bliss and joy come from moments when what we do is consistent with our archetypal depths."

Jean Shinoda Bolen

When I use the term "sexually empowered woman," it may evoke an image of a Sexual Amazon in the minds of some people. If you refer back to the list of words in Chapter 2 that were used to describe "the Sexual Woman," you can see that a sexually empowered woman has a range of expressions. If you refer to the Sexual Essence Wheels in Chapter 7 and travel the four quadrants, you will find sexually empowered women in each one. So what are the fundamental requirements for becoming sexually empowered?

SELF-AWARENESS

The first and most essential element is *Self-Awareness*. The sexually empowered woman is aware of her inner cast of characters related to her sexuality and how they were formed. In reflecting on her life, she has developed her *Observing Self*. Attending to her inner processes becomes a consciousness practice that continues as she evolves. When a woman becomes aware of her inner processes and her self-protective defenses, she can see the places where she needs to grow and heal and the outdated scripts that need to be rewritten. As the mists begin to clear, she can sense her true sexual essence.

Engaging in the processes outlined in my work *Negotiating the Inner Peace Treaty* (Wakefield, 2012) is one excellent way of defining one's inner cast of characters, getting to know them and how they operate, and resolving the inner conflicts that entangle us and keep us from living into our full potential. Dream work is another way of looking inward and being in relationship with the emergent Self, which is always seeking to grow the personality. ISIS wheel work (Ogden, 2013) is another wonderful way of raising sexual consciousness and working through the splits that develop among heart, mind, body, and spirit.

When a woman connects with her sexual essence, her sexuality begins to flow from within. She has now tapped into sources of sexuality and eroticism that can be expressed in her outer life.

Self-Education

Aphrodite women are often interested in sexuality and will seek out sources of sexual education and enrichment for themselves and their partners. Along with attention to their inner processes, they become students of their own bodies, of their sensual and sexual responses. Their interest in pleasure skills is sourced from wanting to deepen sexual pleasure, engagement, and discovery. I particularly love Sheri Winston's (2010, 2014) luscious books on sexual anatomy and "sex craft," and often recommend Ian Kerner's (2004) *She Comes First* for partners interested in mastering the art of cunnilingus.

What Is Sexual Integrity?

As a woman becomes more Self-aware, she begins to feel the misalignment between the scripts she was given and her authentic Self. Many of these scripts were formulated by highly questionable sources, whose original motivation was to control, suppress, and conscript a woman's sexuality. The Self honors none of these constraints, and although a woman may house inner characters who believe strongly in those scripts, the Self is a wiser, deeper force that wants the woman to be all she was born to be. Because the Self is unique to each individual, expressions of Sexual Integrity may take a variety of forms. When people begin to align their outer lives with their inner world, they begin to experience a deep sense of structural integrity, an internal stability, and a "center that can hold."

Sometimes when a woman begins to awaken, she will see just how far she has moved off her true foundation. This can be an anxiety-provoking realization. This is just one of the good reasons why women need to develop practices that calm the reactive nervous system. Our physical bodies do well when we develop "core strength." We need to do the same with our emotional bodies.

MINDFULNESS—GETTING HERE VERSUS GETTING OFF

An increasing number of sexuality practitioners are noting that mindfulness practices are really good for sexuality (Brotto, Basson, & Luira, 2008). This is because one of the core components of a really meaningful sexuality is deep encounter, which can only happen between two people who are fully present to one another.

Being preoccupied with unfinished tasks and unable to focus is a common issue for women. I have heard more than one woman admit to watching the late night news during sex. Whether this is *sexual boredom, emotional disinvestment*, or an *undisciplined mind*, it is a not how one develops an optimal sexuality. Meaningful sexuality requires attention, and mindfulness practices help us to develop the capacity to focus and to actually be where we are. Mindfulness meditation decreases our internal "noise" and self-judgment. It helps to mediate clinical symptoms such as depression, and to increase body awareness and responsiveness (Silverstein, Brown, Roth, & Britton, 2011). Mindfulness practices have also been shown to reduce stress, sexual pain, and the anxiety and sexual avoidance associated with the anticipation of pain (Rosenbaum, 2013).

Somatic Psychotherapist and AASECT-Certified Sex Therapist Maci Daye offers a sexual enrichment program for couples based on the principles of mindfulness. It is called *Passion and Presence* (http://www.passion andpresence.com/index.htm). She asserts that the qualities that ignite passion and heal erotic wounds are curiosity and presence. These are the very qualities that get lost as couples begin to age, succumb to stress and familiarity, or fall into rote sexual practices. Mindfulness allows the energy that is moving through us to be our guide in every moment. Couples learn how to shift states to access more of their pure erotic potential by focusing on "getting here" versus "getting off." In addition to establishing a more attuned and authentic erotic connection, mindfulness is used as a transformational path. Couples work in tandem to heal shame, reintegrate exiled erotic "parts," and embrace the many guises of desire.

Healing Reactive Defenses—Establishing a Calm Core

Our bodies remember both pain and pleasure. Emotionally charged experiences imprint the brain and create neural networks that prime us to react anytime something resembles a painful experience from the past. Getting to a place where we have healed some of this defensive reactivity takes work, but somatic psychologists and neuroscientists like Levine (2010), Ogden (2006), Siegel (1999), Poole Heller (2008), and Ecker, Ticic, and Hulley(2012) all have created treatment interventions that heal these deeply embedded reactive patterns. Although each works differently, what they have in common is working at the intersection of the memory, the brain, and the reactive nervous system.

McKay, Wood, and Brantley (2007), wrote an excellent workbook filled with suggestions on how to *develop mindfulness, interpersonal effectiveness, emotional regulation*, and *distress tolerance*. These practices were originally designed to help clients who struggle with severe emotional dysregulation, but studying these practices would benefit *all women!* When our emotional baseline is calm, and we know who we are, we can become powerful communicators and develop fulfilling relationships.

Once we have calmed the reactive nervous system, it becomes possible to listen and understand and to convey information rather than to defend or blame. Real relationship, presence, and connection become possible. As we engage in practices that calm the nervous system's reactivity, we can integrate heart, mind, body, and spirit. We can move beyond shame into a place of self-acceptance. We begin living from a Calm Core. From here, we can continue to be open to new insights and growth. Our inner stillness allows us to feel our true sexual essence, and Aphrodite's flame begins to inspire and invite us to live meaningful, passionate lives.

Without the development of a Calm Core, clients may have too much self-doubt or anxiety to open up topics or propose something new, fearing rejection, disapproval, or shaming. Operating from a Calm Core, a woman can tolerate vulnerability and continue to move towards what she desires. She can venture out from a stable base into new territory, taking risks, solid enough in herself to manage the outcome, whatever it is. Self-Regulation is the foundation of effective Self-Revelation.

Change Stirs Up the Vulnerable Children

Growth requires change. Sexuality that moves into our depths has the potential to stir up every human emotion, shadow, and light. The Vulnerable Children inside can become highly activated. Gatekeepers would just as soon have things remain the same. Remaining aware of inner processes is important, because these inner characters can stir up some intense body sensations that begin to shape behavior and choices without our even realizing it. The "Goldilocks zone" in the growth process is really that place where we are pushing the edges, but not overwhelming the nervous system so much that it is experienced as traumatic. As a woman begins to heal the wounds of the past, she will begin to differentiate between the Voices of Warning generated by Gatekeepers in alarm, and those appropriate warnings provided by her Wise Sexual Guardian. Certain vulnerabilities that require deeper healing work will become evident only as a client moves more deeply into a relationship and into more engaged sexual experience. Wounds may emerge that were not evident when a woman was operating at a more superficial level. These ancient pleasure thieves need to be exorcized from her psyche. Although this deeper work may be difficult, the rewards of doing it become evident, as a woman experiences ever-deepening levels of pleasure and meaningful relationship.

COMMUNICATION—FINDING YOUR SEXUAL VOICE

Sexual communication between partners has been emphasized as a crucial element of successful sexual relationships since the days of Masters, Johnson, and Kolodny (1982). Kleinplatz et al. (2009) emphasize that people who have optimal sexual experiences don't just communicate—they hold "black belts" in communication. Although we know it is important to "tell your partner what you want and need," a woman who has never wondered about this or attended to her bodily responses won't know. Without sexual Self-awareness, we are having sex in the dark. Without a foundation of inner stability and the capacity to Self-Regulate, a woman may not be able to express what she knows.

Getting Naked in Body, Mind, Heart, and Spirit

Getting naked in body is easy compared with becoming naked emotionally, mentally, and spiritually. That entails the revelation of thoughts, feelings, longings, hopes, expectations, disappointments, assumptions, and concerns. At a deeper level, it means revealing where one finds meaning and how we are moved and inspired. This depth of communication is a tall order for partners who live behind self-protective shields. Likewise, when we are tangled up in caretaking or managing a partner's reactions, we cannot freely and fully express who we are or what we want (Bader, 2002; Bader, Peterson, & Schwartz, 2000; Schnarch, 2009).

Rocking the Boat

A woman who has a big-time Pleaser or Peace Maker in her inner cast will not want to "rock the boat." When her relationship boat starts rocking, all she wants to do is stabilize things and *make peace*. At moments like this, she doesn't care what she feels; she often doesn't know what she thinks. Women like this are easily steamrolled by the emotional intensity of others, and everything that displeases others feels dangerous. She will often backpedal, apologize, and dismiss her desires as unimportant. Women like this always feel guilty for disappointing people and judge themselves heavily as "bitchy" or "mean" if they deny someone something that he or she really wants. Any "no" she gives may be followed by an immediate panic from her Inner Children, who are fearful of being rejected, punished, or abandoned. A practitioner's work with this woman will help her learn to separate out her own personal experience from the people around her and to steady *herself* while she waits for other people's boats to stop rocking.

Here again is where employing a somatically based therapy will be particularly helpful. Beyond talking about it, facilitate her in having the *experience* of holding steady right there in your office. Have her practice communicating from this place, inhabiting the space, feeling clear and confident, and then carrying this experience home. Actually integrating this as "second order change," as part of her *identity*, may require practice over time, with small increments of progress. You can utilize Voice Dialogue to interview Vulnerable Selves, Gatekeepers, and Voices of Warning that get stirred up in the process.

I always check to see if there are any legitimate issues of physical safety that would make it dangerous for a woman to become more vocal or assertive in her relationship. If this exists, she needs a different set of interventions. Barring this, we can work to establish an inner Boat Rocker, who is just fine with shifts in dynamics. This Boat Rocker will become a new supportive figure in her inner cast.

Which "Me" Is Communicating . . . and Who's Agenda Rules?

If we look to the inner self system and all the differing "characters" and agendas within, we can see how a client might become paralyzed trying to figure out "who's in charge." If she doesn't have an awareness of her "inner cast" and doesn't know which inner self should lead, she can become quite confused about what she wants or how to communicate it. A good therapist can help a client sort out this tangle. As the client becomes a more conscious director of her inner cast, she can allow Aphrodite to speak more loudly and to play her important part.

CARMELLA'S CELESTIAL PALACE

My client Carmella hated it when her boyfriend used the word "pussy," but she never explained to him that she had a sexual abuse history and why that particular word was so triggering for her. Instead, she started a fight, which usually ended up with her boyfriend storming out of the house. She was afraid that if her boyfriend knew more about her, he might view her as Damaged Goods. She didn't want to "rock the boat" with a conversation. Instead, she made big waves whenever she derailed one of their sexual experiences. Carmella had lost her power and her capacity to redirect what was happening in a confident, clear way.

Here is an example of a crucial communication, blocked by fear and shame. I affirmed that it was OK for Carmella to care about what someone called her genitals. As we moved behind the inner character that we named the Argument Starter, we drew out and dialogued with that notorious inner character, Damaged Goods. As Carmella began to free herself from the fear and shame that Damaged Goods was generating, she found her center and was able to talk to her boyfriend. Instead of viewing her as "damaged," he was relieved to understand what was going on.

197

He had never been able to figure out where these sudden arguments came from, when things seemed to be going so well.

How we refer to parts of our bodies has meaning for us, and it is important for women to convey what they want their body parts called, particularly if certain names carry a charge. Affectionate couples will often find pet names for their intimate parts. Taoist sexuality has the world's most poetic list of references to the vagina and the vulva compared with the phrases that most women grow up with. In Taoist sexuality they refer to the vagina as "the hidden or celestial palace, the valley of solitude, the path of yin, and the cinnabar or vermilion cave." The penis is referred to as a "jade stalk, yang peak, or ambassador." The clitoris is a "precious pearl, yin bean, jade terrace" and breasts are called the "bells of love." Cunnilingus is "sipping the vast spring" and fellatio is "blowing the flute" and orgasm is "high tide" (Winston, 2014).

Communication From an Archetypal Stance

When we talk about communication we are often referring to *what* is being said. We don't always talk about *where* we are communicating *from*. A woman's *archetypal stance* is equally as important as the words being said! A woman can communicate from many different places in her psyche. Each will have a different impact on the listener. A woman who is in an intense emotional state might be in the archetype of Martyr, Pleading Child, Rebel, or Critical Mother. When a woman is in charge of herself, she can determine what archetypal state will be most effective in getting her communication across.

Women sometimes say to me, "I was just speaking my truth!" Although we need to be forthcoming about the things that really matter, some women come out guns blazing where a clear, confident communication is all that is required. This is not an archetypal stance that invites sexual cooperation. The Warrior Princess may need to put down her sword before her lover can embrace the Soul Mate. The Shrinking Violet may need a few drops of Warrior Princess. The Self-Righteous Saint may need to integrate a bit of Generous Goddess. The Scared Little Girl may need some Playful Elf. The same message communicated from a different archetypal stance will have a very different impact. Help your client find an archetypal stance that feels good and right for what she needs to achieve.

If a woman can't imagine taking a stand, have her *imagine being some-one who can.* Use the exercise of "trying on" an archetype from Chapter 7. Utilize the power of her imagination to activate this energy in her body. Have her speak from this place, so that she becomes accustomed to how it feels. Remind her that she is pulling this archetypal energy up *from her own psyche.* This means that the energy belongs to her. She simply has not activated it until now.

When a woman knows her own capacity to say a solid "yes" and a clear "no," she will have the sense that she can ask for what she wants and set limits regarding what she doesn't want. Anchoring in a place that is strong and clear, but not aggressive or demeaning, requires some personal insight, honesty, and self-regulation. Finding the middle ground between passivity and aggression is hard for many women. This is a capacity that can be developed as a woman learns to regulate her nervous system. In doing so, she will grow in every area of her life.

SANDRA'S SEXUAL PAIN

Sandra came to see me. She was in the archetype of the Pleading Child, wanting me to "fix" her. Her husband was telling her that she was "uptight and hung up," because she didn't want to have sex. She explained that sex hurt.[1]

Sandra had entered into a vicious cycle. She had begun to avoid sexual contact. When she did engage, she was tense and braced herself, anticipating a painful experience. The tension was interfering with desire, arousal, and lubrication, which made intercourse even more uncomfortable. Her husband was frustrated and taking this as a personal rejection. He blamed her for the problem, saying, "Why can't you just relax and enjoy yourself?"

As I asked further questions about the pain, I learned that it began during deep thrusting and was present before the tension or avoidance pattern had begun. I asked Sandra if she had discussed this problem with her gynecologist. She had not. I suggested that Sandra visit her gynecologist and talk to her about the pain she was experiencing. When she did, her doctor explained that Sandra had a "tipped" (retroverted) uterus. The doctor had mentioned this before, but it had never seemed important to Sandra. When Sandra described the pain she was experiencing, her doctor explained that the particular angle of Sandra's uterus could easily make certain angles of thrusting painful. Sandra, who was just beginning to tune in to her own body, had never put these things together before. The doctor suggested that she explain this to her husband and that the two of them experiment with angles and depth that did not have this impact. When Sandra heard this, she began to cry from the sense of relief. She had assumed the whole thing was because she was "uptight and hung up."

At our follow-up session, Sandra was greatly relieved but also concerned about how she would resolve this with her partner. We began to talk about what she wanted to say and to find the archetypal stance from which she would say it. She immediately got the idea that the Pleading Child was not going to get the job done. We talked about when and where she had been confident and clear in her life. She remembered the confidence she once felt participating in student government in college. She had become quite a Diplomat and she wanted to re-anchor this in herself. We spent some time helping her reconnect with that state of being and embodying that archetypal energy. It was an emotionally steady, informational, strong energy, with no defensiveness or aggression. We rehearsed a conversation with her husband, how he might react, and how she could respond from the archetype of the Diplomat. With this preparation, she was able to convey the medical information and ask clearly and undefensively for what she wanted. When her partner understood that her problem was not psychological but anatomical, he changed his sexual expectations and dropped the blaming and shaming. From a place of new cooperation, they redesigned their sexual routine, with signals for keep going, ouch, pause, and "redirect." With lots of good communication, the pain problem began to resolve. In the process, Sandra gained a sense of sexual agency, the experience that she had the power to redirect what was happening in bed. She became much more attuned to the sensations in her whole body, not just her pelvis. As this developed, she moved from hesitant, anxious, and defensive into a place of clarity and confidence, and the couple's sex life became a rich and pleasurable experience.

Ditching Snow White

Some women are sexually experienced. They know what they like and what pleases them, but they don't communicate it because they believe that their sexual sophistication will be intimidating to their current partner. They are also afraid of the names they might be called. I call this "pretending to be Snow White." A woman who is sexually aware and able to convey who she is and how to pleasure her, is a mature, valuable woman. Although some partners have wonderful sexual skills, *relying* on a partner to automatically know what to do is a recipe for frustration and demoralization. Protecting a partner's ego is a sure way into the sexual swamplands. Working from the right archetypal stance is also important, because many partners have sexual performance insecurity and feedback can raise a lot of defenses. Setting up the context of being erotic partners on a path of discovery about each other is a good beginning.

More on Sexual Communication

Show and Tell

There are so many things that need to be conveyed about one's sexual desires and preferences. Talking is good, but sometime showing is better. A sexually empowered woman feels confident enough to do this. She will have already worked with the inner Gatekeepers that may have warned her that it would be way too brazen to guide a lover's hand or to teach by demonstrating!

Affirmation

Affirmation is as important as *information*. Sexuality is a tender topic and egos can be easily bruised. Women need to tell their partners what they are doing right! This kind of affirmation can be really hard for some women. It requires self-revelation and generosity rather than protective withholding. It does a world of good in terms of encouraging a partner who may be a bit insecure or defensive.

Timing

We can all improve in our choice of *timing*. Attempting to make major changes in a partner's sexual approach during a sexual experience, without setting up that context in advance, is *not a good idea and not good timing*. Providing a running critique on your partner's every move during sex is certain to extinguish any sense of mystery, play, self-confidence, and enthusiasm. Agreeing on a time for intimate feedback is a great idea. If a woman's feedback is not well received, she needs to examine the place from which she is saying it, *her archetypal stance*. Speaking from a condescending or critical archetypal stance will not get you where you want to go. Sometimes it is better to talk about sex *out of bed*. A long drive or a walk can be a good time. Walking helps to discharge anxiety, and not being face to face allows partners to react and then take time to calm themselves down and think before responding.

Keandra's Kissing

Gail really cared for her girlfriend Keandra, but she hated a certain way that Keandra kissed. When this happened, she would back off saying, "I hate it when you kiss me that way." For Gail, kissing was one of her primary arousal paths, but instead of helping Keandra to understand exactly what she was doing, from a helpful archetypal stance, she just began to avoid kissing. She told me that she did this because she cared for Keandra, and didn't want to hurt her. "Keandra is just extremely sensitive about things!" Unfortunately, this led to an underlying feeling of disappointment, which caused her to bring less of herself into the relationship. Over time she began to feel increasingly disconnected, and experienced a loss of sexual desire.

I helped Gail learn to find an archetypal stance from which to communicate effectively with her partner. It had never occurred to her that *she* could hold steady while her partner's boat was rocking! We worked on Gail's anxiety and script-based resistance about "teaching" Keandra how she liked to be kissed. Gail also realized that the stance from which she was communicating was a contributing factor in Keandra's "oversensitivity." One day, when they were relating well (good timing), and they were standing around in the kitchen (good place), Gail opened up the conversation. She revealed to Keandra that her sexual avoidance had begun with her inability to communicate about the kissing. She apologized for shutting down and told her partner she wanted to change the direction in which they were drifting. Then she took some time to show and tell how she liked to be kissed. Keandra proved to be an excellent student. She was also grateful, relieved to discover what had gone awry with them, and became hopeful about their future.

Intimate Inquiries

When women talk about their sexual problems, they often speak in generalities. It can be hard to get a clear picture of what is going on.

Sometimes when I am working with a client I will say, "Let's go through that experience in slow motion so that we might discover where things are going awry." I want a detailed, moment-by-moment account, with information about what is happening behaviorally, subjectively, and archetypally. In listening to the progression of events, I can generally ascertain where things went "off the rails." Women can do this on their own, if they will take the time to reflect on where things took a turn for the worse. What was happening and what did "the voices in her head" say that foreclosed on her ability to turn this situation into something more pleasing?

What Are We Listening For?

Although it is not necessary to "overprocess" sex, when things are not going smoothly, I examine scripts, expectations, sexual menu, styles of engagement, core erotic themes, and archetypal orientations. People have very specific "turn-ons" and "turn-offs." Scripts have both process and content material. People can have very different underlying assumptions about how, when, and where sex should occur and how it might best progress. Things like sex toys can create a lot of reaction for some people. All of this requires a certain level of trust and capacity to self-reveal.

The whole topic of orgasm carries a lot of assumptions and expectations, along with performance and response anxiety. Does she need extra stimulation to get over the top and, if so, what kind? Can she show her partner how to best touch her, or stimulate herself? What is the importance of orgasm? Who comes first? What happens after that? Couples need to make sure they communicate about this or they are likely to get stuck in projections about what the other person wants, without actually discussing it. A performance script that measures sexual "success" by whether an orgasm was "achieved," overlooks the dimensions of presence, attunement, and play.

THE ARCHETYPE OF THE INITIATOR

Sex is often considered something that men do to women rather than something that belongs to women, with orgasms as something that men "give" to women. The inference is that women are instruments, played

203

by men (McCormick, 1994). The myth that men are supposed to be the "sexually experienced ones" who teach a woman what to do comes out of a "dominator" relationship model that douses the fire of women's eroticism (Eisler, 1996).

An increasing number of contemporary men are expressing that they are tired of always being the Initiator. They are not satisfied with a woman who is sexually compliant; they want a woman who is engaged. Men are increasingly expressing that *they* want to be an object of desire. One of the ways a man feels desirable is when a woman initiates sex with him (Dworkin & Sullivan, 2007).

Nichols (1995) has written about the problem of "lack of initiation' in lesbian relationships, with *both* women waiting for the other to initiate. This can wind up in a stalemate of eroticism, which has been referred to as "lesbian bed-death."

When I am looking into a woman's inner cast of characters, I look to see if she "houses" an Initiator. If this archetype is missing, she will find it difficult to initiate sex or ask for what she wants. Sometimes the Initiator is being constrained by a Gatekeeper. The Initiator is an archetype that can be awakened and cultivated and added to a woman's inner cast.

Wendy the Waif Becomes the Safe Sex Wonder Woman

My client Wendy, the once upon a time Waif, became a Wonder Woman when it came to the negotiation about her need for sex to be safe physically, emotionally, and spiritually. She began to take her time before jumping into bed, to truly get to know who she was dealing with. When she felt safe to move forward, she got very good at saying, "I like you a lot, and I know we have been moving toward being sexual. Before we are in the moment, I'd like to talk about our sexual health and our histories." Wendy then took out her blood work and began to discuss her sexual health status. She had already moved beyond the shaming, self-blaming litany that Damaged Goods used to heap on her. She could now *initiate* the conversation without shame or hesitation. She would then ask, "What is your sexual health status? Have you had your blood work done lately?" She explained that condom use was mandatory and anyone who was not willing to engage in this conversation was disqualified as a potential lover. Wendy also didn't rely on the other person to carry the condoms. She had one on hand. I began to believe that Wendy was becoming the Poster Woman for the Safe Sex Talk.

MEANINGFUL COMMUNICATION—PONDERING BEFORE PRONOUNCING

Communication can be helpful only when self-reflection has taken place. Superficial communication with no Self-awareness can become very confusing. Here are some precommunication questions for your client to ponder:

- What is my primary sexual essence, and how do I like to experience and express this?
- What archetypes do I inhabit when I'm feeling most confident and positive about my sexuality? How do different archetypal identities affect me sexually? In looking at my inner cast of characters, which archetypes promote pleasure and which ones diminish it? Who else in my inner cast supports my Aphrodite Self, and who restricts her?
- If I were a perfume blend, how many parts of "this and that" (archetypal energies) would be in my formula? How might I like to change this mix?
- What other energies on the Sexual Essence Wheels would I like to explore? How might I do this?
- How do I like to be invited into sexual engagement—the tone, words, energy, non-verbal cues, time, place, situation? What do I like the parts of my body called?
- How do I like to progress from one phase of sexual experience to another? What are the cues I use to signal that I am ready or interested? Is my partner aware of my cues?
- What archetypal energies do I respond to most readily in my partner? What are my biggest turn-ons and turn-offs? What is going on behind the "turn-off?" What might I learn from this in terms of my own sexual template, my sexual scripts, inner Gatekeepers, and unconscious shadow material?
- What am I doing sexually that I wish I were not? What am I *not* doing sexually that I wish I were? What would I do with a "dream lover?"
- What does revealing myself to my partner stir up in me? What projections do I have about how he or she would react to my

becoming more self-revealing in this way? Am I confident enough to suggest something and get a non-supportive re-action? Have I sorted out the best "archetypal stance" from which I might ask? Can I allow my partner's "boat to rock" and hold steady?

- How do I turn myself on? How do I turn myself off?

These last two questions are powerful questions originating from Gina Ogden (2013). When expressed this way, we see that we have a choice in the matter. We can Self-determine. We can redirect situations more to our pleasing. We do not have to get mad, or sad, or shut down. We are directing our inner cast.

Sex and the Single Woman

As a woman becomes more aware of her sexual essence, untangles herself from trauma, and throws off negative sexual scripts, she will begin to experience her innate sensuality and eroticism. She will find that she attracts different partners. The body itself will be drawn to partners who are better matched for this woman's sexual essence. The sexual archetypes a woman inhabits will influence her *choice* of partner.

In attending to her own sexual template, a woman will begin to notice her preferred erotic scenarios (Morin, 1995). She can take a look at what is on her sexual menu (Iasenza, 2010) and determine her sexual path preference (Mosher, 1980). She can also begin to notice the spectrum of archetypal energies she is most responsive to in a partner. Is she drawn to partners who are intense and instinctual; self-reflective and spiritual; easygoing, fun-loving, and spontaneous; ambitious and commanding; intelligent, conversant, philosophical; cultured and worldly wise; rebellious and free thinking; outgoing and witty; dark, sensitive, and brooding; romantic and expressive; kind, loving, and affirmative; heroic and justice loving; adventurous and outdoorsy; earthy and sensuous; idiosyncratic and creative? What gets her motor going?

There is no one way to be sexual, and every partner will carry a different set of archetypal energies, have a different sexual script, and a different arousal template. A sexually confident woman can reveal herself while she continues to learn about her partner, as they negotiate the sexual dance together.

All the Good Ones Are Taken!

When a woman complains to me that there are no potential partners out there, I begin to explore her *expectations, self-defeating scripts,* and *archetypal stance*. Many women believe that their difficulty with attracting someone is because they are "too fat" or "too flat." They are convinced that their inability to find a partner has something to do with their appearance. Despite what the media and the advertising industry would sell us, I insist that "looks" are secondary to archetypal stance. Women who carry Aphrodite energy emanate a sparkle that makes them innately attractive, regardless of their physical "endowments." A woman who is self-confident knows the value she brings as a sexual partner. She knows her special "blend" from the Sexual Essence Wheels and doesn't waste her efforts on those who don't appreciate her blend. Aphrodite women have no shortage of suitors.

Archetypes communicate and evoke responses in others, and many women are unconscious that the archetypal identity they inhabit does not invite people into relationship or attract healthy, available partners. Armored Amazons and Warrior Princesses are hard to get close to. High-achieving Athena women can be so thinking oriented that they exude no sexual energy. Selfless Saints can seem rigid and desexualized and can evoke a fear of judgment. Too much Tigress without a trace of nurture and you've got an alluring but frightening Man Eater. Wounded Women can be fragile or bitter and become Clinging Vines. No one wants to be analyzed by a Psychological Know-It-All. Entitled Princesses are critical, whiny, and perpetually dissatisfied. Shrinking Violets, Wallflowers, Waifs, Orphans, and Poor Little Match Girls don't draw healthy partners to them.

In working with women who are stuck in these sad stories, I try to help them to become conscious of their inner cast and "who" in them is the leading lady when they are on the dating scene. We explore the origins of these domineering non-relational archetypes, Sexual Gatekeepers, Vulnerable Children, and Fairy Tale longings. Conscious awareness brings a woman the power to direct her inner cast, and Aphrodite needs to be part of the cast.

In my office, I have a couple of turtle puppets that I sometimes pull out to demonstrate how no one can know how wonderful we are if we spend our lives pulled back into our protective shells. I explain that we may feel like this is keeping us "safe," but ultimately it keeps us isolated and away from possible experiences of connection and joy.

Jeremy Taylor illustrated Figure 4 for me after a conversation about how carrying different archetypal energies affects how we relate to others and what we evoke in response.

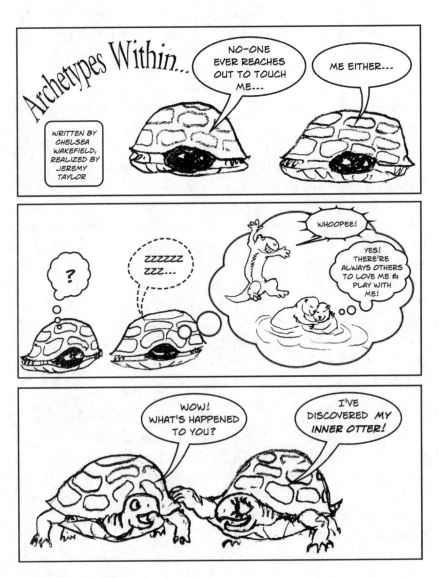

Figure 4

NOTE

1 The *DSM* (APA, 2014) diagnostic for this disorder would be "Genito-Pelvic Pain/Penetration Disorder," or "Dyspareunia."

BIBLIOGRAPHY

American Psychiatric Association. (2014) *Highlights of Changes From* DSM-IV-TR *to* DSM-5. http://www.dsm5.org/Documents/changes%20from%20dsm-iv-tr%20 to%20dsm-5.pdf accessed on 1/20/15.

Bader, E., Peterson, P.,& Schwartz, J. (2000) *Tell Me No Lies: How to Stop Lying to Your Partner—And Yourself—In the Four Stages of Marriage*. New York: St. Martin's Press.

Bader, M. (2002) *Arousal: The Secret Logic of Sexual Fantasies*. New York: Thomas Dunne.

Brotto, L., Basson, R., & Luira, M. (2008) A Mindfulness-Based Group Psychoeducational Intervention Targeting Sexual Arousal Disorder in Women. *The Journal of Sexual Medicine, 1*, 40–48.

Dworkin, S., & Sullivan, L. (2007) "It's Less Work for Us and It Shows Us She Has Good Taste: Masculinity, Sexual Initiation, and Contemporary Sexual Scripts." In M. Kimmel (Ed.) *The Sexual Self: The Construction of Sexual Scripts* (pp.105–121). Nashville, TN: Vanderbilt University.

Ecker, B., Ticic, R., & Hulley, L. (2012) *Unlocking the Emotional Brain: Eliminating Symptoms at Their Roots Using Memory Reconsolidation*. New York: Routledge.

Eisler, R. (1996) *Sacred Pleasure: Sex, Myth, and the Politics of the Body—New Paths to Power and Love*. San Francisco: HarperCollins.

Iasenza, S. (2010) What Is Queer About Sex?: Expanding Sexual Frames in Theory and Practice. *Family Process, 49*, 3, 291–308.

Kerner, I. (2004) *She Comes First: The Thinking Man's Guide to Pleasuring a Woman*. New York: HarperCollins.

Kleinplatz, P., Menard, A.D., Paquet, M., Paradis, N., Campblee, M., Zuccarino, D., & Mehak, L. (2009) The Components of Optimal Sexuality: A Portrait of 'Great Sex.' *Canadian Journal of Human Sexuality, 18*, 1–2, 1–13.

Levine, P. (2010) *In an Unspoken Voice: How the Body Releases Trauma and Restores Goodness*. Berkeley, CA: North Atlantic.

Masters, W., Johnson, V., & Kolodny, R. (1982) *Sex and Human Loving*. Boston: Little, Brown.

McCormick, N. (1994) *Sexual Salvation: Affirming Women's Sexual Rights and Pleasures*. Westport, CT: Praeger.

McKay, M., Wood, J.,& Brantley, J. (2007) *The Dialectical Behavior Therapy Skills Workbook: Practical DBT Exercises for Learning Mindfulness, Interpersonal Effectiveness, Emotion Regulation & Distress Tolerance*. Oakland, CA: New Harbinger.

Morin, J. (1995) *The Erotic Mind: Unlocking the Inner Sources of Sexual Passion and Fulfillment*. New York: Harper Perennial.

Mosher, D.L. (1980). Three Dimensions of Depth of Involvement in Human Sexual Response. *The Journal of Sex Research, 30*, 1, 1–42.

Nichols, M. (1995) Sexual Desire Disorder in a Lesbian-Feminist Couple: The Intersection of Therapy and Politics. In R. Rosen & S. Leiblum (Ed.) *Case Studies in Sex Therapy* (pp. 161–175). New York: Guilford.

Ogden, P. (2006) *Trauma and the Body: A Sensorimotor Approach to Psychotherapy*. New York: Norton.

Ogden, G. (2013) *Expanding the Practice of Sex Therapy: An Integrative Model for Exploring Desire and Intimacy*. New York: Routledge.

Poole Heller, D. (2008) *Healing Early Attachment Wounds: The Dynamic Attachment Re-patterning Experience–Module 1* [manual]. Louisville, CO: Diane Poole Heller.

Rosenbaum, T. (2013) An Integrated Mindfulness-Based Approach to the Treatment of Women With Sexual Pain and Anxiety: Promoting Autonomy and Mind/Body Connection. *Sexual and Relationship Therapy, 28*, 1–2, 20–28. doi: 10.1080/14681994.2013.76981

Schnarch, D. (2009) *Intimacy & Desire: Awaken the Passion in Your Relationship*. New York: Beaufort.

Siegel, D. (1999) *The Developing Mind: How Relationships and the Brain Interact to Shape Who We Are*. New York: Guilford.

Silverstein, R. G., Brown, A. C., Roth, H. D., & Britton, W. B. (2011) Effects of Mindfulness Training on Body Awareness to Sexual Stimuli: Implications for Female Sexual Dysfunction. *Psychosomatic Medicine, 73*, 9, 817–825.

Wakefield, C. (2012) *Negotiating the Inner Peace Treaty: Becoming the Person You Were Born to Be*. Bloomington, IN: Balboa.

Winston, S. (2010) *Women's Anatomy of Arousal: Secret Maps to Buried Pleasure*. Kingston, NY: Mango Garden.

Winston, S. (2014) *Succulent Sex Craft: Your Hands-on Guide to Erotic Play & Practice for Men and Women, Singles and Partners*. Kingston, NY: Mango Garden.

CHAPTER 22

INTERPLAY WITH PARTNERS

"Let there be spaces in your togetherness and let the winds of the heavens dance between you."

Kahlil Gibran

THE INTERPLAY OF TWO INNER SELF SYSTEMS

Part of becoming a woman is navigating the imperfections of human love. The neurochemical cocktail of early love keeps partners in a "mutual adoration society" for a while. After that settles down, they begin to meet "the rest of the cast" that dwells inside their chosen partner. When the fairy tale won't come true according to their longings, they fall into resentment and disillusionment. Many get stuck there. In Hal Stone and Sidra Stone's (2000) book, *Partnering*, they introduce the idea that love relationships are an interplay of *two inner self systems* with all their possible pairings and bonding patterns. The mature, empowered woman understands that there are no "mythical mates," "dream lovers," or "perfect people." It is two sincere adults who co-create a wonderful relationship and sex life, taking into account that human beings have their strengths and frailties.

SEXUAL PROBLEMS CAN MASK DEEPER ISSUES

It is important to note that sexual problems often mask deeper relationship issues. Couples therapy is truly a specialization and sex therapists not trained to recognize toxic couple dynamics can find themselves all wrapped up in the couple's tangled web. Masters and Johnson did not work with troubled couples, Helen Singer Kaplan (1974) did. Many sex therapists refer out for couples caught in toxic relationship patterns. Most of woman's sexual issues have a relational component. If you are working individually with a woman, you can help her develop self-awareness, self-confidence, a sense of agency, strong communication skills, and an awareness of her archetypal profile. You can facilitate her in shifting states and communicating from a variety of archetypal stances. What you can't predict is how her changes will affect the systems in which she is embedded. Systems theory tells us that changes in the woman will result in relational disequilibrium. The response may be positive or negative. If she is challenging "normative" models of relationship or family life, there is likely to be pushback (Walsh & Scheinkman, 1989).

Attachment—Can You Draw Close and Let Go?

The attachment patterns that imprint our early relational experiences shape a woman and determine how easily she can move between connection and separation, closeness and distance. When a woman's early life experiences teach her that people can't be counted on, or perhaps they are even dangerous, she will be wary of closeness. It will be hard for her to surrender herself into a deep, passionate engagement with another. On the other hand, if her early experiences were inconsistent, she may be overfocused on her partner, continually anxious about doing or saying the wrong thing, fearful that she may be abandoned. Her ability to know and reveal herself will be compromised. Women who have a foundation of "secure attachment" are less reactive and can navigate the changing waters of relationship. They are resilient in the face of relational and life stressors. These women travel the sexual psyche with greater ease. This kind of security can be "earned" with personal work that will lay the foundation for extraordinary sex (Cohn, 2011; Fosha, Siegel, & Solomon, 2009; Poole Heller, 2008; Schore & Shore, 2008).

Even Good Things Can Be Too Much

Kaparo (2012) points out that "we are far more trainable toward helplessness and despair than toward responsibility and freedom" (p. 21). We have to allow the body-mind to become accustomed to states of joy and aliveness, to learn to be happy from the inside out.

All of us have a "window of tolerance" for how much emotion we can process at one time. Although it may be hard for some to imagine, good things can be "too much" for some people to take in (Siegel, 1999). People who have experienced dangerous relationships or devastating disappointments find it hard to trust in life's goodness. Being able to tolerate pleasure can be an adjustment. Levine (2009, 2010) discovered that for some people, "titrating" small doses of good things is what helps them move forward, slow movements towards positive engagement, so as not to overwhelm the nervous system.

The Relationship Journey

Relationships are riddled with longings and projections. People "find each other," and in their early limerance (Tennov, 1999) they fall under the spell of the mutual adoration society, believing that this is the partner who will make everything "right." No one is capable of fulfilling the idealized hopes and expectations projected by the other at the beginning of the relationship. As the partners begin to fall off their pedestals, early wounds surface, and negative parental complexes rear their ugly heads. He goes from Hero to Terrible Father and she goes from Angel to Witch Mother. Their inner Vulnerable Children huddle in the background, sad, scared, and lonely. The most difficult part of any relationship is getting beyond early projections and beyond the hurt and anger that the partner will never be who you thought they were, and the answer to everything that went wrong before. If the couple is able to begin to see each other as they are, in their totality, they have a chance to begin building a real relationship. For most couples this is a treacherous journey, but it is filled with invitations for a higher level of relating (Young-Einsendrath, 1984, 1993).

Relationships go through developmental stages, and some couples get stuck along the way (Bader & Pearson, 1988; Bader, Peterson, & Schwartz, 2000). If they get stuck at any one of the stages, they will experience a good degree of suffering and have lots of problems. Some people become so anxious about bonding that they never form the basic foundation of trust. Others are so anxious about separating that they become *enmeshed* and unable to "rock the boat" with truthful disclosures about who they really are. Some are *dependent* on each other, but *furious* about it, especially if they can't get the other person to be who they want them to be. Two people who are growing individually, sharing their individuation journeys with each other, differentiated but emotionally connected, will reach the golden land of relationship. Esther Perel (2007, 2010) reminds us that "fire needs air." Differentiation is the only road to long-term relationship fulfillment and sustained sexual passion (Bader & Pearson, 1988; Bader et al., 2000; Schnarch, 2009).

Couples who keep growing will have much more excitement in their relationship. There will be times when they are not on the same page, but in valuing the relationship for its depth and longevity, they will struggle until they find a new point of balance and cooperation. When they fall into stale patterns, one of the partners will break them out of it (Bader & Pearson, 1988).

Great sex involves negotiation, interplay, and an exchange of invitation and response, leading and following. In being with a partner, there is a movement between an attunement to self and an attunement to the other. There is space for difference. Sometimes this goes smoothly, sometimes not. The moves are not preset, but a grounding in the Self and an underlying respect creates a basis for trust and good will where each partner can respond authentically. In this spacious context, there is freedom for wildness, exploration, tenderness and appreciation, disappointment, and challenge. In being erotic partners, there is permission to oscillate between a selfish desire for satisfaction and an empathic partner sensitivity. In the most exquisite sexual experiences, there is a matchup of the subjective archetypal energies and scripts.

In such relationships, there will be occasional misalignments because people do not grow at the same rate or always want the same things. Learning to navigate these dicey developmental passages is part of a truly evolved relationship, but when two people are in the dance together, it makes the relationship immeasurably valuable. This will motivate them to deal with their differences and work things out.

Sexual Enrichment—The Future of Sex Therapy

Many people believe that drifting into a de-eroticized or sexless relationship is an inevitable part of a long-term marriage. They settle for an absence of erotic life or a droll and unsatisfying sex life because they hope for nothing more. Some people try to communicate needs unsuccessfully and give up without attempting another road in. In recent years, the topic of sexual enrichment has become an emerging focus of sex therapists. There is a new group of clients who have begun to seek sex therapy. Their sexual "functioning" is fine, but they are aware that something is missing. They are bored and struggling with a lack of meaning and enjoyment in their sexual relationships. They want to deepen their experience.

What Long-Term Couples Say About Wonderful Sex

The underlying message of magazines at the supermarket checkout stand is that great sex is for the young, healthy, and beautiful and involves special, even secret, sexual techniques. The couples in Kleinplatz et al's (2009) study defied this paradigm. These researchers were looking at "optimal sexuality" in long-term relationships. They interviewed sexually satisfied couples over the age of sixty, with a variety of sexual orientations and arousal templates, who had been in a relationship for over twenty-five years. For these couples, looking like a movie star or being a sexual athlete was not important. What was at the top of the list for these couples was *presence*, being with one another in a pleasurable communion, attuned to the emotions and to the body of oneself as well as the partner. The next most highly valued quality was *authenticity*, truly opening up and *revealing oneself* to the partner, to know and be known, so that what the partners did in bed had maximum impact. Kleinplatz et al (2009) assert that people who have great sex are *black belts in communication*. These relationships were ones in which partners felt safe to explore, take risks, and have fun. They felt safe to be vulnerable and to surrender to each other and the experiences they shared. Presence, authenticity, and communication allowed the partners to be in sync, *share in an intense connection*, and achieve true erotic *intimacy*. All of these factors led to experiences of *transcendence, bliss*, and *peace*. Although having an orgasm was commonly experienced and valued, it was not a necessary feature, nor was it sufficient in and of itself for great sex to occur.

Intersubjectivity

A lot of what the participants in Kleinplatz et al.'s (2009) study were talking about could be summed up under the label of *intersubjectivity*.

215

Intersubjectivity occurs when two people share their inner experiences with one another: sensations, thoughts, feelings, meanings, anxieties, longings, curiosities. In sharing this information, they begin to really understand each other. They become attuned to each other. This deepens trust, builds connection, and allows for greater risk taking. If a couple continues to share their changing subjective experience with each other, and not fall into fixed routines, they will avoid the stagnation that is so common in long-term sexual relationships.

When we begin to talk about intersubjectivity, it becomes evident that eroticism can be defined in many ways and will differ from person to person. We need to be careful about defining eroticism in a behavioral way that employs any particular sexual script. If we allow for eroticism to be both an expressive as well as a subjective measure, then it refers to the amount of "juice" that flows within a person and between people. It does not necessarily involve intercourse. In talking with one of my highly introverted female friends, she relayed the most erotic experience of her life. It was an early experience with her current partner. They sat reading poetry to each other in front of a blazing fire and fell into a deep and enduring love relationship around those arousing, evocative words. Through their love of words, this couple has also enjoyed a very satisfying sexual relationship.

Forget a New Sexual Position . . . Let's Try a New Archetypal Position!

The supermarket checkout stands are filled with magazine articles on how to "spice up" your marriage. Specially planned evenings, lingerie, improving one's technique, and expanding one's sexual repertoire *can* spice up one's sex life, but what the magazines fail to mention is that it's not just about the lingerie. If the woman cannot carry the archetypal energy that will evoke a response from her partner, she will not carry it off. Helping women learn to shift states out of Eros-inhibiting archetypes, beyond Gatekeepers, and into new archetypal energies represented on the Sexual Essence Wheels, can become a valuable intervention for those who want to expand their practice of sex therapy.

Sexually empowered women draw from all four quadrants of the Sexual Essence Wheels, romancing, nurturing, seducing, and drawing their partners more deeply into the sexual mysteries. Working with sexual archetypes is both creative and inspiring and incorporates the best of script theory, role playing, and symbolic interaction. Approaching sexuality from this perspective invites individuation and self-actualization.

Every archetypal state on the Sexual Essence Wheel will generate a different set of behaviors, sounds, words exchanged, pacing, and so on. *Without the archetypal state the behaviors are contrived*, and they will feel that way; in the archetypal state, it all flows. The same old sexual routines generated from a new archetypal orientation will suddenly feel as if they were being shared with a totally new person. The experience becomes a fresh erotic discovery.

Sexual Evocation

When a woman is no longer enmeshed with her partner, she can shift states more easily. With space to breathe, there can be a call and response. Partners still influence each other, but it feels like dancing instead of unconscious reactivity. The upside of this is a woman's power of *evocation*. In partners that are attuned to energy shifts in each other, every differing archetypal orientation a woman inhabits will evoke a different response in her partner. She is not necessarily *acting* differently, she is *being* different. My client Barbara, in Chapter 9, began to experience the power of *evocation* when she activated the Dream Wench she named "Brandy." When Brandy showed up, Barbara discovered that her Couch Potato husband had more kick to him than she had previously thought.

Making Space for Aphrodite

If a woman wants to enrich her sexual relationship, she may need to adjust her archetypal stance across the board. She will need to recalibrate how she spends her time and energy, at work, with friends, taking care of the house, shuttling children, and so on. She will need to carve out protected time for Aphrodite. The people around her, who benefited from those things, may not like it. One of the things I tell the women in my practice is that an empowered woman doesn't have to explain herself to everyone or account for every minute of every day. When someone calls to invite her to do something, she can say, "Sorry. I already have plans." She doesn't have to justify spending the evening at home, sharing sensual delights with her partner.

The Longing to Be "Met"

As a woman awakens to her own inner fire, she wants to share that fire in a meaningful exchange with a partner. If she has been an Anima Woman, the object of *someone else's* ideal, now she wants to be known for who she really is. She wants to claim *her own* erotic identity, and she wants that identity met with presence and passion. A woman's desire to experience the depth dimension of a sexual and emotional relationship often escalates in midlife. She may find that her partner is not interested in being with an "awakened woman." The balance of power can begin to shift, and this can create serious problems. Women who find their Aphrodite energy become passionately awakened, not just in the bedroom, but in their lives.

Before a woman decides things are hopeless, I want to know from what archetypal stance she has been attempting to move the relationship forward, and if this archetypal stance is one that actually invites communication and change. Is she holding steady and allowing her partner to adjust, or is she reverting to old ways of being when resistance is met? Sometimes a woman needs to shift her archetypal approach into more courageous intensity; sometimes she will be served by nurturing, sometimes by becoming more playful. If I am working with a couple, I begin to look at "who" (in *her* inner cast) is relating to "whom" (in *her partner's* inner cast). When we mix up these pairings, an entirely different situation may emerge. Sometimes a woman can awaken her partner and invite him or her into a time of growth for both of them. If these two people can really encounter each other, as who they are now rather than who they used to be, they will become "beginners" again. They may "find" each other again, in a newly defined relationship, at a higher level. If not, the woman may find herself in the position of having to make difficult choices.

Changing the dynamics in a long-standing relationship is not easy. The system will push back. This requires sincere investment, compassion, and patient determination. I emphasize to women that partners are not "props" on the stage of their lives, responding according to an ideal script. These changes activate a developmental process for both people and introduce a time of "danger and opportunity" as the recalibration takes place. I encourage women to hold steady, sustain a "calm core," and give their partners time to adjust.

The Madonna-Whore Split

There are still men who are incredibly intimidated by a sexually confident woman. This may be a developmental issue for them, wanting a Mother who will care for them but not come at them with any demands. They might also be caught up in the lingering split between Madonna and Whore. They want a sweet, unthreatening Madonna and do not want their Wife to carry too much Seductress energy (Woodman, 1982).

The Fire Cat and the Choir Boy

Francesca was fed up with Steven. Every night he sat up watching the news while she read bodice-ripper romances in bed. She longed for him to come upstairs and ravish her. She told me, "I don't think I can stand it anymore. Ever since we got married, he treats me differently, like a Porcelain Doll. It's his Catholic upbringing. It's like he's a Choir Boy and I'm a Fire Cat! I don't think this will ever work." When Steven came in, and was truly honest, he revealed that he loved and respected Francesca so much that he didn't want to degrade her with his sexual desire. That would be taking her off her high pedestal. Meanwhile, Francesca was at the edge, ready to jump. I found the Madonna-Whore split deeply embedded in Steven's psyche. I began to work with these two estranged lovers to discover a place where they could meet in the middle.

Francesca was willing to do anything, so hungry was she for a passionate engagement. We began to do some Voice Dialogue with her Fire Cat to explore her need for intensity. In the process, we located an early experience in which she had made a life-directing decision to be bold and strong rather than vulnerable and tender. After this, Francesca had always mocked "good girls" and "demure" women. She was proud of being a Sexual Woman. We began to look at the Sexual Essence Wheels and discuss that a truly sexually empowered woman can travel these wheels. I wondered if there was another sexual archetype that she might "try on" that would be less overwhelming for the Choir Boy. Highly motivated to solve this problem, and curious about exploring other aspects of herself, Francesca decided she could shift states from Fire Cat into Kitten. She was also genuinely intrigued by the archetype of the Poet's Muse. This reminded her of the women in the bodice-rippers she had been reading, and so she tucked away her black negligee and bought herself a Victorian Sleeping Gown. Steven liked it a lot.

The couple committed to attending to their inner process and journaling about thoughts, feelings, reactions, as their "inner characters" played out the drama in the bedroom. I began working with Steven's Gatekeepers and the Hell-fire Voices-of-Judgment that plagued him. Francesca was present for one of these sessions and suddenly understood how much her contempt of the Choir Boy had driven Steven further into the world of late-night news. In revealing her own fears of vulnerability to him, they began to connect more deeply and experience each other in a different way. In doing so, they were able to find an overlap in their different erotic templates. As Francesca integrated more Romantic and Muse energies from the Sexual Essence Wheels, Steven began to witness how ethereally beautiful she was in the throes of passion. He now realized that he was not besmirching his beloved with his sexual hunger. They had established a secure base with each other, and from here they began to venture out.

BECOMING CURIOUS INSTEAD OF FURIOUS

We must understand our partner's subjective experience in order to become successful erotic partners. Understanding how *the other person* is interpreting and making meaning in a situation is also necessary to resolve sexual impasses. We don't always understand that *intention* and *impact* are two different things. One partner may mean well, but the impact on the other may be quite different than intended. People interpret situations differently (Stone, Patton, & Heen, 1999). All of us project and amplify, especially when we are feeling vulnerable. It is important for a woman to check if her projections, assumptions, and attributions of motivation are accurate.

As I work with couples, I constantly hear arguments over "what really happened." They don't seem to be able to allow their partner to have a different interpretation of the same event. Couples get caught in pointless power struggles over whose version is "right," never getting to the important underlying issues. They miss the gift of deeper understanding that an exploration of their partner's differing perspective might bring. As couples gain consciousness, they become better able to disentangle themselves from these power struggles. They begin to catch themselves in negative bonding patterns and gain the capacity to move out of them into more productive exchanges. They learn to shift states and engage different "inner partners" within their two inner self systems. In doing so, they learn to dance together.

I always remind women that anger is a powerful defense that is always masking underlying vulnerability. Negotiating meaningful resolutions is made easier by being truly interested in the intentions, meanings, history, and archetypal orientations that shape a partner's inner world. We need to become curious instead of furious. It helps to be aware of when our partner is really extending themselves in order to meet us in a meaningful way and to appreciate those gifts of generosity.

Becoming "Tellable"

In certain relationships, one partner will not reveal themselves to the other because that other partner is not "tellable." Bader et al (2000), reminds women that they become a Lie Invitee when they are so highly reactive that a partner does not dare risk self-disclosure. While I encourage women not to become stuck in this self-defeating pattern themselves, they sometimes contribute to their partner's move into this self-protective stance. There are women who ask questions that function as a setup for an "ambush." An honest answer from the partner will lead them to deep trouble. Partners get wise to this after a while. If a woman has done this a lot in the past, it will take her a while to coax her partner out of hiding.

Partners in Play

The couples I work with in my practice become aware of the bonding patterns that take place between their two inner casts of characters. Some couples can begin to lovingly, playfully name the characters that get into difficult or pleasurable interactions. They can find the partners who can "dance" together. For example, how does she feel about her partner's Puppy Dog sexual approach? Is it cute or a complete turn-off? Can she communicate this? Can she leave her Loyal Employee at the door? Can he shift out of Cynic into something a bit more appealing? Does she respond more to a rough and tumble Swashbuckling approach or a poetic Courtly Lover? Can she shift out of Maid into the Playful Coquette? As they attend to what stirs them, they can develop a deeper synchrony in which there is less "figuring out" and more flow. They can enter into that relaxed sense of play that is so important in an intimate, satisfying sexuality (Kleinplatz et al., 2009; Metz & Lutz, 1990). They can also explore what lies in their sexual shadows. Integrating shadow elements on the Sexual Essence Wheels will grow not only a woman's erotic personality, but also her whole personality. This is how sexuality can become a path of individuation.

Depth Sexuality

Depth sexuality is the product of personal and relationship maturity that encourages the Self-awareness and growth of both partners. Evolved relationships provide a container in which partners can explore and experience new aspects of Self and integrate shadow material. There is a celebration of freedom in sensual, emotional, intellectual, and spiritual pleasure, and a fluidity across the archetypal spectrum. When two partners enter this level of sexual relating, the experience takes on a whole new dimension. The erotic thrives on novelty and the unknown and the psyche is vast with much undiscovered country. When two people are continuing to grow and change, exploring their individual psyches and sharing what they are discovering about themselves, it brings an ongoing freshness to the relationship.

Simple "Feel Good" Sex

I would like to end this chapter by addressing that we live in an age where bigger is better, and the new is always better than the old. We need to be careful about devaluing the sweet and tender sexuality that is the mainstay of sexually satisfying long-term relationships and is part of the sexual spectrum. Barry McCarthy and Emily McCarthy (2004) emphasize that couples who share this kind of pleasure deepen their relational bond and reduce the inevitable stresses of life and marriage. Although a satisfying sex life may contribute only 15–20% to a couple's overall satisfaction with the relationship, when things go bad in the bedroom, this percentage skyrockets, and preoccupation with sexual dissatisfaction can overshadow everything else. Sexual satisfaction is consistently shown to be important for sustaining long-term relationships (Sprecher & Cate, 2004). Couples who are sexually satisfied will tell you that they do not expect for *every* sexual experience to be an expansive exploration or a mind-blowing experience. Although couples desire extraordinary sexual experiences from time to time, Barry McCarthy states that the simple "feel good" sex that sustains a long-term relationship should not be considered boring and passé.

When it comes to family life, a happy, secure marriage makes for secure children. In sensing the sexual bond between the parents, they absorb the message that love, affection, and pleasure are good things that are possible in their future relationships. Couples that sustain a meaningful sexuality over the course of a lifetime value their sexuality and set aside protected time to connect, especially during the challenging years of raising children. Sexually satisfied couples also adjust to changes in life responsibilities, accept the gradual changes in their bodies and in their health, and find new ways of loving in each chapter of life.

BIBLIOGRAPHY

Bader, E., & Pearson, P. (1988) *In Quest of the Mythical Mate: A Developmental Approach to Diagnosis and Treatment in Couples Therapy*. New York: Brunner/Mazel.

Bader, E., Peterson, P., & Schwartz, J. (2000) *Tell Me No Lies: How to Stop Lying to Your Partner—And Yourself—In the Four Stages of Marriage*. New York: St. Martin's Press.

Cohn, R. (2011) *Coming Home to Passion: Restoring Loving Sexuality in Couples With Histories of Childhood Trauma and Neglect*. Santa Barbara, CA: Praeger.

Fosha, D., Siegel, D., & Solomon, M. (2009) *The Healing Power of Emotion: Affective Neuroscience, Development & Clinical Practice*. New York: Norton.

Kaparo, R. (2012) *Awakening Somatic Intelligence: The Art and Practice of Embodied Mindfulness*. Berkeley, CA: North Atlantic.

Kaplan, H. S. (1974) *The New Sex Therapy: Active Treatment of Sexual Dysfunctions*. New York: Brunner/Mazel.

Kleinplatz, P., Menard, A. D., Paquet, M., Paradis, N., Campblee, M., Zuccarino, D., & Mehak, L. (2009) The Components of Optimal Sexuality: A Portrait of 'Great Sex.' *Canadian Journal of Human Sexuality, 18*, 1–2, 1–13.

Levine, P. (2009) *Trauma, Somatic Experiencing and Peter A. Levine Ph.D*. www.youtube.com/watch?v=ByalBx85iC8

Levine, P. (2010) *In an Unspoken Voice: How the Body Releases Trauma and Restores Goodness*. Berkeley, CA: North Atlantic.

McCarthy, B., & McCarthy, E. (2004) *Getting It Right the First Time: Creating a Healthy Marriage*. New York: Brunner-Routledge.

Metz, M., & Lutz, G. (1990) Dyadic Playfulness Differences Between Sexual and Marital Therapy Couples. *Journal of Psychology and Human Sexuality, 3*, 1, 167–182.

Perel, E. (2007) *Mating in Captivity*. New York: Harper.

Perel, E. (2010) The Double Flame: Reconciling Intimacy and Sexuality, Reviving Desire. In S. R. Leiblum (Ed.) *Treating Sexual Desire Disorders: A Clinical Casebook* (pp. 23–43). New York: Guilford.

Poole Heller, D. (2008) *Healing Early Attachment Wounds: The Dynamic Attachment Re-patterning Experience- Module 1* [manual]. Louisville, CO: Diane Poole Heller.

Schnarch, D. (2009) *Intimacy & Desire: Awaken the Passion in Your Relationship*. New York: Beaufort.

Schore, J. R., & Shore, A. N. (2008). Modern Attachment Theory: The Central Role of Affect Regulation in Development and Treatment. *Clinical Social Work Journal, 36*, 9–20.

Siegel, D. (1999) *The Developing Mind: How Relationships and the Brain Interact to Shape Who We Are*. New York: Guilford.

Sprecher, S., & Cate, R. (2004) Sexual Satisfaction and Sexual Expression as Predictors of Relationship Satisfaction and Stability. In J. Harvey, A. Wenzel, & S. Sprecher (Eds.) *The Handbook of Sexuality in Close Relationships* (pp. 235–256). Mahwah, N.J., Lawrence Erlbaum.

Stone, D., Patton, B., & Heen, S. (1999) *Difficult Conversations: How to Discuss What Matters Most*. New York: Penguin.

Stone, H., & Stone, S. (2000) *Partnering: A New Kind of Relationship: How to Love Each Other Without Losing Yourselves*. Novato, CA: Nataraj.

Tennov, D. (1999) *Love & Limerance: The Experience of Being in Love*. Lanham, MD: Scarborough House.

Walsh, F., & Scheinkman, M. (1989) (Fe)male: The Hidden Gender Dimension in Models of Family Therapy. In M. McGoldrick, C. Anderson, & F. Walsh (Eds.) *Women in Families: A Framework for Family Therapy* (pp. 16–41). New York: Norton.

Woodman, M. (1982) *Addiction to Perfection: The Still Unravished Bride*. Toronto, ON: Inner City.

Young-Eisendrath, P. (1984) *Hags and Heroes: A Feminist Approach to Jungian Psychotherapy With Couples*. Toronto, ON: Inner City.

Young-Eisendrath, P. (1993) *You're Not What I Expected: Learning to Love the Opposite Sex*. New York: Morrow.

CHAPTER 23

APHRODITE AND THE LUMINOUS WOMAN®

"The erotic landscape is vastly larger, richer, and more intricate than the physiology of sex or any repertoire of sexual techniques."

Esther Perel

In 2009, I wrote an essay entitled *Becoming a Luminous Woman®*. It begins, "A woman becomes luminous when she begins to live by her own inner light. This light grows as she establishes a taproot into the creative power of her archetypal depths, giving her a quiet dynamism that emanates from the core of her being."

TRAVELING THE SEXUAL ESSENCE WHEELS

To be on the path of Sexual Individuation™ is to be on a path that continues to unfold, exploring the mysteries of the sexual psyche and the wonders of human embodiment.

For many women, the realization that she is not merely a "receptacle" or "responder," but the very source of her sexuality, is a monumental shift that changes her life. She begins to discover the creative power in her archetypal depths and feels this dynamism undergirding her life. Now we have a woman who is in conversation with her instinctual nature. She has discovered that the erotic lives in her and this creative energy will infuse the way she lives, loves and works. This is the telltale indication of the woman who has found Aphrodite.

As a woman begins to travel the Sexual Essence Wheels, she will begin to understand and integrate aspects of each quadrant.

In the sexual essence realm of the Nurturer, she will want to know and understand all aspects of her lover. Who is this person? What do they need and want? In this archetypal energy, her body becomes an extension of the body of the Great Goddess, generous, earthy, warm, sensuous, healing, and responsive. Her greatest joy is to draw her lover close, and to see the happiness and fulfillment in their eyes.

In the sexual essence realm of the Romantic she will enjoy the play of love, the call and response, the seeking and finding, the aching longing and the rapturous fulfillment. When she experiences union, "two hearts beating as one," her joy is boundless. Her desire here is to create a beautiful love story and her sense of hope for the future is enduring.

In the sexual essence realm of the Seductress, she will study the art and strategy of love, and learn about her particular power of allure, developing her capacity to intuit the sexual psyche of her lover, to captivate them, and if she wishes, to hold them. Here she will gain confidence in her power to create experiences of passion and pleasure and to remain intriguing throughout her life.

In the sexual essence realm of the Mystic/Muse, a woman will anchor herself in her luminous depths. In the archetype of the Muse her inner light will inevitably draw others to her and inspire them to greatness. As the Sexual Priestess, she will come to understand the power of her sexuality to inspire, heal, deepen, and transform. Communion and union with this woman will invite a lover into sexual mysteries and a profound soul-to-soul connection.

Each woman has a sexual "home land" that can be found on the Sexual Essence Wheels. She also has a passport to visit other lands from which she can come home bearing gifts. Women possess all of this potential and they can explore it and cultivate it when they pull themselves out of the dark corners of the Sexual Essence Wheels and begin to travel *around* them.

A woman can visit the "essence" home land of her partner in order to understand his or her subjective experience while still retaining "citizenship" in her preferred quadrant of the wheel. Although an established arousal template might be thought of as a "birth language," she can learn new languages. She can learn to dance the dances of other cultures.

THE JOURNEY OF SEXUAL INDIVIDUATION

When we begin to view sexuality as a path of growth and individuation, it takes on a whole new dimension. Approaching sexuality in this way brings creativity and discovery to it. Sexuality is multidimensional and women can enjoy the dimensions of sensuality and eroticism at *any* age, with or without a partner.

Women's sexual fulfillment comes from many sources: being Self-aware, Self-accepting, and joyfully embodied; having the capacity to manage strong emotions; developing excellent listening and communication skills; revealing who she is as a sexual being and asking for what she wants, clearly and unapologetically. Women who begin to attune deeply to their bodily responses know what kind of sexual exchanges feel good to them. They can convey their pleasure and desires to a partner whom they can engage with flexibility, curiosity, compassion, and a sense of humor. This is a woman who is able to play, as well as redirect situations that might derail less sexually adept women. She can have her own subjective experiences, yet seek to know who her partner is. She can listen and relate without becoming reactive, she can bond without becoming enmeshed, she can appreciate what is, rather than longing for what might have been. She can be in the present moment. She can take risks, learn, and grow.

As a woman learns and grows, her goals will change. The woman who came into treatment wanting to please a partner will learn that she can also please herself. If she was a little waif who believed she had little to offer, she will come to understand the beauty and light of her blossoming Aphrodite nature. Now we have a woman who is interested in sexuality for its own sake, for its pleasure, for what it opens up in her.

The more courageous and willing a woman is to encounter her Self, shadow and light, to heal lingering wounds from the past, and to remain in an ongoing process of growth, the more light she will carry, and the more meaning and pleasure she will find. The process of claiming herself sexually will cause her to grow, and live a larger, more inspired life. In the flush of her Aphrodite energy, she will create things she previously never dreamed of.

For the woman who has found Aphrodite, sexuality itself becomes a pathway of Self-discovery. Much of a woman's individuation journey can occur through the growth that is generated in her sexual development. Sexual experiences can teach us things about ourselves that we did not know before, opening places in the psyche where we have never traveled. A woman's sensual and sexual identity can continue to evolve over the course of her life. As she continues to explore her archetypal depths, the fire of Aphrodite will light her path, and she will experience an ever deepening degree of freedom and pleasure, meaning and joy.

APPENDICES

THE SEXUAL ESSENCE WHEELS

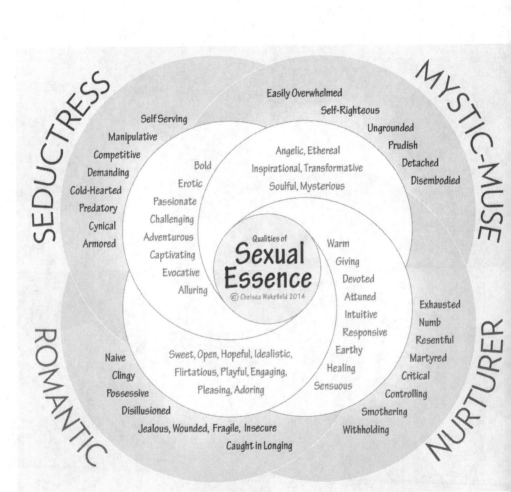

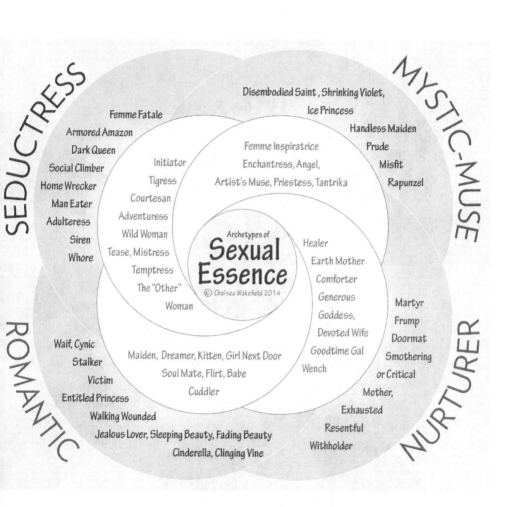

SEDUCTRESS

MYSTIC-MUSE

ROMANTIC

NURTURER

Femme Fatale
Armored Amazon
Dark Queen
Social Climber
Home Wrecker
Man Eater
Adulteress
Siren
Whore

Disembodied Saint , Shrinking Violet,
Ice Princess

Handless Maiden
Prude
Misfit
Rapunzel

Initiator
Tigress
Courtesan
Adventuress
Wild Woman
Tease, Mistress
Temptress
The "Other"
Woman

Femme Inspiratrice
Enchantress, Angel,
Artist's Muse, Priestess, Tantrika

Archetypes of
Sexual Essence
© Chelsea Wakefield 2014

Healer
Earth Mother
Comforter
Generous
Goddess,
Devoted Wife
Goodtime Gal
Wench

Martyr
Frump
Doormat
Smothering
or Critical
Mother,
Exhausted
Resentful
Withholder

Waif, Cynic
Stalker
Victim
Entitled Princess
Walking Wounded
Jealous Lover, Sleeping Beauty, Fading Beauty
Cinderella, Clinging Vine

Maiden, Dreamer, Kitten, Girl Next Door
Soul Mate, Flirt, Babe
Cuddler

THE NEW VIEW MANIFESTO

http://www.newviewcampaign.org/manifesto4.asp

A New View of Women's Sexual Problems

by The Working Group on A New View of Women's Sexual Problems:
*Alperstein, L., Fishman, J., Hall, M., Handwerker, L., Hartley, H., Kaschak,
E., Kleinplatz, P., Loe, M., Mamo, L., Tavris, C., Tiefer, L. (2000)*

WOMEN'S SEXUAL PROBLEMS: A NEW CLASSIFICATION

Sexual problems, which the working group on *A New View of Women's Sexual Problems* defines as discontent or dissatisfaction with any emotional, physical, or relational aspect of sexual experience, may arise in one or more of the following interrelated aspects of women's sexual lives.

I. SEXUAL PROBLEMS DUE TO SOCIO-CULTURAL, POLITICAL, OR ECONOMIC FACTORS

A. Ignorance and anxiety due to inadequate sex education, lack of access to health services, or other social constraints:
1. Lack of vocabulary to describe subjective or physical experience.
2. Lack of information about human sexual biology and life-stage changes.
3. Lack of information about how gender roles influence men's and women's sexual expectations, beliefs, and behaviors.
4. Inadequate access to information and services for contraception and abortion, STD prevention and treatment, sexual trauma, and domestic violence.
B. Sexual avoidance or distress due to perceived inability to meet cultural norms regarding correct or ideal sexuality, including:
1. Anxiety or shame about one's body, sexual attractiveness, or sexual responses.

2. Confusion or shame about one's sexual orientation or identity, or about sexual fantasies and desires.

C. Inhibitions due to conflict between the sexual norms of one's subculture or culture of origin and those of the dominant culture.

D. Lack of interest, fatigue, or lack of time due to family and work obligations.

II. SEXUAL PROBLEMS RELATING TO PARTNER AND RELATIONSHIP

A. Inhibition, avoidance, or distress arising from betrayal, dislike, or fear of partner, partner's abuse or couple's unequal power, or arising from partner's negative patterns of communication.

B. Discrepancies in desire for sexual activity or in preferences for various sexual activities.

C. Ignorance or inhibition about communicating preferences or initiating, pacing, or shaping sexual activities.

D. Loss of sexual interest and reciprocity as a result of conflicts over commonplace issues such as money, schedules, or relatives, or resulting from traumatic experiences, e.g., infertility or the death of a child.

E. Inhibitions in arousal or spontaneity due to partner's health status or sexual problems.

III. SEXUAL PROBLEMS DUE TO PSYCHOLOGICAL FACTORS

A. Sexual aversion, mistrust, or inhibition of sexual pleasure due to:
1. Past experiences of physical, sexual, or emotional abuse.
2. General personality problems with attachment, rejection, co-operation, or entitlement.
3. Depression or anxiety.

B. Sexual inhibition due to fear of sexual acts or of their possible consequences, e.g., pain during intercourse, pregnancy, sexually transmitted disease, loss of partner, loss of reputation.

IV. SEXUAL PROBLEMS DUE TO MEDICAL FACTORS

Pain or lack of physical response during sexual activity despite a supportive and safe interpersonal situation, adequate sexual knowledge, and positive sexual attitudes. Such problems can arise from:

A. Numerous local or systemic medical conditions affecting neuro-logical, neurovascular, circulatory, endocrine or other systems of the body;

B. Pregnancy, sexually transmitted diseases, or other sex-related conditions.

C. Side effects of many drugs, medications, or medical treatments.

D. Iatrogenic conditions.

THE LUMINOUS WOMAN®
WEEKEND

The Luminous Woman® Weekend is an experiential weekend in which a woman can learn about archetypes of the feminine and discover who sits at her "inner round table." We look at the developmental passages of a woman's life and how she can avoid the common quagmires, moving from the archetype of Daughter into Fully Enfranchised Woman. The weekend empowers women to cross thresholds of limitation, release things that have bound them, expand their range of archetypal energies, and live more inspired, joyfully embodied lives. They learn that their archetypal stance is more powerful than their history or any barrier that stands before them and connect with deep resources that help to move them forward. When a woman begins to live by her inner light, connected to her deep wisdom and archetypal potential, possibilities open up for her that were not available before. The weekend is filled with laughter, tears, music, poetry, stories, nourishing food, and women together in genuine mutual appreciation, going deep, sharing their wisdom and hope, and "listening each other into life." For more information on these transformational weekends see www.chelseawakefield.com.

INDEX

Lover 21, 47, 81, 93, 112, 116, 138, 144, 177, 178, 184, 198, 204, 205, 221, 226
Luke, Helen 43
Luminous Woman 23, 177, 225–8, 234
Luminous Woman Weekend 177, 234

McCarthy, Barry 128, 148, 222, 223
McCormick, Naomi 24, 31, 111, 129, 165, 181, 204
McKay, Matthew 194
MacNaughton, Ian 175
McNeely, D. A. 43
Madonna 14, 130, 219
Madonna-Whore split 130–1, 219
Maiden 84, 110–11, 114, 120, 126
Maines, Rachel 15
Maltz, Wendy 18, 84, 152, 187
Man Eater 163, 207
Marie's Lioness (archetypal dream work) 92–3
Marriage Shock: The Transformation of Women Into Wives 143
Martyr 74, 75, 198
Masters, William 7, 16, 28–30, 32, 35, 54, 65, 145, 195, 212
Masters and Johnson era: direct/indirect clitoral stimulation 29; Freud's unenlightened perspective 28; "in vivo" laboratory study 28; Kaplan, Helen Singer 29–30; "non-demand" touching exercises 29; premature ejaculation and anorgasmia 32; Sensate Focus 29; sex education 29
"mature" and "immature" orgasm 16
meaning 1, 38, 25, 31, 32, 34, 53–5, 59, 96, 123, 126, 134, 178, 185, 189, 196, 198, 215, 220, 227, 228
memory reconsolidation 64
Menarche 23, 57, 123–4
menopause 57, 125, 180
menstruation 27, 53, 123, 124
Meston, Cindy 25, 167, 169, 181
Militant Feminists 102
mindfulness 29, 139, 175, 193–4
Mintz, Laurie 128
Mistress 145, 164–5, 183
Mistress Lorelei 166
Molly the Maid (Eros-Inhibiting archetypes, shifting states) 86
Moore, Thomas 165, 188–9
Morin, Jack 5, 32, 83, 165, 206
Moser, Charles 165

Mosher, Donald 80, 145, 206
Mother: devoted 93, hovering 60, 86, 96, nurturing 144
Mother's Daughter 126
Mount Olympus 116
Multidimensional aspects of sexuality 5, 227
multiple orgasms 134
Muse 71, 72, 77, 84, 114, 120, 121, 183, 219, 220, 226
Myers-Briggs Type Indicator 38
Myss, Carolyn 41, 66, 157
Mystic 71, 72, 76, 81, 82, 114, 177, 190, 226

Nan and the Chastity Belt (The Inner Patriarch) 143
Narrative Therapy 53
native land 72–3
Negotiating the Inner Peace Treaty 7, 67, 192
Nelson, Gertrud 110, 120, 126
nervous system 107, 149, 150, 158, 193–5, 199, 213
neural connectivity patterns 159–60
New View Manifesto 31, 232–4
New View, The 13, 31, 129, 130, 231
Nichols, Margaret 165, 204
Nobody's Fool 183
non-sexual women 22, 156
Noricks, Jay 68
Northrup, Christine 62, 180
Nun 14
Nursemaid 166
Nurturer 71, 72, 75, 82, 123, 144, 226
Nurturing Mother 144

Obedient Child 60
objectification 111, 115, 121–2
Observing Self 57, 60, 68, 88, 93, 95, 191
Ogden, Gina 2, 5, 18, 24, 25, 31, 32, 35, 55, 66, 96, 114, 128, 129, 131, 135, 157, 177, 181, 192, 194, 206
Old Maid 182
optimal sex 26
orgasm 2, 8, 16, 18, 24–6, 29, 30, 32, 35, 112, 128, 134–7, 139, 153, 198, 203, 215; counting and measuring 135; distraction 136; hierarchy 134; intense emotions 136–7; interference list 135–6; self-pleasuring 138–9
Outlaw 84

Pandora archetype 188
Paris, Ginette 43, 46

242